Human Sexuality for Health Professionals

MARTHA UNDERWOOD BARNARD, R.N., M.N.

Faculty-Nurse Clinician, School of Nursing,
University of Kansas Medical Center, Kansas City

BARBARA J. CLANCY, R.N., M.S.N.

Associate Professor, School of Nursing,
University of Kansas Medical Center, Kansas City

KERMIT E. KRANTZ, M.D.

Professor and Chairman, Obstetrics and
Gynecology and Dean of Clinical Affairs,
University of Kansas Medical Center, Kansas City

W. B. SAUNDERS COMPANY Philadelphia   London   Toronto

W. B. Saunders Company: West Washington Square
                            Philadelphia, PA   19105

                            1 St. Anne's Road
                            Eastbourne, East Sussex BN21 3UN, England

                            1 Goldthorne Avenue
                            Toronto, Ontario M8Z 5T9, Canada

Human Sexuality for Health Professionals   ISBN   0-7216-1544-9

Last digit is the print number: 9   8   7   6   5   4   3   2

DEDICATION

*To the members of our families
whose understanding and patience were
necessary in the completion of this book.*

Howard
Amanda
Rebecca
Richard
Elizabeth
Stephen
Doris

CONTRIBUTORS

CLAUDIA ANDERSON, R.N., M.N.
Doctoral Candidate, School of Nursing, University of Texas — Austin
Sexuality During Pregnancy

ROSE THERESE BAHR, R.N., Ph.D.
Associate Professor, Department of Community Health Nursing, School of Nursing, University of Kansas Medical Center, Kansas City
Sexuality Education: A Need in Health Care

MARTHA UNDERWOOD BARNARD, R.N., M.N.
Faculty-Nurse Clinician, School of Nursing, University of Kansas Medical Center, Kansas City
Introduction

ANN WOLBERT BURGESS, R.N., D.N.Sc., F.A.A.N.
Professor of Nursing, Boston College, Chestnut Hill; Visiting Privileges, Boston City Hospital, Boston, Massachusetts
Rape Counseling: Perspectives of Victim and Nurse

KATHRYN ELLEN CHRISTIANSEN, R.N., M.A.
Assistant Professor, Department of Community Health Nursing, School of Nursing, University of Kansas Medical Center, Kansas City
Sex Education: Whose Responsibility Is It?

BARBARA J. CLANCY, R.N., M.S.N.
Associate Professor, School of Nursing, University of Kansas Medical Center, Kansas City
Introduction; Counseling and Abortion; Sexuality During Pregnancy

R. L. CLANCY, Ph.D.
Associate Professor of Physiology, University of Kansas Medical Center, Kansas City
Sex for the Cardiac Patient

M. EDWARD CLARK, Ed.R.D.
Instructor in Sexual and Marital Counseling, Department of Obstetrics and Gynecology, University of Kansas Medical Center, Kansas City
Sexual Counseling

ROBERT D. CRIST, M.D., Ph.D.

Associate Professor of Obstetrics and Gynecology, University of Kansas Medical Center, Kansas City

Problems in Adolescent Sexuality

LUCILLE D. GRESS, R.N., B.S.N., M.A.

Associate Professor, School of Nursing, University of Kansas Medical Center, Kansas City

Human Sexuality and Aging

GLENN L. HASWELL, M.D.

Associate Professor of Obstetrics-Gynecology, University of Nebraska College of Medicine, Omaha

Chronic Illness and Sexuality

PAUL A. HENSLEIGH, M.D., Ph.D.

Associate Professor of Gynecology and Obstetrics, Stanford University; Attending, Maternal and Fetal Medicine, Stanford University Medical Center, Stanford; Attending, Santa Clara Valley Medical Center, San Jose, California

Infertility

GALE B. HICKENLOOPER, R.N., B.S.

Graduate Student, University of Pittsburgh Graduate School of Public Health, Pittsburgh, Pennsylvania

Problems in Adolescent Sexuality

JANE F. HUNTINGTON, B.A.

Graduate Student, Graduate Program in Criminal Justice, American University, Washington, D.C.

Rape Counseling: Perspectives of Victim and Nurse

LINDA K. HUXALL, R.N., B.S.N., M.N.

Instructor of Family Child Nursing, University of Missouri – Columbia

Counseling Regarding Birth Control Methods

KERMIT E. KRANTZ, M.D., LITT.D.

Professor and Chairman, Department of Obstetrics and Gynecology; Professor of Anatomy; Associate to the Executive Vice President for Facilities Development, University of Kansas Medical Center, Kansas City

Female Reproductive Anatomy and Sexual Response

MANI M. MANI, M.D.

Assistant Professor of Surgery, University of Kansas Medical Center, Kansas City

The Role of Reconstructive Surgery in Human Sexuality

FRANK W. MASTERS, M.D.

Professor and Chairman, Department of Surgery; Chief, Section of Plastic Surgery, University of Kansas Medical Center, Kansas City

The Role of Reconstructive Surgery in Human Sexuality

ROSEMARY J. MCKEIGHEN, R.N., M.S.

Associate Professor; Director, Mental Health Graduate Program, College of Nursing, University of Iowa, Iowa City

Drives, Differences, and Deviations

MARY QUINLAN, R.N., B.S.N., M.S.

Assistant Professor, School of Nursing, University of Kansas Medical Center, Kansas City

Sex for the Cardiac Patient

BARBARA LONG QUIRK, R.N., M.N.

Assistant Professor, School of Medicine, University of Kansas Medical Center, Kansas City; Clinical Nurse Specialist, Department of Obstetrics and Gynecology, Truman Medical Center, Kansas City, Missouri

Sexuality During Pregnancy

SUZANNE SAWYER, B.S.N., N.P.

Director of Medical Services, Counseling and Health Service, University of San Francisco, San Francisco, California

Counseling Regarding Birth Control Methods

F. JANE SEMMENS, B.S., CERT. SEX THERAPIST

Instructor in Counseling (Sex), Department of Obstetrics and Gynecology, Medical University of South Carolina, Charleston

The Sexual History and Physical Examination

JAMES P. SEMMENS, M.D., F.A.C.O.G., F.A.C.S.

Associate Professor of Obstetrics and Gynecology, Medical University of South Carolina; Attending, Charleston County Hospital, Veterans Administration Hospital, Charleston

The Sexual History and Physical Examination

REV. JERRY L. SPENCER, B.A., M.A.

Associate Professor of History and Philosophy of Medicine, University of Kansas Medical Center, Kansas City

Old Morality Vs. New Morality

RICHARD O. SWORD, D.D.S., M.D.

Clinical Professor of Psychiatry, School of Dentistry, University of Missouri—Kansas City; Staff Psychiatrist, Veterans Administration Center, Leavenworth, Kansas

Sexual Deviancy

CAROL TAYLOR, B.A.

Anthropologist in Residence, College of Nursing, University of Florida, Gainesville

Cultural Aspects of Human Sexuality

SISTER MARY EMMANUEL THOMAS, R.S.M., M.S.N.

Graduate Student, Rehabilitation Psychology, University of Kansas, Kansas City

Old Morality Vs. New Morality

CESAR VILLANUEVA, M.D.
    Assistant Professor of Gynecology and Obstetrics, University of Kansas Medical Center, Kansas City
Counseling and Abortion

ANITA L. WINGATE, R.N., Ph.D.
    Assistant Professor, School of Nursing, University of Kansas Medical Center, Kansas City
The Male Reproductive System and Sexual Response

LORRAINE WOLF, R.N., M.A.
Homosexuality: Especially in Adolescence

PREFACE

During the past several years a new attitude toward sex and sexuality has surfaced. People are more open to discussing all aspects of sexuality. In the past, those who sought help from health professionals were chiefly seeking counseling for sexual problems. Now people are exploring ways to better understand their own sexuality and to enhance sexual relationships. The study and expression of sexuality are being thought of as a normal and healthy fact of life.

Many books in this area have been published recently, ranging from sophisticated pornography to textbooks written for members of the various professions. Most of these books have been prepared by one person or by several persons within the same profession. Other books have dealt with one specific area of sexuality, for example, the techniques of sexual intercourse or descriptions of therapy for particular sexual dysfunctions.

Until recently, sexual knowledge, counseling, and therapy were thought to be the province of the obstetrician, psychologist or psychiatrist, minister, and marriage counselor. It is agreed that sexual therapy should remain in the realm of the specialists; however, sexual knowledge and counseling can and should be provided by a variety of educated and trained health professionals so that the human being can be potentiated as a sexual being.

This book treats several facets of sexuality from a multidisciplinary approach. All of the professionals who have contributed to its content are experts in their respective fields. The book deals with a variety of topics that will be of interest to many different health professionals. Historical and religious aspects as well as psychophysiological disorders that can affect a person's sexuality are included.

The editors' intent is to present in one volume a variety of subjects pertaining to sexuality and to assist students of the health professions to gain an understanding of these subjects. With such knowledge and application they can better understand their own needs as well as the needs of those consumers who seek health care.

To these students, and other concerned professionals, young and old, we present our views and the ideas of others regarding the aspects of sexuality.

MARTHA U. BARNARD, R.N., M.N.
BARBARA J. CLANCY, R.N., M.S.N.
KERMIT E. KRANTZ, M.D.

CONTENTS

CHAPTER
1

INTRODUCTION

Martha U. Barnard, R.N., M.N.,
and Barbara J. Clancy, R.N., M.S.N.

It is not surprising that, in our rapidly changing society, ideas about sexuality have changed radically, and the term itself has taken on new definitions and new connotations. Education, health care, entertainment, the make-up of the family, and the many factors that enter into modern society are in a constant state of flux. Sexuality and its effects on society are not exceptions. Sexual attitudes among the public and professionals alike have changed over the last two decades and probably significantly more over the last decade. A variety of reasons can be identified as being partly responsible, but it is very difficult to identify the single factor that has had the greatest impact on the sexual revolution.

BACKGROUND FOR CHANGE

Historically speaking, the Bible was the first book to refer to sexual matters, and Biblical scholars often note that The Great Book was remarkably sensual in expression.

Queen Victoria made history by being attended in childbirth by a male and was therefore thought to be "daring." Today sexual attitudes referred to as Victorian are thought to be outmoded or prudish.

Before the 1940's publications appeared dealing with sexuality but few were intended for the public. Some were written for professionals and others for the clandestine sellers and readers of pornography. Men read such information but usually in privacy, perhaps followed by some discussion with a male companion. Little if anything was discussed with a female companion, and if a woman read sexual literature the matter was kept totally in the privacy of her thoughts. A woman who did discuss sexual matters was thought to be a "not nice" person. Comments with a sexual connotation were thought to be in the poorest of taste and looked upon as being "dirty." Unfortunately these attitudes still prevail in the minds of some persons today.

1

Kinsey's surveys of males and females in the late 1940's and 1950's made the public and health professionals aware of the concerns, problems, and feelings of a large number of people regarding aspects of sexuality. Discussions, books, and films related to sex were still considered taboo by a large portion of the public, however.

After the Kinsey report the next major influence on the attitudes of the public and health professionals was the research and writings of Masters and Johnson. Their experiments with live subjects and the subsequent report of their findings, entitled *Human Sexual Response* and *Human Sexual Inadequacy,* opened the minds of many. Masters and Johnson initiated new types of research, new therapeutic groups, new modes of treatment, and new attitudes toward sexuality itself. Many, for the first time, sought treatment for their sexual problems. Those not considered to have sexual problems sought increased sexual fulfillment through special counseling and experimental groups conducted by Masters and Johnson. Equally important, special seminars were conducted for a variety of health professionals that would begin to densensitize them to their sexual hangups and begin to educate them toward helping patients with their sexual problems as well as toward a greater sexual fulfillment.

In the 1960's and early 1970's literature, entertainment, education, and community programs all took on a new look. The time had arrived for sexuality to become something more than a bedroom topic or underground entertainment. People enjoyed getting lost in the fantasies of novels, ballets, Broadway musicals, films, and television productions with sexual connotations. No longer was it necessary for the public to base its knowledge about sexual matters on a long list of assumptions and old wives' tales. Now factual information was being received through the media and put to use. The public was demanding more information. No longer were fantasies enough. Now the question was asked: Who would work with people with sexual problems and informational needs? It seemed that the demand would be met by a variety of individuals.

INVOLVEMENT OF HEALTH PROFESSIONALS

The new curiosities, concerns, and questions are now coming in droves. Many individuals go to books for answers but others want someone to talk to and get counseling from. The physician and often the nurse have been suggested as the most knowledgeable persons in this field. After all, the thinking goes, they are familiar with the anatomy and certainly are trained not to be embarrassed by asking questions or answering questions related to sexuality. If this assumption is correct, why haven't people found answers to their sex-related questions? Probably because the assumption is very incorrect.

There are exceptions to the rule, of course, but on the whole, outside of obstetrics, gynecology, and psychiatry, few members of either the nursing or medical professions have found it important to delve into the sexual problems of their patients or provide any kind of educational material related to this matter. Like the public, the health professional has been caught up in his own questions and answers, and only a few have had the personal resources to develop the appreciation and knowledge that is needed to help others, much less themselves.

Now, as part of the vast changes in medical and nursing curricula, courses dealing with human sexuality are being taught to the professionals who will be most involved with these human needs. Classes, seminars, sensitivity groups, and personal counseling are now a part of many health professionals' educational experience. Through an early introduction of these subjects (many times prior to the clinical years) students learn that attention to sexual concerns is a necessary part of giving total care to their patients. No longer will the meeting of sexual needs be the privilege of a few, mainly outpatients; hospitalized patients with acute and chronic disease will now also share in this widened scope of care.

Students who do not receive this information in their health education have begun to clamor for a change in their curricula. As a result of the humanistic trend in care of their patients and themselves they are coming to realize how important the fulfillment of sexual needs is in achieving the total health of the individual. Some faculty members are hearing the students' desires and are now requesting and giving more seminars that will begin to help prepare them in this field. Some are taking the opportunity to learn with their students.

Higher education curricula are thus beginning to close the gap in education related to sexuality. Graduate schools educating health professionals will not be the only institutions offering these courses. Undergraduate curricula now include topics related to sexuality as an important component in the educational experience aimed at preparing our youth for modern and full living. People need to be made aware that it is not sick to have sexual experiences, sexual thoughts, and sexual fantasies, or to read pornography and see sexual films. Sex is no longer for the dirty old man but can be something acceptable and beautiful for all ages, classes, colors, and intellects. The idea that the expression of one's sexuality through sexual experience is as normal a function as eating and sleeping is beginning to take hold. Because of this, new curiosities have evolved and the youth of America are becoming better equipped to cope with them. They have developed personal resources for helping themselves as well as learning to call on outside resources when the need arises.

COMMUNITY INVOLVEMENT

Where, when, and how do people learn about sex, sexuality, or what it really means to be a sexual person? All too frequently it is not in school, at home, or in organized community programs. These resources are not able to provide the facts in the proper perspective, if they can provide them at all. Most parents have only limited sexual knowledge but are afraid or ashamed to admit it. Primary and secondary school systems in general are archaic in the dissemination of family living education, in particular sex education, which is only one small aspect of the entire program. School boards make judgments on the inclusion of sexual information in the curricula, often to the detriment of the student. Such decisions often are not based on rational information or consultation with the school nurse or other experts in the field. Frequently decisions concerning health programs are based on emotional responses and nothing more.

Churches are beginning to provide programs for both adults and youth, but unfortunately the masses who need such information are not reached. As the trend continues and more of these community programs are offered, subsequent educational experiences will have to be developed that will build on the foundation knowledge. Some day not the minority but the majority of educational institutions will offer sex information in their curricula. Healthy children and youth will emerge. In the future the family will have the knowledge for their offspring as the questions arise.

THE FUTURE

Life styles have changed and will continue to change. The family may be a single person or a multifamily group. Entertainment, education, marital counseling, and life styles are all centered around sexual connotations. No longer is the homosexual viewed as pathologic but instead he is accepted as someone with an altered life style who has the right to live the life he chooses. No longer are parents appalled when their three-year-old masturbates; instead their health professional prepares them for this normal event and for ways of handling it. Pregnancy is now looked on not as something that requires forfeit of all sex and sex play but as something that should enhance these feelings. It is being seen as not just the mother's experience but as a period that both parents can enjoy as being beautiful and meaningful and most of all the product of a beautiful experience — the sexual act.

It is and it will be the belief that being a sexual person to any degree (for the meaning of sexuality is not restricted to intercourse) is an integral part of being a healthy person. Sexual problems can be intense enough to cause personality or interpersonal or psychiatric problems. Intensive therapy may be needed, and part of the therapy will be centered on the client's sexual needs. However, the majority of sexual concerns can be handled by health professionals who stress the normal state of being a sexual person, who give sexual information, and who make specific suggestions to enhance a sexual relationship.

Could it be true that as society begins to become more educated regarding sexual curiosities and problems, human beings will become healthier and ultimately there will be healthier couples and, most important, healthier offspring? This could be one clue to the mystery of the extreme unhappiness that the average human being is now experiencing both within himself and with others.

2

SEXUALITY EDUCATION: A NEED IN HEALTH CARE

Rose Therese Bahr, R.N., Ph.D.

At present, few health care settings provide sexual teaching as an integral part of the total health care delivered to the patient and his family. Primarily such teaching may be found in mental health centers and clinics, youth centers, problem pregnancy clinics, and women's health clinics. Because of the work assignments and complexities of institutional systems (hospitals, nursing homes), the taking of health histories in the area of sexuality is seldom done. This may be due to two factors: first, the staffing pattern of the institution; and second, the difficulties encountered by health professionals who have not been given an adequate formal educational program preparing them to deal with the subject of human sexuality.

Some nursing education programs and medical schools do provide courses on human sexuality with an application to the clinical setting. Not all courses on the subject are adequate, however. Often insufficient time is devoted to probing in a constructive manner the feelings of the health professional student in terms of his own attitudes and values concerning sexuality.[9] Health professionals are people and as such are products of their own culture. In addition, the fact that nurses and doctors are products of the subculture of nursing and medicine poses additional problems for them.

Assessment tools utilized for purposes of gathering data on sexuality have been emerging but need much refinement, particularly in the area of phraseology. That is, the questions asked of the client must be relevant and open-ended so that the client feels free to discuss, without reservation, his needs, his conflicts, and his interests in the area of sexuality.

HEALTH CARE INCLUDES SEXUALITY EDUCATION

Health care is a product sanctioned by society. In reviewing its health needs, however, it becomes apparent that "society has not yet achieved a healthy acceptance of sexuality." Witness of this fact is the frequently encountered playboy philosophy that treats sexuality as a "desirable accessory which can be changed according to the whim of the moment,"[6] or the religious view whereby sex is treated as a function of the body that can be readily disciplined. Peoples of all cultures have many ideas of what sexuality is and how to impart this information to their children. Health professionals know that many misconceptions and much embarrassment and denial or masking of sexual feelings occur within the clients seen in the various health care settings each day. The changing reactions are due partly to "a conceptual confusion between sex and sexuality, and partly to a crisis of beliefs."[9]

If one believes that a person's sexuality is an accepted element in human living, then it should be an integral part of the health care given to clients. In reality, however, little attention is given to this aspect in health teaching by the very professionals who should be the most knowledgeable regarding human growth and development. Health professionals can be challenged with the question: "If you don't include sexuality content in your health teaching, then how can you believe that sex is part of the natural physiological functioning of the human being?"[9]

The three major components of human sexuality appear to be gender identity, gender role behavior, and eroticism. Each of these components is intrinsic to being a sexual human being. The challenge to society today is how to provide each individual, from the moment of his birth, with the best possible environmental learning and experiential sequences for his orderly sexual evolution and fulfillment during his life span.[2]

In the past it was thought that "a great deal of sexual activity was more an outlet for psychic tension than a genuine sexual drive, and was therefore to be regarded more as a sedative than a genuine enjoyment of happiness."[8] Denber notes that today the use of sexuality has become a way of triumphing over the ancient enemy, whether male or female. The search for freedom has cast aside mores, values, and traditions, while hedonism is accepted as the new "value-line." At every level of society, gender confusion, the unisex trend in appearance and clothing, unrestrained public nudity, and group sexual living, all characterized by a severely intense compulsiveness, have made sex the mutually generalized "do-it-yourself" psychotherapy. This use of sex is a response to a deep need for release of emotional energy that is built up by the sequence of day-by-day tension-producing events. Consequently, the health professional may encounter the individual who is experiencing such tension and may be looking to sex for a solution. Sex becomes the sole bridge to others: physical in nature, devoid of its human, warm, and empathic qualities, it becomes a nonemotional vehicle for expressing feelings. It seems to be a way of reaching out physically through a spurious type of fusion while remaining emotionally detached.[4]

Sex is used sometimes as a very potent means of externalizing inner conflict. Aside from its roots in visceral function and its relationship to fundamental instinctual drives, sexuality deeply reflects the inner psychological being. As such, it is very likely to be used as a means of expressing inner battles through a shorthand of symptoms. Professionals who accept sexual problems at face value without "inquiring into the total personality picture and the interrelationships render a disservice to the patient."[4]

Educating regarding sexuality, therefore, is a helping situation in which the helping professional establishes a trustful, open communication with the client. Through problem-solving, a resolution of difficulties combined with an increased capacity for coping with life results for the client. The need for sexual education is paramount. The health professional should assess the whole person by identifying: (1) areas of concern or conflict, (2) extent of knowledge or misconceptions, and (3) need for health teaching that the client feels may assist him to perform on a higher plane of wellness.

FOCUS ON PATIENT AND FAMILY NEEDS

The health team members are in a unique position for intervening in an individual's sexual concerns in health and illness. Clients seek out those whom they believe to be knowledgeable in the area of human sexuality. Psychologically, sex involves powerful pressures and relationships that may not be understood by the client.[3] The health professional should understand that sexuality arouses forceful and meaningful emotions that can make life worth while but at other times can destroy it. Sexual relationships can evoke both the best and the worst in human beings. Jealousy, revenge, loyalty, and sharing are some of the harmful and enobling emotions which are associated with sex as well as with love itself. These emotional reactions may be hidden in many guises and must be identified through counseling for the benefit of the client.

The health professional must understand further that, psychologically, sex is very complicated. The sexual relationships between man and woman call forth many earlier relationships and experiences in the lives of each. The very ability or inability to be warm and loving and appreciative is based on the personalities involved rather than on the anatomy and physiology involved. An individual whose personality makes it difficult for him to have successful nonsexual relationships will have difficulty achieving a successful sexual relationship.[3] Identification of the depths of a relationship should be explored to bring about a positive adjustment for the person so that adaptation to his circumstances may result.

The client's family life, in which sexuality is a central theme, should be explored as well. The physical relationship of sex is the central fact that differentiates marriage from most other relationships in an individual's life. The partnership and love of husband and wife, which include sex, are based on their roles of man and woman. In addition, male and female roles influence how all members of the family act toward each other throughout their lives.

From the moment of a child's birth, parents have expectations of how he or she will act, based partly on the child's sex. These signals—spoken, conscious, or unconscious—are transmitted to the child quickly and instill a definite concept of what it means to be a boy or a girl—and a man or a woman—early in life. These ideas or "parent scripts" may need to be identified for the person to aid him to a more freely chosen approach to relationships with others.

The following assumptions, listed by Ard in relation to marriage counseling, are equally applicable in assisting a client in identifying his need for sexuality education:

1. *Anxiety, tension, guilt feelings or concern is usually the driving force that motivates clients to seek information.*
2. *Sexual maladjustment and problems can be alleviated or worked through by using methods, knowledge, and techniques to bring understanding to the client.*
3. *Most, but not all, of the ways of behaving which are adopted by the client are those which are consistent with his concept of self.*
4. *An aim of sexual teaching is to help the client perceive reality more accurately.*
5. *The client has the capacity to problem-solve if given adequate information.*
6. *Through sexuality education the client is encouraged to communicate his question and knowledge thereby bringing more of his significant feelings and experiences into the realm of awareness.*
7. *The drive or tendency toward psychological health is within most clients.*
8. *The ultimate goal of sexual education is the optimal development of the individual's potentialities.*
9. *Sexuality education is a worthwhile and helpful activity.*[1]

THE ROLE OF THE HEALTH TEAM

In reviewing the importance of comprehensive and inclusive health care for all clients entering the health care delivery system, it is a key consideration to provide a climate for sexual education that is supportive and accepting. In the past the medical and nursing professions have coped poorly with problems of sexuality of clients. We have neglected the patient's sexuality, which is such a vital part of human nature. The concept of rehabilitation should be built on helping the total personality to a point of maximal functioning.[7] Sexuality is critically important to the client's self-image and to feelings of self-worth and accomplishment.

Therefore, the role of the health team should be to:

1. *Take a history of the client, and remember that it is a conversation between two or more people and anxiety may be present.*
2. *Listen and watch nonverbal communication; avoid note taking.*
3. *Provide privacy and insure confidentiality.*
4. *Allow enough time to discuss and explore needs, attitudes, feelings, values, expectations, practices, anxieties, fears, and problems.*
5. *Be frank, warm, objective, respectful, unembarrassed, open, nonevasive, nonmoralistic, reassuring, and empathetic.*
6. *Clarify vocabulary. Words have different emotional connotations to each person. Help the patient to describe his or her sexual life accurately. Note the patient's choice of words. Don't overgeneralize or oversimplify.*
7. *Help patients arrive at their own answers when exploring moral issues. Don't tell the patient what is right and wrong. Don't judge the patient by norms held by the health team members.*
8. *Be aware of anxiety — silence, jokes, covert complaints, testing, distortions, trying to please. Don't take sides as this may reinforce a patient's defenses and misinterpretations.*
9. *Bear in mind that several interviews may be necessary to complete the history in order to initiate sexual education.*[5]

CONCLUSION

Sexual education is more and more becoming a prominent element in providing comprehensive physical and mental health care to clients of all ages and cultures. It is imperative that health professionals remember that their major responsibility in delivery of health care is to provide the necessary framework for total health need resolution. Society is being bombarded with sexual stimuli which may cause sexual conflicts due to the lack of understanding and lack of education. Human lives are programmed for a rapid pace and continual change, which can ultimately create voids between persons. In filling these voids people sometimes fail to consider the consequences of imposing different values systems upon others. This often results in deterioration of personal relationships, guilt feelings, and conflicts between individuals and family members.

Health professionals are in key positions to help clients become more fully functioning individuals by alleviating the anxiety built up over the period of years that eventually results in lessening of health. Health team members have a role in sexual teaching and it is hoped this role will be implemented positively.

The importance of sex and sexuality is paramount for both the individual and society. The client's achievement of a well integrated, positive well-being on all levels of living will result in more peaceful family life and a more productive and peaceful society.

REFERENCES

1. Ard, Ben and Constance Ard. *Handbook of Marriage Counseling*. Palo Alto, California: Science and Behavior Books, Inc., 1969.
2. Calderone, Mary. What Has Been the Most Important Discovery or Innovation in the Field of Sexuality During the Past Thirty Years? *Medical Aspects of Human Sexuality*, 6:52–65, 1972.
3. Dalrymple, Willard. *Sex is For Real: Human Sexuality and Sexual Responsibility*. New York: McGraw-Hill Book Company, 1969.
4. Denber, H. C. B. The Use of Sexuality to Externalize Inner Conflict. *Medical Aspects of Human Sexuality*, 7:44–63, 1973.
5. Elder, Mary Scovill. The Unmet Challenge, Nurse Counseling on Sexuality. In: *Human Sexuality: Nursing Implications*. New York: The American Journal of Nursing Company, 1973, pp. 39–46.
6. Hettlinger, R. *Living With Sex: The Student's Dilemma*. New York: The Seabury Press, 1966.
7. Hanlon, Kathryn. Maintaining Sexuality After Spinal Cord Injury. *Nursing '75*, 5:58–62, 1975.
8. Horney, Karen. *Self Analysis*. New York: W. W. Norton, 1942.
9. Krizinofski, M. Human Sexuality and Nursing Practice. *Nursing Clinics of North America*, 8:673–681, Dec. 1973.

3

THE MALE REPRODUCTIVE SYSTEM AND SEXUAL RESPONSE

Anita Wingate, R.N., Ph.D.

MALE ANATOMY

The male reproductive system consists chiefly of the male gonads, which produce both the germ cells and various hormones, and the duct system, which transports the germ cells to the exterior. Other structures, such as glands, contribute to the function of the male reproductive system, which is to produce mature germ cells and deposit these in the female system for propagation of the species. The male copulatory organ, the penis, is used to inject sperm into the female vagina, making fertilization of an ovum (or egg cell) possible.

TESTES

The male gonads, the testes, are suspended in a sac called the scrotum. The scrotal sac consists of muscle fibers, fascia, and overlying skin, which is continuous with that over the abdomen. There is one testis in each of the two compartments of the scrotum, the compartments being formed by a septum. The two sets of muscle fibers in the scrotum, the tunica dartos and the cremaster, act to wrinkle the scrotal wall and to shorten the length of the scrotum, respectively; both actions, reflex in nature, move the testes upward toward the warmer environment of the pelvis when the scrotum is exposed to cold temperatures. Sperm cells cannot survive in temperature that is either too cold or too warm. The descent of the testes from the abdomen into the scrotum, usually before birth, serves to protect the testes from the higher temperatures in the abdomen.

Germ Cell Production. The male germ cells, the spermatozoa, develop in the area of the testes called the seminiferous tubules. Each testis is an ovoid body that measures about 5 cm. by 2.5 cm. Each testis is divided into several compartments by numerous connective tissue septa. Each of about 250 lobules contains one to four tightly coiled seminiferous tubules, which are lined throughout with a layer of germinal epithelium. The process of sperm formation, spermatogenesis, takes place in this germinal epithelium.

The germinal epithelium contains two types of cells. The Sertoli cells, columnar cells with oval nuclei, produce secretions for nourishment of the spermatozoa during their development. The other type of cells are the spermatogenic cells, which pass through several stages before becoming mature spermatozoa.

The process of spermatogenesis involves meiotic divisions that result in sperm with a haploid number of chromosomes, that is, 23 chromosomes. When the sperm fertilizes an ovum, which also carries the haploid number of chromosomes, the zygote (or fertilized egg) will then bear the normal, diploid number of chromosomes.

The spermatogenic cells are arranged in several rows beginning peripherally at the basement membrane and extending inward to the lumen of the tubule. The cells furthest from the lumen are the most immature, the spermatogonia. These stem cells, formed during fetal life, divide mitotically to form other spermatogonia, resulting in an almost limitless supply of stem cells. At puberty, the spermatogonia begin to differentiate and some of them form primary spermatocytes, the next stage of spermatogenesis. The primary spermatocytes pass through a meiotic division, resulting in a halving of the diploid number of chromosomes; this division, in which two haploid secondary spermatocytes are formed, is also called a reduction division. Each secondary spermatocyte carries 22 autosomes plus either an X or a Y sex chromosome, which will determine the sex of the zygote resulting from fertilization by the eventual spermatozoon developing from that spermatocyte. Each secondary spermatocyte undergoes a division that results in two haploid spermatids. Each spermatid in turn undergoes a metamorphic process called spermiogenesis, which results in a spermatozoon. Among the maturational changes that occur are disappearance of most of the cytoplasm, elongation of the cell, and development of a tail piece with a cilium capable of propelling the sperm. It is while these maturational changes are occurring that the Sertoli cells appear to nourish the sperm.

The spermatogenic process takes about 60 days in the seminiferous tubules and results in sperm that are still incapable of fertilizing an ovum. After further time in the epididymis, the sperm become motile and truly viable. After removal from the male reproductive tract, sperm die probably within 48 hours. The path that sperm follow after leaving the seminiferous tubules will be discussed shortly.

Hormone Production.   Between the coiled seminiferous tubules in the testes are groups of interstitial cells that are the endocrine portion of the testes. The interstitial cells (Leydig cells) produce the male sex hormone, testosterone. Unlike the case in the female, hormone production in the male is not cyclic. However, as in the female, hormone production is affected by gonadotropic hormones from the anterior pituitary, which in turn is stimulated by the hypothalamus.

The follicle-stimulating hormone (FSH) portion of the gonadotropins acts on the seminiferous tubule to stimulate spermatogenesis. The luteinizing hormone (LH) in the male is more accurately termed the interstitial cell stimulating hormone (ICSH), as it stimulates the production of testosterone. Testosterone is released into the bloodstream for delivery to target tissues.

Male sex hormone (testosterone) maintains the process of spermatogenesis, promotes growth by effects on protein anabolism, and causes the development and maintenance of secondary sex characteristics. Thus testosterone is responsible for the male pattern in hair growth, for the male body build of broad shoulders and narrower hips, for growth of the external genitalia, and for vocal cord changes resulting in a deeper voice, to mention a few. The protein anabolic effects result in a larger muscle mass in males than is seen in females. The male hormone increases sex drive in both heterosexual and homosexual men. As in women, the sex hormone in the male has only a supportive role in sexual behavior, with psychological factors having great effect on such behavior. Male sex hormone production by Leydig cells does not decrease dramatically at a male "climacteric" but may decrease gradually in later years.

DUCT SYSTEM

The duct system through which sperm are transported to the exterior begins with a tubular system in the testes and terminates at the distal end of the penis. As sperm are formed in the testes, some are forced through the rete testis into the convoluted epididymis, a tubule of small diameter but about 20 feet long if it were straightened out. The epididymis lies on the upper posterior superior portion of the testes. The sperm gain motility as they pass through the epididymis into the ductus deferens (vas deferens). The ductus deferens, one of several structures within the spermatic cord, leads upward from the testis to the pubic bone where it enters the inguinal canal; other structures accompanying the ductus are blood vessels, lymph vessels, and nerves bound together with fascia. Upon entering the pelvic cavity the ductus deferens passes posteriorly and laterally to the urinary bladder and downward to enter the prostate gland. At this point, each ductus deferens joins an ejaculatory duct of a seminal vesicle posterior to the urinary bladder. The two ejaculatory ducts open into the prostatic portion of the urethra. The urethra passes on through the prostate to enter the penis.

Accessory Structures of the Duct System.   Several glands contribute secretions that, together with the sperm, constitute semen. The seminal vesicles, placed between the fundus of the bladder and the rectum, are small pouches about 7 cm. long. They secrete a slightly alkaline fluid containing fructose, as an energy source for sperm, and prostaglandins, which may stimulate contractions of the female genital tract. Over half of the total semen volume is derived from the seminal vesicles.

The prostate gland, pear-shaped and walnut-sized, lies below the bladder and anterior to the rectum. Many tiny pores open from the prostate into the urethra, which the prostate surrounds. Prostatitis, not uncommon in advanced years, may result in enlargement of the prostate with at least partial closure of the prostatic urethra. The prostate gland contributes about 20 per cent of the seminal fluid, adding more alkalinity to the fluid.

The bulbourethral glands (Cowper's glands) are a pair of pea-sized structures lying along the lower lateral portion of the membranous urethra. They secrete a slightly alkaline fluid during sexual stimulation and may help neutralize any acidic urine that might be present in the urethra.

Semen.   Semen (or seminal fluid) is made up of several hundred million sperm per discharge, along with secretions of the seminal vesicles, prostate, bulbourethral glands, and glands that secrete mucus along the urethra. Semen is milky in appearance and is thick in a fresh ejaculate but becomes watery within an hour as a result of the action of hydrolytic enzymes from the prostate. The typical volume of seminal fluid ranges from 2 to 6 ml., depending on the length of time between ejaculations. A semen sample can be useful for estimating male fertility, since it is known that the average normal sperm count is about 120 million per milliliter.[1] An increase in the percentage of sperm with abnormal forms, a decrease in sperm motility, or a decrease in sperm count is suggestive of decreased fertility.

PENIS

The male copulatory organ, the penis, varies in size in different individuals, but usually is about 6 inches long and 1 inch in diameter when in a state of erection. It is attached to the front of the pubic arch by fascia, which also partially separates the three columns of erectile tissue that largely construct the penis. The three cylindrical masses of tissue contain a large number of blood sinuses, which upon filling account for the enlargement of the penis at erection. The erectile columns are the

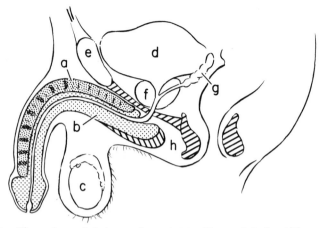

Figure 3–1.   The male genitals in a quiescent state. The penis is flaccid because there is relatively little blood in the corpora cavernosa (*a*) and in the corpus spongiosum (*b*). The testes (*c*) are in their normal low position during quiescence. (*d*) represents the urinary bladder and its anatomic relationships to (*e*) the pubic bone, (*f*) the prostate, and (*g*) the seminal vesicles. (*h*) is a schematic representation of the bulbocavernosus and perineal muscles. (From Kaplan, H. S. *The New Sex Therapy.* New York: Brunner/Mazel, 1974.)

upper two corpora cavernosa penis and the one lower corpus spongiosum, which contains the penile urethra, the common passageway for urine and semen.

The skin covering the penis is thin, loose, and devoid of adipose tissue. At the distal part of the penis, the skin becomes folded upon itself to form the foreskin or prepuce, which in its natural state covers part of the distal end of the corpus spongiosum, the glans penis. Cutting of the prepuce is called circumcision and is often done to avoid the accumulation of smegma, the cheeselike substance secreted by small glands around the base of the glans. The proximal portion of each corpus cavernosum is called a crus penis and is firmly bound to the ischium and pubis.

Figure 3–1 shows the penis and the other male genitalia in a quiescent state.

PHYSIOLOGY OF ERECTION AND EJACULATION

In the male, sexual stimulation leads initially to erection. Psychic as well as tactile stimuli can cause sexual excitation, but tactile stimulation in the pubic region and especially the glans penis, the skin of which has numerous tactile receptors, is most effective. Afferent input from tactile, auditory, visual, and olfactory senses is integrated in the cerebrum, with subsequent increase of parasympathetic outflow from the spinal cord along the pelvic splanchnic nerves. This results in arteriolar dilation in the penis and filling of the venous sinusoids in the erectile tissue, the corpora cavernosa and corpus spongiosum. As the erectile tissue fills, venous outflow is further impaired and the penis becomes hard and elongated or erect (Fig. 3–2).

If further stimulation occurs, an additional reflex brings about ejaculation, the forceful expulsion of semen. In the male, ejaculation is part of the larger response called orgasm, and it involves spinal reflexes in the lumbar segment of the spinal cord. Afferent impulses initiate rhythmic sympathetic discharge in the hypogastric nerves, causing contractions of smooth muscles in the testes, epididymis, ductus deferens, seminal vesicles, and prostate gland to force sperm and semen into the urethra. Pudendal nerves supplying skeletal muscles at the base of the penis aid in the forceful expelling of the semen to the exterior (Fig. 3–3). Other orgasmic responses include increased heart rate and blood pressure, cutaneous vasodilation, and heightened emotions.

Shortly after ejaculation, the sympathetic outflow causes vasoconstriction of arteries of the penis so that inflow of blood lessens and penile turgor decreases, or detumescence occurs. After orgasm and ejaculation occur, the male passes through a refractory period, during which he will not be able to ejaculate in response to sexual stimulation. Detumescence occurs more rapidly in older men than in younger men; in the latter the total decrease in penile size may take up to a half hour.

As described above, the male sexual response is biphasic in nature (as is the female's). The first phase, erection, is normally followed by the second phase, orgasm involving ejaculation. The first phase can be

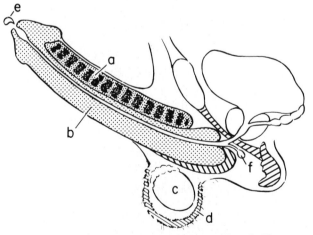

Figure 3–2.   The male genitals in a highly aroused state (plateau). The corpora cavernosa (*a*) and the corpus spongiosum (*b*) are filled with blood, causing erection of the penis. The testes (*c*) are also engorged and increase in size and just before orgasm rise against the perineal floor. The dartos tunic (*d*), which covers the testes, is thickened and contracted. A drop of clear mucoid secretion (*e*) from Cowper's gland (*f*) appears at the urethral meatus during intense excitement. (From Kaplan, H. S. *The New Sex Therapy.* New York: Brunner/Mazel, 1974.)

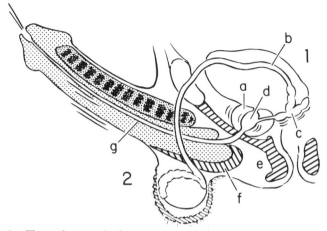

Figure 3–3. The male genitals during orgasm. Phase 1—Emission: This phase is perceived as the sensation of "ejaculatory inevitability." The internal male reproductive viscera [prostate *(a)*, vas deferens *(b)*, seminal vesicles *(c)*] contract and collect the ejaculate in the urethral bulb *(d)*. Phase 2—Expulsion: The perineal *(e)* and bulbocavernosus *(f)* muscles contract with a 0.8 second rhythm, causing pulsations of the penis and expulsion of the ejaculate. The penile urethra *(g)* also contracts. (From Kaplan, H. S. *The New Sex Therapy.* New York: Brunner/Mazel, 1974.)

maintained for variable lengths of time and is parasympathetically mediated. Even if erectile tissue is present and adequately supplied with blood, autonomic nerves, and sensory nerves, the male may fail to have an erection because of psychogenic factors; more typically, the patient may lose his erection after having achieved it but before penetration of the female tract or ejaculation. The second phase of the male sexual response, ejaculation, is sympathetically mediated and this reflex may also be inhibited, causing clinical difficulties with reproduction and sexual activity. Most men are better able to achieve voluntary control over the ejaculatory reflex than over the erection reflex; lack of such control results in premature ejaculation. Age affects the ejaculatory response more than the erection reflex; the frequency of ejaculation decreases with age, while the capacity for erection is relatively unimpaired.[2]

SUMMARY

In summary, the male sexual response, like the female's, is a complex, orderly sequence of events that results in preparation of the genital organs for coitus. The male gonads produce both hormones and sperm, the duct system conducts sperm to the exterior of the body, and accessory structures contribute to the semen in which sperm are carried. Properly stimulated, the penis achieves erection and ejaculation, making possible the placement of sperm in the female reproductive tract. Clinical implications result when there is failure of any of the events leading to the successful placement of sperm in the female tract.

REFERENCES

1. Bishop, David W. Biology of Spermatozoa. In *Sex and Internal Secretions,* Vol. II, 3rd ed. William C. Young (ed.). Baltimore: Williams & Wilkins Co., 1961, pp. 707–796.
2. Kaplan, M. Singer. *The New Sex Therapy.* New York: Brunner/Mazel, 1974, Chapter 1, pp. 5–33.

4

FEMALE REPRODUCTIVE ANATOMY AND SEXUAL RESPONSE

Kermit E. Krantz, M.D., Litt.D.

A prerequisite of an adequate discussion of sexual response is a definition of relevant anatomical terms. This will allow a better understanding of the bodily functions involved in sexual activity.

FEMALE ANATOMY

The vulva of the female comprises the external genital organs, which include the mons pubis, labia majora, labia minora, clitoris, Bartholin's glands, and Skene's glands opening into the vestibule. The hair distribution, size, shape, and coloration of these structures vary among individuals and among racial groups. Pubic hair normally appears in an inverted triangle, with the base centered over the mons pubis.

The various structures of the female have their counterparts or homologues in the male (Fig. 4–1). The labia majora correspond to the scrotum of the male; the posterior commissure to the scrotal raphe; the glans clitoridis to the glans penis; the labia minora to the penile urethral area; and the corpora cavernosa of the clitoris to the penile corpora cavernosa. The vestibular bulbs of the female find their counterpart in the corpus spongiosum of the male; the middle portion of the vestibule is similar to the male's membranous urethra; and the Bartholin glands are homologous to the bulbourethral glands. Both sexes contain identical structures in early embryonic development; the difference at maturity is predicated upon hormonal development of either male or female structures.

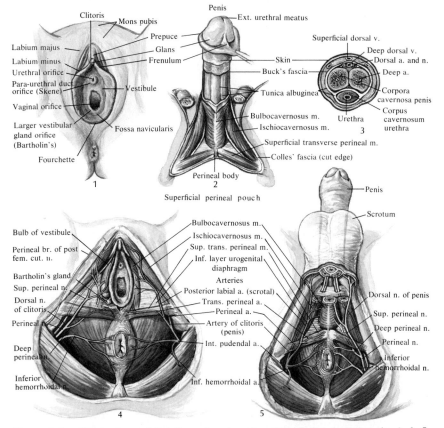

Figure 4–1. Comparison of female and male external genitalia. *1, 4,* Female; *2, 3, 5,* male. (From Healey, J. E., Jr. *A Synopsis of Clinical Anatomy.* Philadelphia: W. B. Saunders Co., 1969.)

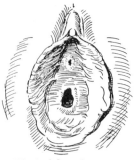

Virginal Introitus

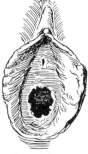

Marital Introitus

Parous Introitus
Showing Myrtiform
Caruncles

Figure 4–2. The intact hymenal ring, the marital introitus, and the parous introitus with "carunculae hymenales." (From Bookmiller, M. M., and Bowen, G. L. *Textbook of Obstetrics and Obstetric Nursing,* 5th ed. Philadelphia: W. B. Saunders Co., 1967.)

The labia majora, originating from the mons pubis and terminating in the perineum, appear as two mounds lying on either side of the labia minora. The labia minora are two hairless folds of skin that lie on either side of the introitus. They are variable in length, thickness, and width and contain corrugations over their surface. Their upper surface is on the clitoris, fusing with the foreskin and frenulum. The labia minora contain glands called the lesser vestibular glands, or glands of Littre, similar to those in the penile portion of the male urethra. The clitoris itself is a homologue of the terminal end of the penis and consists of two small erectile cavernous bodies terminating in the glans clitoridis. Variations in size and length occur from individual to individual. The vestibule is bordered on either side by the labia minora. Two small glands also enter the vestibule on either side, at approximately five and seven o'clock. These glands are called the larger vestibular, or Bartholin's, glands.

Deeper than the superficial structures just described are the bulbocavernosus muscles and vestibular bodies and the ischiocavernosus muscles and their cavernous tissue. The former surround the lateral aspects of the vestibule, while the latter occupy a more lateral and superior position. Where the vestibule joins the vagina appears an inconstant membranous structure — the hymen (Fig. 4–2). The hymen varies in size and shape, depending upon age, parity, and sexual activity. If it has been ruptured, the small remaining tags of tissue are termed the carunculae. The hymenal opening may range in pattern from septate to stellate to crescentic and may, occasionally, be totally imperforate. The length of the vagina varies from 2.7 to 3.9 inches, with the posterior surface the longer because of the additional space behind the cervix. It is without glands, contains folds that are termed "rugae," and varies in shape from similar to an H in its lower portion to crescentic in its upper portion. It is intimately involved with the urethra in its lower third.[2]

FEMALE SEXUAL RESPONSE

INNERVATION

The innervation of the external genitalia is supplied from two sources. The first, supplying the upper portion of the vulva, consists of segmental fibers originating from the last thoracic and the first and second lumbar nerves. These nerves traverse the abdomen along the pelvic border to supply the mons pubis, the labia majora, and part of the labia minora. They are termed the iliohypogastric, ilioinguinal, and genital femoral nerves. In addition, nerves from the sacral plexus form fibers that descend through the pelvis and enter the perineum in the region of the junction of the rectum and the introitus. Termed the pudendal nerves, they send fibers onto the perineal area, the labia minora, and the clitoris itself.

The nerve bundles and fibers just described contain both sensory and motor elements. The vagina receives its very sparse innervation from fibers of the parasympathetic and sympathetic systems, through ganglia that lie adjacent to the uterus and bladder. These nerves are primarily motor in nature, with a very minimal number of sensory elements. The microscopic innervation or types of free nerve endings, as well as their distribution, are of significance. These nerve endings are divided into four distinct groups: touch, pressure, pain, and special types.

The endings modulating touch are Meissner's corpuscles, Merkel's tactile disk, and peritrichal endings. Touch fibers supply the mons area, labia majora, labia minora, and clitoris, but are noticeably absent in the vagina.[1]

The pressure-sensitive endings are the pacinian corpuscles, which control the sensation of deep-tension pressure. They are large enough to be seen by the naked eye and are present in great abundance in the external genitalia, the mons area, the labia majora, the labia minora, and the clitoris. They are also seen within the genital area but are absent in the hymenal ring and the vagina. Pacinian corpuscles play a significant role in sexual activity. As engorgement increases, pressure within the nerve bundle is transmitted to the deep-pressure–sensitive pacinian endings, reducing the participation necessary for discharge. Participation in this process constitutes their primary function within the corpus cavernosum of the clitoris and the vestibular bulbs on either side of the introitus during orgasm.[1]

The third modality of nerve ending is the free pain ending. The sensation of pain is achieved through these endings, and they are distributed equally over the mons veneris, labia majora, and labia minora and, in greater numbers, in the hymenal ring. Free pain endings are unique in that, as sparse as they are, they represent the only kind present within the vagina.

There are also other types of specialized endings. Ruffini's corpuscles lie deep in the skin or in the subcutaneous connective tissue. Their exact role is not known but is believed to be related to that of the Dogiel-Krause type corpuscles discussed below. Ruffini's corpuscles are seen abundantly in the mons veneris, and in above average amounts in the labia minora, but are absent in the hymenal ring and the vagina. Some investigators believe that they perceive warmth, and others that they play a role in the perception of sexual stimulation. The Dogiel-Krause corpuscles (or genital corpuscles of Krause) vary tremendously in size and shape. They appear to be degenerated pacinian corpuscles, except that there is extensive arborization within their capsule. As previously stated, they may be in close proximity to Ruffini's corpuscles. Many workers feel that Dogiel-Krause corpuscles act as thermal receptors or receptors for sexual stimuli. These corpuscles are seen in small amounts in the mons pubis and the labia majora, and in large numbers in the labia minora. They are absent in the clitoris, the hymenal ring, and the vagina.[1]

The distribution of the endings just described is approximate. There is distinct variation in the number and distribution of the various types of endings from female to female. In fact, studies cite some individuals with total absence of deep-pressure specialized endings in either the clitoris or the labia minora and others without such endings in the labia minora but with an abundance of them in the clitoris. Displacement of the greater number of endings to the area of the posterior commissure has even been reported. These variations would therefore suggest that sexual stimulation of the erogenous zones may also vary from individual to individual. Deep-pressure specialized nerve endings are also seen in abundance in the area of the lips, the areoli of the breasts, and the plantar and palmar surfaces. Aggregations of the various types of endings may be found localized in the neck and axillary area and displaced along the breast line from the axilla to the inguinal region.[1]

PHYSIOLOGICAL COMPONENTS OF SEXUAL RESPONSE

Understanding the physiological responses to sexual arousal requires a review of the most significant work completed on this subject—that of Masters and Johnson.[3] These authors have described various areas of the body during the excitement phase, the excitement plateau, and the orgasmic and resolution phases of the sexual response cycle. General changes that take place during this cycle in the human female include hyperventilation, an increased respiratory rate (as high as 40 breaths per minute during the orgasmic phase), and an increased heart rate of 110 to 180 beats per minute. Variations in the intensity of the female orgasm in turn reflect variations in the heart rate, with an increase during the plateau phase. Cardiac demand correlates directly with the rate of rising tension in sexual excitement. Similarly, blood pressure also becomes elevated during excitement, plateau, and orgasm, registering at 20 to 80 mm. of mercury diastolic. A natural consequence, therefore, is widespread perspiration over the body, not only during, but also following orgasm.

The nipples become erect with progressive turgidity during excitement, the size of the breast increasing during the plateau phase and gradually decreasing during resolution. A maculopapular rash descends from the face, over the neck, to the chest during excitement, evolving into a well developed flush over the entire body during the plateau. This also increases in intensity in direct correlation with the extent of orgasm. Muscle tension during excitement and plateau are dependent upon the degree of excitement, with loss of voluntary control culminating in clonic and tonic spasms during orgasm and relaxation following orgasm. Both voluntary and involuntary contractions of the anal sphincter also occur during orgasm.

ORGAN RESPONSE

The vulval response to sexual stimulation begins with vascular engorgement in the area of the mons pubis, accompanied by perspiration from the sweat glands. According to Masters and Johnson,[3] the labia majora thin and flatten out against the perineum, with a slight elevation upward and outward from the introitus, depending on the parity of the woman. During prolonged sexual excitement, the labia majora may become markedly engorged with the venous blood and may become edematous. Resolution follows orgasm, though the congestion may persist for a period of two to three hours. The labia minora distend to two or three times their normal size. The tumescence of the labia minora at the peak of the excitement phase results in a definitive color change from pink to bright red, accompanied by secretion from the surface glands. This specific change has been termed the "sex skin change" by Masters; the degree of this response is, in part, dependent upon the parity of the individual, being less intense in the parous than in the nulliparous female. No woman has been observed by Masters to attain orgasm without first displaying this specific sex skin or labia minora color change.[3]

The greater vestibular glands (Bartholin's glands) respond to sexual stimulation by secreting a small amount of mucoid material, which is deposited in the fossa navicularis, a groove between the hymen and the labia minora. The amount secreted in the excitement phase appears to play an insignificant role in coitus. Following the age of 30, the Bartholin glands display little if any function.

The prepuce of the clitoris reacts similarly to the labia minora — with tumescence. The clitoris itself, specifically the glans, demonstrates vasocongestion with tumescence, usually persisting so long as any significant degree of sexual excitement is present. The changes cited by Masters and Johnson that occur within the vagina during sexual excitement include the production of copious transudate. Tumescence in the bulbocavernosus and ischiocavernosus bodies forms the orgasmic platform during the plateau phase and is accentuated during orgasm, with dilation of the upper two thirds of the vagina, full vaginal expansion, and lengthening of the posterior fornix. During resolution, the vagina is no longer distended.[3]

Vascular engorgement within the pelvis during the excitement phase also involves the nerve bundles. Pacinian corpuscles within these bundles are susceptible to vascular changes and probably play a significant role in tripping the orgasmic phase.

Each woman must learn which body areas are most erogenous and most capable of precipitating increased excitement for her. These areas may be learned by the individual only through experimentation. Whenever possible, they should be utilized to heighten the excitement phase in order that the plateau level may be achieved and single or multiple orgasms realized. Woman is capable of multiple organisms of varying intensity, depending in part upon her own mental and emotional outlook regarding the sexual act. Therefore, examination of her own attitude, as well as that of her partner, can help a woman to realize her full capacity for sexual pleasure.

REFERENCES

1. Krantz, K. E. Innervation of Human Vulva and Vagina. *Obstetrics and Gynecology*, 12:382–396, 1958.
2. Krantz, K. E. The Gross and Microscopic Anatomy of the Human Vagina. *Annals of the New York Academy of Science*, 83:89–104, 1959.
3. Masters, William H. and Virginia Johnson. *Human Sexual Response*. Boston: Little, Brown and Company, 1966.

CHAPTER

5

THE SEXUAL HISTORY AND PHYSICAL EXAMINATION

James P. Semmens, M.D., F.A.C.O.G., F.A.C.S.,
and F. Jane Semmens, B.S.

What constitutes a good sexual history? Can the general rules of interviewing be applied to obtaining a sexual history? Can the physical examination be used as an extension of the sexual history? What methods of history-taking are most effective? What are the indications, advantages, and disadvantages of the various methods? Who should take a sexual history? What attitude is best for professionals to assume when discussing sexual problems with a patient or client? How can professionals prepare themselves to be more effective when obtaining a sexual history and discussing sexual problems? These are some questions that those engaged in health care delivery must answer if they are to become effective in providing total patient care, which includes the treatment of psychological as well as somatic manifestations brought about by stress.

The objective of a sexual interview is to obtain an in-depth history of the patient's problems—physical, emotional, and social—and to determine how they are interrelated. Besides obtaining information, the interviewer must provide empathy, comfort, and trust in order to encourage the patient's cooperation. This is equally as important in obtaining a good history as it is in insuring cooperation in the course of treatment. The location of the interview, the surroundings, and the attitude of the interviewer must convey an atmosphere of privacy; otherwise, the patient will not be comfortable and open when invited to talk about personal problems.

INTERVIEWING TECHNIQUES

The sexual interview should begin in such a way that all bits of relevant information have a chance to emerge. The interviewer should ask open-ended questions that invite the patient to explain the problem but that do not indicate the type of response expected. He should word the questions in such a way that in answering, the patient has a broad spectrum of selections from which to choose. Closed questions that imply that the response should be one of only two correct choices, such as "yes" or "no," should be avoided. The history taker should encourage the patient verbally by repeating a key phrase, which suggests that more explanation or clarification is necessary. Nonverbal responses should be used, such as a nod or questioning look, to signify that the response is understood or that further explanation is needed. Direct attention to important themes will elicit pertinent information and not waste time with superfluous data. However, it may become threatening to pursue one line of questioning to the exclusion of other topics, and the patient may withdraw into silence if this imparts the feeling that the interviewer has become biased, judgmental, or personally curious.

OBSERVATION OF BODY LANGUAGE

The key to effective history-taking at the onset is close observation of the patient's behavior, general appearance, dress, and attitude toward the interviewer. The latter should take the time to introduce himself and to invite the patient to identify herself as a person — by name, by her role as wife, mother, professional, and so forth — to help make her comfortable. Often during these first few minutes one can gain more information by observing the appearance, attitude, and mannerisms of the patient than could be obtained in the answers to time-consuming direct questions. Mannerisms such as wringing of the hands, twisting a handkerchief, swinging a foot, shifting from one position to another, chain smoking, chin quivering, and watering eyes should be observed.

CONFRONTATION

There are many techniques that can be employed to elicit information based on observation of outward manifestations of nonverbalized emotions. One of these, confrontation, is a way of encouraging the patient to speak openly about something that is being communicated nonverbally. In a nonthreatening way, the history taker tells the patient about something he is observing in the patient's actions that expresses emotions inconsistent with the words being said. Overt turning away from the interviewer or other partner is an outward sign of nervousness, anxiety, and inner emotional conflict. The patient may be silent, evasive, contradictory, or overly talkative. Tactfully commenting on the evidence of this unexpressed emotional state may precipitate the patient's expressing his true feelings. Emotional outbursts such as anger or tears may be of therapeutic value if they lead to an understanding of the reasons for these feelings. When a message is ambiguous, the interviewer may clarify it by confronting the patient with what he understands to be the meaning by repeating in his own words what he is hearing as it is colored by the outward signs observed.

SUPPORT

Support as an interviewing technique consists of responses that create an atmosphere of understanding, interest, and desire to help. Actions and statements that reassure the patient and relieve uncomfortable emotions may in themselves be therapeutic. If the patient is on the verge of tears, the situation will not be relieved if the interviewer seems embarrassed or hurried or tries to ignore this show of emotion. The interviewer can convey empathy either by quietly allowing the patient time to regain composure or by giving the patient permission to express the intense emotion without guilt or shame. Either method is supportive when used in conjunction with helping the patient explore the reasons for the frustration. The interviewer must convey self-confidence in his ability to handle emotional situations and in making the right decision regarding whether it is better for the patient to vent the emotions or to attempt to regain composure before continuing the interview.

LISTENING

Critical attentive listening is essential as an interviewing technique. One should listen not only to what is said, but also to the tone of voice, choice of words, length of sentences, and hesitations. The interviewer should observe body language so that he can interpret how honestly the patient's feelings are being expressed verbally. The interviewer who makes the patient feel shut off before having a chance to tell about a complaint may miss valuable information and lose the advantage attained by permitting the patient to take an active role in the diagnostic process. History-taking in which the patient actively participates lays the foundation for a good relationship, which may in itself have therapeutic value.

Silence is the most important technique utilized by the interviewer to be a good listener when the patient is speaking freely and informatively about relevant subjects. The history taker should avoid the trap of using silence to organize his own thoughts about how to phrase the wording of his next sentence. Silence should be used as a technique to convey understanding and interested listening.

DIRECT QUESTIONING

Direct questions are used to obtain any pertinent information the patient has not volunteered. Questions should be phrased in such a manner that the patient will be unable to evade the issue. When the patient is speaking freely, the interviewer should try not to suggest the response he wants to hear by unwisely interrupting to ask a question, unless the patient has wandered off the track with superfluous information.

PHYSICAL EXAMINATION

The physical examination should be used as an extension of the interview proper. It may reveal new, significant behavioral observations as well as pertinent physical data. It should be used as a forum in which the history taker educates the patient, answers questions, explodes erroneous myths, and explores fantasies and superstitions concerning real or imagined physical problems.

Discussion of the interviewer's findings is a significant part of the interview process. This involves a concise nontechnical summary of conclusions, a statement of what remains unclear, and a supportive manner that indicates interest in the patient's well-being as well as realistic optimism about the success of therapy. A clear plan of action should be proposed, and the treatment should be undertaken only after there is mutual agreement on the goals. The patient and the interviewer should together decide when the latter will treat, when he will refer, and to whom he will refer.

METHODS OF TAKING A SEXUAL HISTORY

Sexual history-taking can assume many forms. One of the simplest methods is the compilation of data, starting with the chief complaint, the time of onset, and the degree of concern or desire to secure help. It is usually wise to ask about less personal things first and to assess emotional and functional problems later. If the patient is female, it is appropriate to begin with her menstrual history, including the onset of menarche, regularity and duration of periods, and presence or absence of discomfort associated with menses. The next topic might be dating patterns, including parental advice concerning sexual activity. It should

SEXUAL HISTORY

Female

Name _____ Age _____
Single _____ Married _____ Divorced _____ Widowed _____
Occupation _____
Age at onset of menses _____
Emotional preparation for first period _____
Periods regular?_____ No. of days flow_____
Do you have any problems related to menstruation? _____
    Pain or discomfort? mild _____ moderate _____ severe _____
    At what time of your period? Before _____ During _____ After _____
    Periods too heavy _____
    Passing clots _____
    Irregular periods _____
    Need medicine for pain_____
    Stay in bed first day_____
Have you ever had an abnormal Pap smear? _____
Any difficulty in being able to get pregnant? _____
Have you had any gynecological surgery? _____
    If so, what was the operation? _____
    What was the diagnosis? _____
Have you had problems with a discharge? _____
    Itching? _____ Irritation? _____ Odor? _____
Did you see a doctor about it? _____
Diagnosis? _____ What treatment was prescribed? _____
    Did you follow through the treatment? _____
Do you douche? _____ If so, how often? _____ With what? _____
    Any special time? _____
Have you ever been treated for an infection in your tubes or ovaries? _____
    Diagnosis? _____
Have you ever had a venereal disease? _____ Diagnosis? _____
    Treatment? _____
Do menstrual problems, discharge, cramps, etc. affect your sexual
    communication? _____ To what degree? _____ No effect _____
    Slight effect _____ Moderate _____ Always _____
Number of pregnancies _____ Number of live births _____
    Number of miscarriages _____ Number of therapeutic abortions _____
Type of contraception used _____
Is the method satisfactory to prevent pregnancy? _____
    Does it interfere with sexual pleasure? _____
    Are you concerned that it endangers your health? _____
Are you concerned that it interferes with your future fertility? _____
Have you noticed any change in your ability to lubricate during sexual arousal?
Increase_____ Decrease_____
Comment: _____

Figure 5–1.

be determined whether she has any problems with vaginal discharge, such as itching, irritation, or offensive odor, and if at any time she has been treated for infection of her fallopian tubes or ovaries. Questions about douching and personal hygiene may give clues to the patient's comfort with her female role.

Next would be an obstetric history regarding pregnancies and contraceptive methods employed. The patient's comfort with her present method of contraception is very important, especially her attitude toward its risk to her personal health versus risk of pregnancy. This can lead into exploration of her concept of her sexual role, frequency and degree of orgasmic satisfaction, and to what extent the latter may relate to her sexual complaint. In questioning about orgasm, the interviewer must be sure to ascertain when the woman is orgasmic: during coitus, autostimulation, manual manipulation, oral stimulation from her partner, or any combination of these.

Usually, sexual history-taking for males will be more direct, with the chief complaint being either the inability to achieve erection or the inability to control ejaculation. Men seldom complain of dyspareunia, penile irritation, or discharge. Male orientation equates sexual prowess and function with masculinity. Past history of venereal disease may be difficult to obtain, but a history of prostatitis, dysuria, or frequency may permit an in-depth search into genitourinary problems. Guilt regarding past infection may contribute to male dysfunction, especially if the couple is currently working through problems related to infertility.

SEXUAL HISTORY

Male

Name _____ Age _____

Single _____ Married _____ Divorced _____ Widowed _____

Occupation _____

Do you have any problems in achieving erection? _____

Do you have a problem controlling ejaculation? _____

Have you had any urinary tract infections? _____

    What treatment was prescribed? _____

    Did you follow through the treatment? _____

Have you ever suffered trauma to the testicles? _____ Treated by a doctor? _____

Have you had any prostate infection? _____

Are you bothered with urinary frequency? _____ Urgency? _____

    Burning? _____

Have you ever been treated for a nonspecific urethritis? _____

Have you ever been treated for a venereal disease? _____

    Diagnosis? _____   Treatment? _____

Figure 5–2.

Both Partners

Age of earliest sexual activity _____
Premarital sexual activity limitations:

    Masturbation _____   Oral genital sex _____

    Petting _____   Intercourse _____

Were your parents affectionate? _____
Were they touchers? Father _____ Mother _____
Were they a sharing, sexual couple? _____
Is it acceptable for adolescents to stimulate themselves sexually? _____

    For single adults? _____   For married couples? _____

    For yourself? _____   For your partner? _____

Is oral sex acceptable for adolescents instead of intercourse? _____

    For single adults? _____   For married couples? _____

    For yourself? _____   For your partner? _____

Currently are you satisfied with your sexual response? _____

    Are you able to climax? _____

    As frequently as you would like? _____

    As easily as you would like? _____

Do you feel that your partner is satisfied with your sexual interest level? _____

    With your response? _____

    With his (her) capability? _____

Do you have any concern with your ability to respond to your partner's

    sexual needs? _____

Excessive use of alcohol:

    Self _____   Partner _____

Is there a history of diabetes in either family?

    Self _____   Partner _____

Medication for diabetes:

    Self _____   Partner _____

Medication for hypertension:

    Self _____   Partner _____

Grade your relationship as it currently exists in regard to:

    Social communication and interaction 0 1 2 3 4 5

    Verbal communication 0 1 2 3 4 5

    Touching communication 0 1 2 3 4 5

    Affection for each other 0 1 2 3 4 5

    Your sexual needs being met 0 1 2 3 4 5

    Partner's sexual needs being met 0 1 2 3 4 5

    Frequency of sexual communication 0 1 2 3 4 5

Do you think your partner may have a physical problem? _____

    If so, what? _____

Figure 5–2 *Continued.*

COTHERAPY TECHNIQUE

When a relationship is being evaluated, both partners should be present to hear each other express individual points of view, needs, and preferences. Together they should explore how the sexual dysfunction affects their relationship by discussing its onset, the circumstances surrounding it, and any concerns they may experience about their fertility as a result of the current problem. Probably the greatest breakthrough in sexual counseling is the utilization of a cotherapy team, which can provide professional interpretation from both a male and a female orientation. The advantages far outweigh the disadvantages, which might include cost and availability of a skilled cotherapist.

One therapist on the team should be a physician or nurse who is willing to conduct physical examinations of both partners as an extension of the interview to permit the treatment of organic as well as functional problems, which frequently coexist. In our clinic this is referred to as the "sexological examination," and it is conducted with both partners present. It provides a learning experience for the couple as well as an opportunity to treat or rule out specific organic problems. We have found that the sexological examination creates an atmosphere of openness and honesty that often marks an important turning point within the therapeutic module. Many minor problems corrected during this procedure result in maximal benefit because they grant permission for change, the major goal in behavioral modification.

The extremes of types of history-taking are represented by (1) a nonpersonalized data accumulation that the patient may complete with or without the assistance of a nurse or social worker and (2) the interview and history with both partners of the relationship present as well as a cotherapy team.

The interview as an integral part of the therapeutic module is discussed next, along with an explanation of the terms "sex value system" and "comfort index."

ATTITUDE OF THE INTERVIEWER

Which type of sexual history is appropriate? That really depends upon the circumstances and upon the person taking the history. It may be a simple inquiry regarding problems with physical and emotional response. Frequently, direct questioning invites a "yes" or "no" answer and fails to establish communication because it does not allow the patient to express attitudes and feelings. An atmosphere must be created in which the patient feels that the interviewer will not be judgmental but will help explore alternatives and provide enlightenment. Caution should be exercised to avoid seeking information about a specific episode within a relationship and dwelling on it unless the episode is illustrative of the relationship in general, since this may overemphasize its importance. Verbalizing about certain sexual practices with which the patient may be uncomfortable and about the disparity in sexual needs and desires of the partners can be helpful in exposing underlying causes of conflicts and differences. Specific information may be elicited by inquiring whether the person is comfortable within the relationship and whether each partner is meeting the needs of the other. It takes more than a casual inquiry tossed out in an unrelated part of history-taking to obtain the type of information that will be of therapeutic value.

Unfortunately, many professionals assigned the task of taking a sexual history persist in direct questioning that invites "yes" or "no" answers, because subconsciously they do not want detailed information that exposes their own frustrations and sexual attitudes. Patients can sense the comfort of the interviewer very quickly. It is suggested that the interviewer exercise a certain degree of introspection and honesty in an attempt to understand the comfort index within his or her personal sex value system.

LOCATION

Where one obtains a sexual history can be important. Certainly, privacy and comfort are aspects of the most acceptable environment. The office setting conveys a message that expresses the comfort index of the physician or interviewer. One physician who by his own admission was uncomfortable discussing sexual problems with his patients spent little time with them in his consultation room but chose to discuss most of their complaints or needs in an examining area, which was composed of thin-walled cubicles separated from a connecting hallway only by curtains at the door. This arrangement provided privacy for the physical examination but was a deterrent to the discussion of personal matters—patients were forced to make a special request for a more private discussion, and few did. There are other subtle protective mechanisms for the professional who is uncomfortable with his sexuality, such as the familiar statement, "My patients don't have any sexual problems. At least, they're not important enough for them to ask about them in my office."

QUESTIONNAIRES

One "cop-out" is to hand patients a questionnaire that is so lengthy and involved that it would make a Kinsey interview seem like an abstract. Usually the terminology is too sophisticated for most people, and if answers are given at all, there will be a number of contradictions. The sexual history needs to be more open and inclusive if it is to become a part of the therapeutic module. We do not take written notes during our intake, and we assure each couple that our referral sources expect no written report, which would be an invasion of the privacy that the therapists and couple must have in order to be totally open. The patient is far more at ease when little or no note-taking occurs during the discussion of personal and sexual content. If it is a necessity to maintain records, a short dictation following the interview with a client or couple can be accomplished after they have left the room. When we record a session, it is only to prepare a cassette tape for the couple to take home and use as they attempt to better understand their individual differences and expectations for the relationship. This technique opens many lines of communication that the clients have avoided in the past and permits reinforcement of suggestions offered by the therapists.

SEX VALUE SYSTEM

In evaluating patients with sexual dysfunction, Masters and Johnson stressed the importance of interpreting the sex value system each partner brought into the relationship. They define "sex value system" as "all those components important to the individual that are erotic to that individual."[2] Sex value system encompasses the attitudes and emotions resulting from the individual's experiences within a sociocultural structure. Sexuality is that dimension of an individual's personality through which maleness or femaleness is expressed in interaction with other people. This most vulnerable form of human communication is expressed as sexual function in sociocultural relationships, in pair-unit interaction, and in self-gratification.

Sexual functioning is a natural psychophysiological process in which the target organ responsivity may or may not be part of the individual's conscious awareness. Personal needs may be in conflict with societal needs. These sexual values have been referred to as "intrinsic" when derived by individuals from within themselves relative to their personal situations or experiences, and "extrinsic" when related to accepted standards of society concerning right and wrong, good or bad. The ideal situation would be one in which both personal and societal values are the same, rather than one in which the personal values are in conflict with societal values, resulting in the individual's having to sacrifice his needs to fulfill those of society, or vice versa.

Rene Guyon, in *The Ethics of Sexual Acts,* lists four basic handicaps of sexual morality as used in our society:[1]

> 1. False association of ideas: *namely, that one cannot logically attribute moral values to physiological organs. The penis, testicles, vagina, etc. cannot in themselves be good, bad, pure or impure. Such an association contributes to a mental relationship of two facts which are in reality unrelated.*

2. False reasoning from false association: *that society con-demns people who exercise their sexual capabilities as being morally inferior even though this exercise does not interfere with or take advantage of others. A woman's "honor" seems to be based in her sexual organs. False associations of this type either ignore or distort the true nature of the individual.*

3. Conventional classifications which cannot be justified scientifically: *the foremost example of this is to suggest that masturbation is a route to insanity or contributes to female frigidity or male infertility, facts which have been scientifically disproven.*

4. Confusion between physiology and morality: *to assume that the sexual act is a moral or immoral act is to assume that there is no honor or dishonor when two people share sexual pleasure. The act itself is a deliberate exercise of physiological and psychological needs. Only the situation surrounding the act or the persons involved can be judged as moral or immoral.*

In *Introduction to Sexual Counseling*, Robert R. Wilson suggests that the foregoing is not meant to imply that all value systems are always corruptive forces working against an individual's basic freedoms, or that sexuality is value-free.[3] When many of our societal values concerned with human sexuality are definitely misplaced, they become a contributing cause to sexual inhibition and, in extreme cases, to sexual dysfunction. Many people are directed by such standards and consider them to be moral, ethical, normal, mature, or simply the way things are.

INITIAL INTAKE

In the cotherapist approach to treatment of sexual dysfunction, the initial intake is a session during which the couple's sexual histories are developed. The therapists attempt to interpret each partner's sex value system by exploring and discussing childhood, adolescent, dating, and premarital experiences; the differing sexual attitudes of being reared as a male or a female child in a particular cultural setting; comfort in touching and being touched; and both partners' concept of their parents as a sexual couple. These learning experiences, in combination with the clients' interpretation of societal standards, constitute the sex value system that each individual brought into the relationship. One valuable technique we employ during this initial intake is to ask both partners to relax, close their eyes, take themselves back to their midteens, and try to visualize their parents in the privacy of their room, unclothed, in a torrid embrace as a warm, sharing sexual couple. The clients' responses to this type of information become a vital part of the therapeutic module and open lines of communication and understanding for the dysfunctional couple.

INDIVIDUAL CROSS-INTERVIEWS

Each partner is interviewed separately by each cotherapist. During these interviews, private information concerning past sexual experiences which may contribute to a sense of guilt, insecurity, or inferiority are discussed. These may include rape, incest, masturbation, venereal infections, and extramarital affairs, as well as attitudes, differences, and fantasies that the client feels may be detrimental to the relationship. Often, this is material that the client feels the other partner cannot handle. Although it may represent an invasion of individual privacy initially, sharing it with an empathetic therapist can be of therapeutic value.

COMFORT INDEX FOR THE CLIENTS

Another dimension of the interview with both partners is determination of the comfort index of each as a sexual person who gives as well as receives sexual pleasure and communication within the relationship. When both partners are able to verbalize their feelings, this index permits insight into hostile etiologic factors that may contribute to the current problem. The true therapeutic value of the comfort index and sex value system is best understood when the dysfunctional couple becomes fully aware of what each partner brought into the relationship and what his or her expectations were. What has become increasingly evident to us is that even though these differences are suspected or known, little had been accomplished in negotiating individual needs and differences prior to seeking counsel. Instead, each partner waited for the other to change, which is unrealistic, since patterns of human behavior and sexual needs often represent years of conditioning. A great degree of cooperation and effort is required on the part of both individuals to bring about change. Before behavioral modification is attempted, the individuals within the relationship must accept who and what they are and must develop mutual trust and understanding. Their primary goal should be enrichment of the relationship.

CLASSIFICATION AND CONCEPT OF SEXUAL DYSFUNCTION

Inability to cope with the stress of everyday living may assume neurotic manifestations of varying degrees of anxiety or depression, which may be expressed by one or both partners in their interpersonal relationship as sexual dysfunction. If the dysfunction is not recognized and treated, it is possible for the neurosis to deepen into psychosis;

ANXIETY

♂	♀
Premature ejaculation	Primary nonorgasmia Vaginismus
Ejaculatory impotence	Dyspareunia
Decreased sexual interest	Decreased sexual interest
Seminal seepage	Sexual withdrawal
Impotence	Secondary nonorgasmia

DEPRESSION

Figure 5–3. Forms of sexual dysfunction correlated with anxiety and depression.

however, in our clinical experience, 95 per cent of couples with sexual dysfunction present with symptoms that can be classified as minor forms of situational neuroses that are amenable to short psychosexual therapy.

Anxiety represents a triggered, excitable, uncontrollable response, whereas depression represents withdrawal and insecurity. It is possible to correlate these extremes of neurotic behavior with sexual dysfunction. For the male, premature ejaculation is associated with anxiety and insecurity, while impotence is associated more frequently with depression and loss of personal esteem and sense of self-worth. When due to psychological causes, ejaculatory impotence, seminal seepage, and decreased sex interest can be classified along the scale between premature ejaculation and impotence (Fig. 5–3). Female dysfunction is classified as forms of anorgasmia, loss of libido, dyspareunia, and vaginismus. Primary nonorgasmia and vaginismus are associated with anxiety, immaturity, and insecurity, while secondary nonorgasmia, dyspareunia, and loss of libido are more likely to be associated with depressive reaction, loss of self-esteem, frustration, disappointment, and personal insecurity within the relationship. Women who are occasionally orgasmic with autostimulation, oral techniques, or vibrators and who are uncomfortable giving or receiving affection from another person would be classified at midscale, because they can respond only in impersonal situations.

COMFORT INDEX FOR THE INTERVIEWER; SEX ATTITUDE REASSESSMENT

Sex attitude reassessment programs for professionals and patients permit them to examine their own values and their comfort with various types of sexual behavior. An effective therapist, counselor, or interviewer taking any kind of sexual history must possess the capability to understand and accept the patient's right to whatever form of sexual expression he or she prefers. If patients feel that the nurse, doctor, or social worker cannot understand their needs or desires for homosexual or bisexual expression, oral or anal sex, or any other form of sexual behavior, they will be unable to engage in meaningful dialogue. The principal reason for this inability would be the patient's desire to avoid causing embarrassment to the interviewer. Also, the therapist who lacks empathy and understanding is seldom able to offer any therapeutic help.

A high comfort index and openness in sexual attitudes are a must for the interviewer. Most professionals are introspective enough to know that the principal reason they do not get involved in sexual history-taking is their own lack of comfort with sexual content. It may be possible for their attitudes and comfort levels to change with attendance at professionally sponsored sex attitude reassessment programs specifically designed to allow the interviewers exposure to a variety of audiovisual sexual materials. Facilitators encourage attendees to express their reactions and work through their positive and negative feelings in relation to what they have seen. These sessions are not designed to change one's own sex value system but to create a capacity for greater understanding, empathy, and acceptance of the sexual practices of others. The interviewer may be uncomfortable or repulsed by such practices as oral sex or homosexuality, but in order to be effective, he must become accepting and sympathetic with the patient who finds these pleasurable. It has only been recently that homosexuality has become an accepted method of sexual expression rather than being considered pathologic behavior. The majority of society, however, as manifest by existing state laws, remains intolerant of the practice.

Sex attitude reassessment can also be accomplished by increased reading to help the interviewer better understand most sexual practices. The process will lack the impact of an audiovisual program conducted by professionals, but it may be the most comfortable way for some to become more knowledgeable and to work through their feelings. Sexual values, needs, fantasies, and feelings are a very private part of our emotional self and need to be worked through privately. The important thing is not *how* professionals prepare themselves to become more comfortable with sexual material, but rather *that* they prepare themselves so that they do not appear judgmental or rejecting of patients and clients seeking their help.

LANGUAGE IN SEXUAL HISTORY TAKING

Medical terminology cannot always be used with all clients. Professionals should familiarize themselves with slang and jargon expressions for sexual material so that they understand the meanings and can be comfortable when they are used by clients. To register horror or disgust when a client uses such slang, to suggest the use of medical terms instead, implies that the client's language is inappropriate and unacceptable, which may be interpreted as a form of rejection. The result is usually embarrassment to the client, who will become defensive and refuse to discuss important subjects for fear of not meeting the interviewer's standards. Allowing clients to use their own language and giving them permission to be unfamiliar with medical terminology is one way to show acceptance. Imposing a new vocabulary on them has the same effect as forcing a totally new value system upon them.

PHYSICAL EXAMINATION

The physical examination should be an extension of history-taking in the delivery of health care. The term "sexological examination" has been applied to that portion of the physical examination of the sexually dysfunctional couple during which attention is directed toward the genitalia and pelvic structures as well as other areas of the body considered capable of erotic stimulation and physiological response. This type of examination permits the professional to ask specific questions relative to degrees of pleasurability or discomfort and to ascertain to what extent the effects of surgery, disease processes, congenital abnormalities, or loss of pelvic muscle tone and turgor contribute to sexual dysfunction.

We have found that the sexological examination provides a meaningful area for honesty and dialogue between therapists and clients. A recent example was that of a dysfunctional male who had sustained a spinal cord injury and who was able to achieve only partial erection. At the time of the examination, his spouse was found to have a virginal introitus, which indicated to the therapists that the couple had never consummated their marriage, although the dialogue in history-taking had suggested otherwise.

It has been our practice to precede the sexological examination with instruction about it in the office setting, utilizing those means of communication that are best adapted to the clients' intellectual capacity. The approaches that we use most frequently include illustrations from the text *Human Sexual Response* by Masters and Johnson,[2] which one of the therapists draws on 3 × 5 cards, or video tapes that illustrate all aspects of male and female sexual physiology. The couple is informed that the sexological examination will permit them to better understand what they have learned as it applies to themselves: their individual differences, capabilities, and responses.

Sexological Examination of the Male

The sexological examination of the male must include an evaluation of the external genitalia, with attention to evidence of local disease and abnormalities that would contribute to male dyspareunia or impotence. Particularly important is any evidence of scar tissue or fibrosis of the corpus spongiosum of the penis, which may contribute to special problems for the uncircumcised male, and hypospadias, which may result in spraying or ejaculation outside of the vaginal barrel, contributing to infertility and leading to avoidance of sexual communication. We observed one male client with a scar extending from the dorsal coronal ridge to the shaft of the penis who experienced dyspareunia with erection, and sufficient pain with intromission to cause impotence.

Examination of the testes and scrotum should include attention to the possible presence of hydrocele or varicocele, disparity in the size of the testes, and any excessive tenderness, which may be indicative of old trauma or tumor. In the older male, it is important to evaluate the prostate gland and to rule out prostatitis, benign hypertrophy, or a possible neoplastic lesion. During the perineal examination of the male, we illustrate the squeeze technique for controlling premature ejaculation, if necessary, and teach the couple the location of specific areas of response posterior to the scrotum in the median raphe, anterior to the anus, that are pleasurable. The cremasteric reflexes are checked. The responsiveness of male nipple and breast to stimulation is also taught as part of the indoctrination of a female partner who has not been comfortable touching her partner during sexual communication. Special instructions of this type are particularly important in therapy of the impotent male.

Sexological Examination of the Female

The sexological examination of the female is usually initiated with examination of the breast and nipple response. It is sometimes possible to illustrate the cutaneous flush that occurs on the anterior chest wall and neck and occasionally spreads to the face. The breasts are examined for masses, lumps, cysts, abnormal vascular patterns, and evidence of nipple discharge or irritation. It is important to rule out neoplastic breast disease, and to assure clients that breast stimulation does not contribute to cancer and that oral stimulation is safe for the non-nursing female. A number of women have been taught to avoid breast stimulation, especially oral stimulation of the nipples, with the warning that it may cause infection or cancer.

During pelvic examination, the female partner uses a mirror so that both partners can familiarize themselves with the anatomy of the genitalia. Particularly important are a discussion about the clitoris, determination of the presence or absence of adhesions about the glans of the clitoris, and an appraisal of clitoral size, since many women feel that their clitoris is too small. Occasionally, adhesions may be present or the prepuce may be extensive enough to interfere with visualization or stimulation. We explain that the clitoris is a nonlubricating organ whose only function is sexual pleasurability. We emphasize that continued stimulation causes drying and irritation of the glans, producing sufficient discomfort to inhibit orgasm.

Other lesions of the female external genitalia capable of contributing to dysfunction are urethral caruncles, bartholinitis, and scarring of the perineum from pelvic surgery, episiotomy, and obstetric lacerations. Pressure is placed in the scarred areas of the vagina and the hymenal ring, and any clinical evidence of vaginismus is noted.

The internal pelvic examination is essentially the same as any bimanual and speculum examination, except that the mirror is used during the speculum examination, offering both clients an opportunity to visualize the cervix and vaginal walls. With the patient still in lithotomy position, the tone of the pubococcygeal and levator muscles is evaluated, and Kegel exercises are taught (see Chapter 13). The male partner is now asked to examine the female partner, as the female may have done if she so chose during his examination. It is important that the sexual partner evaluate the degrees of sensitivity to pleasure, particularly in areas of old scar formation. The male partner is instructed to ask the female to communicate the degrees of pleasurability versus discomfort in her vagina, since it has been shown that if the nerve supply has been interfered with and turgor is lost, scars may be painful enough to contribute to loss of sexual interest or response. The bimanual examination completes the female sexological examination and rules out any deep pelvic pathologic process capable of causing discomfort during sexual arousal or coitus.

Summary

It is important that any patient experiencing sexual problems have a thorough sexological examination. The intent of this history and examination should not be solely data collection, but also the education of the patient and partner, so that misunderstandings can be avoided.

REFERENCES

1. Guyon, Rene. The Ethics of Sexual Acts. In *Studies in Sexual Ethics,* Vol. 1. New York: Knopf, 1948. Reprint: New York: Octagon, 1972.
2. Masters, William H. and Virginia Johnson. *Human Sexual Inadequacy.* Boston: Little, Brown and Company, 1970.
3. Wilson, Robert R. *Introduction to Sexual Counseling.* Chapel Hill, North Carolina: Carolina Population Center, 1974.

CHAPTER
6

SEXUAL COUNSELING

M. Edward Clark, Ed.R.D.

THE NITTY-GRITTY OF COUNSELING

Counseling is the process by which the counselor enables the client to become his own counselor. It is not giving advice or telling the client about himself or what to do. It is, rather, an educational process in which the counselor teaches the client how to discover things about himself — things that have not been a part of awareness previously.

Clients who come for counseling with the belief that the counselor is possessed of some sort of magic or esoteric wisdom are doomed to disappointment. The only skill that the counselor has is the skill of helping the client in the hard work of self-healing. Clients who come for counseling with the implicit request, "Do me something, counselor," are asking for the impossible. Such clients reveal themselves in short order. It soon becomes apparent to them and to the counselor that no work is taking place between counseling sessions.

When that happens, as it often does, it is the function of the counselor to confront the client with the fact of his inactivity and his desire for magic. Such confrontation will elicit some kind of reaction. It may cause the client to withdraw from counseling or to go on looking for magic by counselor hopping. It may awaken the client to the reality of the counseling process so that he begins the work process both in and out of the counseling sessions. It may not have much effect at all, so that the confrontation by the counselor will have to be repeated. This leads us to say, therefore, that confrontation is an integral part of the counseling process.

THE DECISION TO SEEK COUNSELING

Typically, the counseling process goes through three stages. The initial stage is one of relief that the help-seeking decision has been made and the process is started. There may have been a great deal of turmoil of mind and emotion prior to the decision. Our culture implies that people should be able to solve their own problems and, therefore, that seeking help is a sign of weakness. This is especially true among

44

men who have the injunction to be strong and self-sufficient. Women may hesitate to seek counseling because of the same injunction or because they feel that it will be a reflection on the manhood of their spouse.

The first great step forward, therefore, is the decision to seek counseling. The counselor has the opportunity in the initial session to give the counselee strong support for the decision. People who come for counseling very often ask the specific question, "Do you see any hope?" The response of the counselor is obvious: "You are in my office seeking help. That is the first great sign of hope."

WHO IS TO BE CHANGED?

The second phase that usually occurs in counseling is that in which it becomes apparent that the counselee wants the change to take place in some other person. In the counseling of married couples this is almost inevitable: "If only he/she would . . . ." In the terms of transactional analysis this is a discount of the other person and indicates that one of the games being played is "If it weren't for him/her." It is also an indication of life position: "I'm O.K. Spouse is not O.K." Or, in other terms, it represents a "one-up" position, which by implication put the other person "one down."

All games begin with a discount. It may be a self-discount or a discount (real or imagined) from another person.

Self-discounts are also destructive of healthful interpersonal relations. The person who comes to the health professional saying: "It's all my fault or it's all my problem," is in a self-discount, one-down position. His life position, therefore, is in the "I'm not O.K. He/she is O.K." The game here may be "Kick Me" or it may be a "Humility" or "Guilt" racket.

THE CLIENT NEEDS TO BE CHANGED

In some respects it may be easier to move from the "I'm not O.K.; he/she is O.K." to the third phase of counseling, which is the recognition on the part of the client that change within himself is necessary. Along with this realization should come a complementary realization that each person is responsible for his own change. No one person can change another person. We can only change ourselves. We can, however, decide what we want from another person in a relationship and communicate that want to the other person. He then can respond either by giving what is wanted, if that is possible, or by giving part of what is wanted, or by refusing to give what is wanted.

For many people in counseling, coming on straight about what is wanted is one of the internal changes that needs to take place. In our culture it is "not nice" to ask for anything for ourselves. Others are supposed to be mindreaders and guess what our wants and needs are and then meet those needs or satisfy those wants. Sometimes this works; more often it doesn't.

To express our needs and wants does not necessarily mean that all our needs and wants will be fulfilled. It does mean that we are no longer engaged in guessing games. Also, if wants and needs are out in the open, it is then possible to consider them objectively (from our Adult ego state). This greatly increases the possibility of fulfillment, or of an understanding of why fulfillment is not possible at the particular time.

When phase three in counseling is reached, the prospects of success in the counseling situation are greatly enhanced. The situation is then reminiscent of the nest of quails in the farmer's wheat field. The baby birds heard the farmer say that tomorrow his neighbor would come to cut the wheat. All the young birds were fearful and anxious to move out of the field. The mother bird was calm, however, and insisted that there was no hurry. The neighbor did not show up the next day, as the mother bird had foreseen. The farmer came again to the field and was overheard to say: "Tomorrow my brother will come to cut the wheat." Again the baby birds wanted to move. Again the mother said, "There is plenty of time." Of course the brother did not come to cut the wheat either. So it went until finally the farmer said: "Tomorrow I will cut the wheat myself." Then the mother bird said: "Now it is time to move."

When clients decide that the changes have to take place within them and that each individual is responsible for his own change, then the counselor can be assured that the time for movement toward wholeness and interpersonal growth and communication has arrived.

THREE BASIC RESOURCES OF THE COUNSELOR

It is important for anyone engaging in counseling to be aware of the three basic ingredients that make for success in counseling. Those basics are knowledge, rapport, and counselor comfort.

Knowledge. It goes without saying that anyone who wishes to engage in counseling has an ethical responsibility to engage in education and training before hanging out a shingle or announcing the intent to counsel. This is not to say that no counseling is done by people who have had no formal training. On the contrary, informal counseling is carried on almost universally. Some informal counseling is helpful and therapeutic. Some of it is not therapeutic but harmless. Some may be harmful. This kind of informal counseling is going to continue. However, if a person intends to counsel in a professional way, it is imperative that he or she acquire the necessary professional credentials.

There are many avenues through which credentials may be obtained. Many universities offer courses and advanced degrees in counseling. There are, of course, advanced degrees in psychology and in social work. The medical and nursing professions offer degrees in psychiatry. A great many theological seminaries require courses in pastoral counseling and offer courses in clinical pastoral education. A few universities offer specialized training in marriage and sexual counseling. Masters and Johnson, at the Reproductive Biology Research Foundation in St. Louis, offer specialized training in sexual counseling. Medical schools and nursing schools now include required courses on marital and sexual counseling as part of the curriculum. There are currently many sources of training in the fields of transactional analysis, gestalt therapy, and reality therapy in almost every large city. There is no excuse, therefore, for untrained counselors. The fact is that those who are seriously engaged in counseling, regardless of the degrees they may have earned, continue to seek out ways to improve their knowledge and skills.

Anyone engaged in the counseling profession is continually in the process of gaining more knowledge and skills. Clinical experience and research are constantly providing fresh information and insights that can increase the effectiveness of the counselor. The continuing pursuit of knowledge is one of the things that make counseling an exciting profession.

Rapport. Knowledge, to be useful, has to become incarnate in an individual. Computers can store more knowledge than the human brain. They can give out information and even respond to questions. But only the human personality has the ability to empathize with and respond to another human personality.

When counselor and clients meet there are literally thousands of nonverbal and verbal interactions that will have a bearing on the outcome of the counseling. Given the wide diversity among human beings, it is inevitable that certain people respond differently to a given counselor. In cases in which there is a strong initial negative response on the part of the client, the probability is that not much will happen in the counseling sessions, regardless of how successful that counselor may have been with other clients.

This sense of mutual trust and regard is referred to as rapport. It is generally agreed that rapport is an essential ingredient in counseling. Without at least a minimum of rapport, counseling is apt to produce no positive results and may, in fact, have a negative effect.

Rapport is not something that you either have or you don't. The ability to create a setting where rapport can be established with a client can be learned. There are a few simple rules. The client can be put at ease by the friendliness of the counselor, by smiling and keeping eye contact, and by letting the client express his feelings (at the beginning of the first session) about coming to a counselor. It is also important that the counselor show concern for the client as a person and express confidence in his own ability to be helpful.

Rapport grows stronger as the client begins to feel that he is not placed in a "one-down" position. Communication at any depth will not take place until rapport is established. Regardless of the training of the counselor or the particular counseling approach he uses, rapport is an absolute necessity. It is as important as, or even more important than, the counseling method used.

Comfort. Closely related to rapport is the comfort level of the counselor. This involves the counselor's ability to listen to the client with his Adult ego state, that is to say, without judgmental inner or outer responses. Clients seem to have an intuitive sense about the freedom with which they can speak to counselors, and they refrain from telling the counselor anything that they feel he will be unable to handle emotionally. It may be kind of the client to spare the counselor an emotional response, but the chances are that the client will seek another counselor who he senses will be comfortable with whatever he may want to reveal.

The proof of the importance of counselor comfort, or lack of it, is abundantly apparent if one talks with women about how they feel about discussing sexual questions with their physicians. It is rare indeed for a woman acquaintance or client to say that she feels comfortable in talking openly about sexual subjects with her doctor, even with her gynecologist. One client related that when she went for a physical examination prior to her marriage, the doctor met with her in the office following the physical, sat at his desk with head bowed and eyes averted, and mumbled: "You're all right 'down there'." That was the extent of his report.

Another woman stated that though she felt she had a good relationship with her doctor over a period of several years, she could never bring herself to discuss a sexual problem that she had in her marriage. Because of this, she finally changed to a woman physician, who then referred her to a counselor. This woman's intuition told her that she could not discuss her sexual problem with her doctor without making him uncomfortable. She could have been mistaken, but she was probably right.

Counselor discomfort reveals the areas where the counselor needs counseling or information or both. The two most frequent areas of discomfort are those of human sexuality and death and dying. Our own attitudes about sexuality are so much a part of us that we assume that they are right and ought to be universally accepted. If any discussion of sexuality was a "no-no" in our family as we were growing up, and it was and still is in most families, then we, very likely, will be uncomfortable if the subject is brought forward for discussion by a client. Death is often a taboo area even in counseling situations. If one is doing counseling and has discomfort in discussing sexuality or death or any other area, he should recognize it as a signal and get some counseling.

Transference and countertransference (not in the Freudian sense) also enter into the picture. In simpler terms, this amounts to the emotional responses between client and counselor. As Masters and Johnson have demonstrated by research, we are all sexual beings. Every counseling situation, therefore, has a sexual component to a greater or lesser degree.

What's the procedure when a counselor becomes "turned on" by an attractive client or when the client experiences sexual feelings? Ethics as well as good counseling procedure indicate that restraints are essential. In some instances it is well to acknowledge the attraction involved and then go on to say that any sexual involvement under the circumstances would be destructive rather than therapeutic. One may lose a client, but it is better to lose a client than get involved in a situation that might destroy a practice or endanger one's certification as a counselor.

IDENTIFYING THE PROBLEMS

It is not unheard of for people to seek counseling and at the same time not be able to tell the counselor what the problem is. In most instances the client will be able to state in general terms what the problem seems to be. This is referred to as the "presenting problem." It may or may not be the only problem or the real problem. This is particularly true if the presenting problem is indicated as sexual. Apart from some physical disability or illness, it is safe to say that there are no purely sexual problems.

The presenting problem, however, is a starting point. Each counselor will decide on what seems then to be the appropriate procedure. Regardless of the procedure, the counselor will be aiming at establishing a contract with the client.

CONTRACTS

Briefly stated, a counseling contract involves what the counselor is prepared to contribute to the counseling situation and what the client is prepared to contribute. In most instances, the counselor contributes skill and concern in exchange for some monetary reward by the client or by the organization he represents. The client is also asked to make contracts about the changes he wishes to make. Contracts need to be specific. "I want to be happy" is not a contract. "I will own my own feelings and tell my spouse when I am angry" is a contract. "I will write a story about my favorite animal" is a contract. "I will think good thoughts" is not. "I will try to stop watching T.V. all day Saturday" is not a contract. "I will stop watching T.V. on Saturday" is.

The questions that need to be repeated at frequent intervals, then, are these: What is it that you want to change in your attitude or behavior? What kind of contract do you wish to make in order to bring about these changes? The role of the counselor is to give the client permission to make the changes he wishes to make, to be potent and positive in his support of the client in making the changes, and to offer protection to the client during the change process. Protection consists of being available for support when the client needs that support to fulfill the contract.

If a client is suicidal, the immediate contract is "Don't kill yourself." In support of that contract the counselor gives protection by being available by phone or in person if necessary. A counselor with an unlisted phone number is not in a position to offer protection when and if it may be needed.

Contracts, if they are to work, must be made by the Adult ego state. They are positive statements of what the client is agreeing to do or not to do. It is generally helpful if the client writes the contract down and takes a copy with him. If the contract is not carried out according to plan, the logical question is "How did you stop yourself from doing what you said you would do?"

Contracts are, of course, renewable and changeable, and new ones are appropriate at any time. Obtaining positive, specific contracts is sometimes quite difficult and may take several sessions. They are the best grounds for success in the counseling situation.

THE MIDDLE

Thus far we have been speaking primarily of the beginning stages of the counseling process. That is, the initial phase of counseling consists of establishing rapport, identifying the problem(s), deciding on a counseling approach (tentative), and securing a contract. There is also a middle and an end.

The middle phase of the counseling process consists of fulfilling the initial contract, making new contracts, and fulfilling them, until the client is satisfied that he has attained his goal. The nature of the problem will determine the length of the counseling.

Eric Berne had as his goal the curing of the patient in the first session. If he was unable to do that, then he wanted to cure him in the second session, and so on. Cure in one session may be possible if, for example, a couple comes with the presenting problem of premature ejaculation on the part of the male, but even then it is unlikely, for it will take a number of practice sessions on the part of the couple before the problem is solved.

In most instances a series of sessions is required. It may take three or more sessions to establish rapport, identify the problem, and establish a contract. One of the problems that the counselor faces is that many clients expect to work out their difficulties in a very short time. That is understandable but not realistic.

The middle phase of counseling in many instances seems the most difficult, for there are times when progress seems at a standstill. It is important, then, to continue to work on "mini-contracts" that can be carried out successfully within a short time. Confrontation needs to be balanced with support. It is good to remember that the goal of counseling is to remove the "pain," not just to lessen it.

It is during the middle stage of counseling when the side effects begin to show up in the persons with whom the client is interpersonally related. It is a truism that if one person in a family of two or more changes, the others in the family are forced to change also. It may even be that if one member of the family gets well, another member of the family will become ill. A common example of this is seen in the situation in which a woman comes in for counseling because she has been nonorgastic in her sexual experience and nonmotivated toward sexual activity with her spouse. In the course of counseling she has a change of attitude and increases her sexual desire and she becomes orgastic. So now instead of being resistant to her husband's sexual approaches she becomes the aggressor. Quite a change! In prospect the husband felt this would be terrific. In actuality he finds his manhood threatened and in a short time becomes impotent. This becomes a new facet of the problem that must also enter into the counseling.

This may be the appropriate time to indicate that there has been a significant change in the way counseling is done. Until recently it was thought that each member of the family should have a separate counselor, rather than conjoint counselors. This is no longer the case for an increasingly large number of counselors and therapists. Conjoint and family counseling has proved to be much more effective. This does not mean that individuals are never seen on a one-to-one basis. It does mean that a significant portion of the counseling is done on a conjoint or total family basis. When both spouses or an entire family is present, the counselor has the opportunity to observe patterns of communication and relationships as they are happening. This brings the counseling situation into the immediate present.

THE END OF COUNSELING

If the counselor has a firm contract with the client, then the client will know when the contract has been fulfilled. The counselor will generally know also when the goals of the counseling are being reached. This is something that the counselor will check out frequently as the counseling progresses. It is desirable to discuss with the client the termination of counseling. Thus some notice can be taken of what has happened and the changes that have taken place can be recognized and affirmed. It is a time, also, when the clients can become more aware of their ability to be their own counselors.

GROUP COUNSELING

What has already been said, for the most part, has application to one-to-one counseling, conjoint counseling, family counseling, or group counseling. More and more counselors are engaging in group counseling for a number of reasons.

First of all, it is a more expeditious use of the counselor's time. The mathematics of this are obvious. One-to-one counseling with eight people would require the time of a counselor for a very full day. Conjoint counseling with couples (four) would require approximately 4 hours. One group session with four couples or eight people would require an hour and a half.

Time, however, is not the greatest advantage. The greatest advantage is the contribution that the other members of the group can make to the counseling session. Their insights are often right to the point. It also happens that people will relate to other members of the group (or play the same games with them) in the same way that they relate in the family situation.

Still a third advantage is that many counselors work with a co-counselor in a group situation. If possible, a co-counselor should be of the opposite sex so that both male and female insights are available to the group. And it is easier for two people to observe what is happening in the group than it is for one person to see it. Co-counselors need to work out in advance their own relationships so that they do not fall into competitive games in the counseling situation. A part of the training of counselors, group or otherwise, is that of being supervised by a qualified counselor. The training of group counselors requires this kind of supervision.

MOTIVATION TO SEEK COUNSELING

Anyone doing counseling would be wise to remember that people seeking counseling do so for a variety of reasons. Very often people come in order to involve the counselor in a game of "courtroom." In this game the counselor is expected to declare one party right and one party wrong. If the counselor allows this to happen, the only result can be that someone is confirmed in a "one-up" position and someone is left in a "one-down" position. The one-down position, I'm not O.K., is a victim or discount position and the platform from which all games start.

Others come to a counselor as a gesture to prove that nothing can be done. In such cases, one or both partners in a marital situation may want out but there will be less guilt if some token attempt is made at working out the problems. Once a few sessions with a counselor have taken place and no progress is made, then it is O.K. to terminate the relationship. The title of this game is "Look how hard I tried." The observant counselor can usually spot this game very early and not get involved as a participant in the game.

Another common motivation for seeking counseling by couples or parent and child, as mentioned previously, is the desire for the other person to change. The point to remember in such situations is that the counselor does not have the power to change anyone but himself, and the parties in a counseling situation are in the same situation. Change comes from within, and it is up to each individual to determine what, if any, change is desirable and then to determine to make it.

Not all people who seek counseling come for such devious reasons. Very often people come because they are hurting and they genuinely wish to do something about themselves and the relationships they have with others. These are the people who keep counseling appointments and work on their contracts between counseling sessions. Working with such people is a rewarding experience for the counselor as well as for the people involved.

TEENAGE COUNSELING

Someone has made the cynical but perhaps astute observation that raising a child in Western society is like putting a jigsaw puzzle together and finding that regardless of how it is put together, it turns out to be wrong.

Certainly there are hosts of parents who have tried very hard to put everything together in the right way only to discover that something went wrong. Our society tends strongly to hold parents responsible for the behavior of their children. If a child, especially a teenager, isn't doing well in school or if the teenager is a "trouble maker," then bring the parents in and face them with the problem. It must be their fault. If a teenager lands before the juvenile judge it is often the same thing: Bring the parents in. In some instances the judge may "sentence" the parents to take the teenager to church and Sunday School.

And, even more often, parents blame themselves. What did we do wrong? Why would a child of ours, upon whom we have lavished love and affection as well as material things, behave in such a way? Where did we fail? Along with the guilt there is anguish and tears.

How can society account for Alice?[1] Her father was a university professor, her mother a woman of talent and high moral standards. Yet Alice drifted into the drug culture and her life ended tragically before she was 20. Who is to blame for such a tragedy? Society? Her parents?

The schools? Alice herself? No doubt her parents are tormented with guilt and self-blame and continue to ask: What did we do wrong? Where did we fail?

There are no easy answers to explain Alice and the thousands like her. Perhaps it is one of those situations in which no one is to blame and yet everybody is to blame, including Alice herself.

Teenage Culture

It becomes obvious, then, that to engage in the counseling of teenagers is to open a very large can of worms. That there is a teenage culture in America is apparent. That it is in the process of constant change is also apparent. To attempt to counsel with teenagers without some familiarity with what may be currently going on in the local youth culture would be foolhardy. The problem for counselors of mature years is that while we were once young, we can never be young in the same context in which the present teenager is now young. However, if we can sit where they sit, we can have some understanding of the problems and the desires with which they are trying to deal.

Crisis of Identity

Perhaps to some extent there has always been a crisis of identity for the teenager. It certainly is a crisis for many teenagers in today's society. In spite of the fact that there is a great emphasis on youth in our culture, the mainstream of culture really has little place for youth. Youth are discounted in our society (as are the elderly). That is to say, they have no place of value in their own eyes. They are herded into classrooms where they are regimented into rows of seats and lectured at. They are conditioned to respond to whistles and bells in the same manner as Pavlov's dog. Decisions that affect their future are made for them in Washington, in the state capitol, in city hall, and in school board meetings, without their knowledge or consent. The commercial vultures flood the air waves in a constant attempt to capture the earned or unearned youth dollars: Buy this record, or this shampoo, or this car and you will have it made, you will be "in," and your identity will be established.

In counseling with teenagers it is imperative to recognize that there are very few of us, teenagers or otherwise, who have the strength to stand alone. We all need a support group in which we are accepted, are counted as valuable members, and are needed. Since the nuclear family is not always able to fill these needs, the teenager searches elsewhere. A lot of other teenagers are also looking, so it is not surprising that groups get together to meet their needs.

Peer Groups

Groups in themselves are neither good nor bad. They can be either or neither. The peer group takes on much of the function of the Parent ego state and, temporarily at least, dictates the value structure for the individuals in the group à la *West Side Story, Go Ask Alice, or Lord of the Flies.*

To the involved teenagers there is not likely to be such a thing as "the wrong crowd." If it is a crowd that accepts him, it is "the right crowd." The Jesus freaks or the drug culture, for the young, is not very different from the country club set or the jet set or the church groups of adults. In each instance the individual is awarded acceptance "if." This is a *conditional* acceptance. In each case the conditions are different but the principle is the same: buy into our value system. If you don't buy into our value system, then you will not be accepted.

No one wants to be an isolate (or at least very few do). It is not a healthy state. We really can't be human alone. The trick is to find the kinds of people who will not only accept us but will also be a resource for our self-actualization. Self-actualization is the process of growth that brings about the increasing fulfillment of our individual potential.

Change, Change, Change

If teenagers seem to be, as Churchill once said about Russia, a mystery wrapped in an enigma, it should not surprise us. The fact is, of course, that all kinds of things are going on within them physically as well as emotionally. To top it off, there is a wide variance in the ways that teenagers develop.

Dr. Derek Miller of the University of Michigan in Ann Arbor says that during puberty there is an impairment of the capacity to consider the future. This means that teenagers (during puberty) have little ability to forego present desires for future gains.

Radical changes in body image are also taking place for both boys and girls. As a rule, girls are 2 years more advanced than boys. Voice changes, a new awareness of girls, and appearance of pubic and facial hair are changes that boys experience. Girls develop in even more radical ways: the breasts enlarge, menstrual periods begin, and other sexual characteristics appear. At this age, like spring in the popular song, sexuality is "busting out all over." It is difficult for many adults to handle their sexuality. Imagine how difficult, confusing, and frightening it is for teenagers who have little knowledge and no experience.

Aggressive behavior is characteristic of this age of development. A boy or girl who has been a "model" child up to this time may now become aggressive, secretive, and petulant. According to Dr. Miller, the girls may attack the mother (nurturing) functions of the mother. Boys may provoke the mothering of the mother and then scornfully reject it. The norms of the family are often looked upon as shopworn "hand-me-downs" and are, seemingly, rejected. To most parents this is, to say the least, less than gratifying.

In counseling adolescents it is important to think in terms of maturation rather than of calendar years. There are essentially three stages of adolescence. Puberty, the first stage, lasts approximately 3 years. This is the time when the most rapid physical and emotional changes occur. The middle stage also lasts approximately 3 years. In addition to some physical and emotional changes that continue in this period, it is the time in which the earlier learnings of childhood that were taken on without question are now evaluated and accepted as one's own or rejected. It is a time when the adolescent is looking for people "to be like." The third stage is of indeterminate length and blends into adulthood. It is a time of identity testing, of, so to speak, trying one's life style on for size and making adjustments so that the fit is more comfortable.

Separation and Identity

Most parents find it difficult to understand the need for children to separate themselves from parents in order to establish their own identity. The relatively recent development of the nuclear family has added to the necessity for such separation. This is scary not only for the parents but also for the adolescents. Parents still have a very significant role to play, but teenagers need someone, or several someones, in addition to the parents to whom they can relate. Dr. Ross Snyder of the Chicago Theological Seminary refers to such persons as "guarantors." A "guarantor" is a mature person other than a parent who can serve as a friend, a listener, a confidant, an "advisor," or the like. Such a person, chosen by the teen himself, acts as a reference point for the adolescent's own ideas and behavior. On the whole, teenagers are inclined to choose "guarantors" who will meet a specific need at a specific time and move on to other "guarantors" as the need arises. School teachers, neighbors, friends, and now and then a relative play the "guarantor's" role.

It is imperative to remember when counseling adolescents that they are always struggling for their own independence. Since this is the case it is necessary to see the individual in the context of the family. Individual counseling can be helpful with some kinds of teenage problems. Family counseling offers greater hope of success in most instances. For one thing, family counseling takes the stigma of being the "sick one" from any one individual. This in itself is very therapeutic. It is also almost a certainty that if one individual in a family situation is experiencing abnormal difficulties, there is something in the family situation that is contributing to the difficulties.

Does the family, for example, need a "sick one" in order to function in its long accustomed way? Numerous counselors have given testimony to the fact that in a given family situation if the "designated sick one" begins to "get well," another member of the family will "get sick." As Dr. Miller says, the improvement of the child may be an intolerable threat to the parents!

Ego States

In counseling with teenagers it will be helpful to look at the ego structure à la Eric Berne and the transactional analysis model. The ego structure of a prepubescent child can be approximately represented as in Figure 6–1.

Possibly nearly all of the Critical Parent (CP) of the child would be a direct takeover from natural parents or other parent figures. There would likely be a "leak" between the Critical Parent and the Adult ego (A) state, with the result that opinions would be confused with facts. The Nurturing Parent (NP) would function most frequently in relation to peer groups, companions, or pets, and to some extent with parents, especially in times of illness.[2, 3]

The Adult ego state, logically, would be drawn as a smaller component, since it has not reached full development as a computer.

The Child ego state would be composed of a significant amount of Natural Child (NC), perhaps 50 per cent, the obedient Adapted Child (AC), 40 per cent, and the rebellious Adapted Child (RC), 10 per cent.

Figure 6–1.

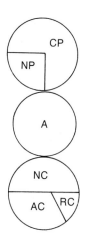

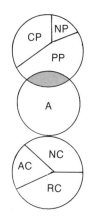

Figure 6–2.

At the time of adolescence, significant changes in the ego states take place. A new factor is introduced into the Critical Parent in the form of Peer values and into the Child ego state in the form of a greater portion of rebellious Adapted Child. The ego structure of the pubescent adolescent would be more properly represented in Figure 6–2.

The Peer Parent (PP) value structure carries a lot of weight and the Critical Parent or the Nurturing Parent less weight. There is still a leak, a rather large one now, from the Peer Parent into the Adult, where opinion is taken as fact.

In the Child ego state there has been a decrease in the obedient Adapted Child and a large increase in the rebellious Adapted Child.[2, 3]

It may be realistic to assume that during the adolescent years the quantities of Critical Parent, Peer Parent, Nurturing Parent, Adult, Natural Child, Obedient Child, and Rebellious Child are in almost constant flux. The counselor must be aware of the changes in ego states as the counseling takes place.

Reality Clarification

One of the important elements of counseling with teenagers (and also with adults) falls under the heading of reality clarification and testing. Very often there is a war going on among the ego states. Critical Parent and Peer Parent both seek control. Critical Parent and Rebellious Child stage numerous battles. This may take place to the degree that the Natural Child gets squeezed out and the adolescent becomes hostile, sad, and depressed, except, perhaps, when the child is surrounded by the peer culture.

It is the function of the counselor to help the adolescent strengthen the ring around the adult ego state. This will help the person decide what the facts of the situation are, what the alternatives are, and the possible outcome of certain types of activities or behavior. It will decrease the possibility of confusing opinion with fact (leaks from Parent to Adult). This is the process of reality clarification and testing.

All of the ego states of the counselor are useful in a counseling situation. With teenagers, however, special care must be taken when using the Parent ego state. A teenager who gets the feeling that he is being treated as a child is almost certain to rebel. The Parent ego state is valuable, however, in permission-giving by the counselor. The counselor can give the teenager permission to have all sorts of feelings such as anger, fear, tenderness, joy, and love. The counselor can also make it plain that there is a great difference between awareness of feelings and behavior relating to such feelings. Feeling anger in one's awareness is not the same as behaving in an angry way.

Sexual Counseling with Adolescents

One of the axioms of jurisprudence is that ignorance of the law is no excuse. Ignorance in sexual matters is often used as an excuse, but there is no longer any excuse in our culture for sexual ignorance.

Ignorance continues to exist because adults are uncomfortable about their own sexuality and are therefore uncomfortable in imparting information to their children. Children sense this lack of comfort and look elsewhere for information. Often what they get is misinformation from their peer group. What was said earlier about counselor comfort needs to be doubly emphasized with reference to teenage counseling.

The counselor has the opportunity to be a source of factual information. It goes without saying that the counselor must be sure of the facts and not assume that what he or she learned as a child or teenager represents factual information. Probably more misinformation about sex than factual information is passed around. Here are just some samples:

A woman cannot become pregnant if she has intercourse standing up.
Pregnancy will not occur unless the woman has an orgasm.
A woman will not become pregnant the first time she has intercourse.
Masturbation causes warts or mental illness or pimples on the face.
Simultaneous climaxes are necessary for conception to take place.
Urination by the woman after intercourse will prevent pregnancy.
Humans can get "hung up" (experience penis captivity) during sexual intercourse.
Babies are born through the navel.
Kissing can cause pregnancy.
Venereal disease can be contracted from dirty toilet seats.
The few drops of lubricating fluid that seep from the penis during sexual excitement are a sign of some sort of malfunction.

The list could go on and on. The misinformation that is current in the teenage culture is symptomatic of the misinformation that is abroad in the adult culture.

No discussion of teenage counseling would be complete without some mention of "the pill," the liberation movement, and changing sexual mores. From infancy onward, the present-day teenager has been saturated via the mass media with sexual stimuli. K. Anna and Robert T. Francoeur refer to our culture as a "hot sex" culture.[5] In their terminology "hot sex" is contrasted with "cool sex," à la McCluhan's "hot" and "cool" media. "Hot sex" is concerned with performance and quantity, and centers in the genitals.

"Cool sex" is concerned with relationships, communication, love, and caring. It is obvious that there is now a great deal of emphasis on "hot sex," and it would be strange indeed if this concept did not have a strong influence on the young. The pill, by removing the risk of pregnancy, tends to support the "hot sex" concept. In so far as the liberation movement emphasizes the immediate "now" pleasures, it also may be supporting "hot sex."[5]

Teenagers, especially those who have bought into the "hot sex" culture, will be seeking contraceptives. When this happens the counselor has a number of choices. The Parent ego state of the counselor will probably say "no pills." The Adult ego state, however, if in executive control, will seek to discover what the facts of the situation are. This means reality testing and value clarification with the teenager. In a "hot sex" culture such as ours, it is safe to assume that a substantial percentage of teenagers will experience genital sex. As long as the "hot sex" emphasis is continued, teenage sex is inevitable. To many counselors as well as parents, it may seem less than desirable to advise birth control pills. It is, however, even less desirable to contemplate teenage pregnancies.

The pros and cons of teenage premarital sex are widely discussed from a number of points of view: morals, emotions, economics, health, religion. Historically, in the United States, teenage premarital sex has been "forbidden." The trend within the past decade has been toward a greater acceptance of premarital sex among the older, more mature teenagers.

Inseparable from teenage premarital sex is the large number of teenage premarital pregnancies. That they are the cause of much grief and unhappiness few would question. Once the pregnancy occurs each alternative seems less than promising. Teenage marriages are least likely to succeed. The teenage woman who marries and has a child is almost certain to short-circuit the normal developmental process that is so important in gaining independence and identity. Carrying the child to term and raising it as a single parent puts an adult responsibility upon a person who is not yet equipped to handle it. In most cases the parents of the teenager become the "parents" of the newborn child. In some subcultures this is relatively acceptable. In white, middle-class America it is not.

The third alternative is to carry the child to term and give it up for adoption. This also exacts an emotional price on the part of the teenage mother as well as her family. It may well be the most satisfactory solution with respect to the child. The fourth alternative is abortion. Abortions for therapeutic purposes during the first trimester are now legal in many areas. The legality of the procedure does not necessarily avoid the emotional problems that the teenager may encounter. The realities of individual circumstances will dictate what appears to be the least destructive course to be followed.

In the light of the undesirable choices that are available once conception has taken place, it seems a logical necessity to provide access to the pill or other reliable methods of contraception in a society that is enamored of "hot sex."

The logical time for teenage sexual counseling is early in the puberty period. Knowledge and reality testing at that time may be the means of avoiding many difficulties and heartaches later on.

If the counseling of teenagers sounds formidable, it is. At the same time, it can also be very rewarding, for teenagers are already in the process of change, so change is not foreign to them. There is, therefore, more flexibility and openness than is normally encountered in counseling with adults.

PREMARITAL COUNSELING

Generally speaking, what passes for premarital counseling is less than adequate. Often it consists of two or three sessions with the minister or rabbi in which few, if any, of the real problems are dealt with in any significant way. This is not always the fault of the counselor. Very often a couple who have decided to marry are sure that love will solve all their problems. Therefore premarital counseling is looked upon as a waste of time and is participated in reluctantly, if at all.

Paradoxically, if a couple seeks professional counseling from a marriage counselor prior to marriage, the rule of thumb for the counselor is that one or the other of the pair wants out of the engagement. This is not always the case, but it happens often enough to alert the counselor to that possibility.

Premarital counseling that is done a few days or weeks prior to the wedding is, no doubt, better than no counseling. It has become apparent, however, that very often in such near-term counseling both individuals are in their Child ego states and are not willing to exercise their objective Adult ego states. To do so would be too threatening to their romantic fantasies.

The time for premarital counseling, then, is before emotional involvement has reached the point at which it is no longer realistic to expect objectivity. It *is* possible for the skilled counselor to use his own Adult ego state in such a way that the couple may respond from their Adult ego states. Counseling is much more successful, however, when it is done long before the wedding plans have been made. In an ideal society, premarital counseling would be a regular part of the formal and informal educational process from childhood onward.

Individual Uniqueness

Even if such long-term educational counseling were to come about, there would still be a need for premarital counseling for the specific couple. Not only is every person born unique; so also is the situation in which he is reared unique. Uniqueness is one of the prize possessions of every individual. It is what makes for variety and richness in a culture. Uniqueness is more easily "worn" by single persons, since commitment and proximity do not bulk as large in day-to-day relationships. It is not uncommon to find that ideas, attitudes, and behavior that were acceptable (or even unknown) before marriage become difficult to live with on a day-to-day basis after marriage.

Mr. and Mrs. B., twice married to each other, came in for counseling in an effort to avoid a second divorce. Their uniqueness as individuals was pronounced. Mr. B. was the youngest of 11 children of Irish Catholic parents. His mother was a hard-working woman who kept going under any circumstances including illness and childbirth. The household was pretty rough and tumble, loosely organized, and wanting in neatness. Mr. B. grew up as an independent person who could take care of himself. Tenderness was not in large supply in his family.

Mrs. B. was born of middle-class parents and had one sister. In her family, any hint of illness brought large amounts of sympathy and attention. The house was always well ordered and clean. Mrs. B. was always kept clean and well groomed. The household ran on schedule.

Both Mr. and Mrs. B. were highly intelligent people who held responsible, well paying jobs. After they married, when Mrs. B. did not feel well, instead of sympathy and attention, she got ridicule. When Mr. B. left his clothes or the newspaper scattered over the house, he got screamed at. When Mrs. B. took hours to get dressed, with every hair in just the right place, Mr. B. was so tired of waiting that he was angry. Here were two unique, likable people whose developmental backgrounds were so different that living in the same house was anything but easy.

Premarital counseling in which the Adult ego states were functioning would have helped Mr. and Mrs. B. to understand the ways in which they were unique and the areas in which conflict most likely would arise. Mrs. B. wanted a nurturing Parent who would take care of her "little kid." What she got was a critical Parent with a "be strong" driver. Mr. B. wanted a playful Child combined with a noncritical Parent plus a very adapted Child. The combination was very susceptible to cross-transactions that stopped communication and caused frustration and anger to be stored up.

What happened with Mr. and Mrs. B., not just once but twice, was that they married without a full appreciation of the ways in which their uniqueness as individuals would lead them into destructive games with each other. Fortunately not all couples who "fall in love" have as wide a difference in their uniqueness, but *every* couple has considerable difference to adjust to. Awareness of the differences can make the necessary adjustments less painful. Premarital counseling can increase the awareness of the couple and enable them to have a clearer picture of themselves and their options. Uniqueness is not the problem. In fact it can be a plus. The problem arises in the inability of one or both persons to accept the differences without judging one's way right and the other's way wrong.

Synergic vs. Symbiotic Marriage

Synergic and symbiotic are terms with which every counselor should be familiar. Applied to interpersonal relationships between two people, synergic means that the functioning of each person contributes in a helpful way to the ability of the other to function. In other words, the functioning of either person does not exact a price from the other but instead provides a payoff or dividend. To put it another way, by being what I want to be, I contribute to what you want to be, and vice versa. Merle Shain puts it this way: "People who are loving toward each other set up their marriage so that it is possible for both partners to get what they need from life and so that no one is expected to give up his need to meet those of his spouse, and when their partner meets one of their needs, they accept it as a gift instead of viewing each unmet one as if it were a betrayal."[11]

A symbiotic relationship is a quite different one, in which I try to complete my "wholeness" by borrowing a part of you, and you complete your "wholeness" by borrowing a part of me. The result is a highly dependent relationship that leaves each person in a very vulnerable position with at least one ego state that does not function properly.

Figure 6–3 depicts the symbiotic relationship in terms of the transactional analysis model. In this situation the woman, on the left, has a Parent and an Adult ego state that function very poorly in the

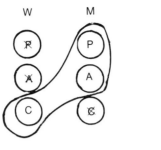

Figure 6–3.

dyadic relationship. The Child ego state, however, is fully cathected. The man, on the right, has Parent and Adult ego states that are fully functioning but little or no Child in the interacting relationship. Thus each person is deprived of one or more functioning ego states in *this* relationship. This makes for all kinds of problems. Healthy marital living requires that both persons have fully functioning egos at the Child, Adult, and Parent level. Each person has boundaries that can be opened or closed at the appropriate times.

In our society it is not unusual for pair bonding to take place on a symbiotic level. Younger women, especially those who wish to get away from their parents' home, seek out a man who will "take care of me." If a woman finds such a man, it is, of course, one who wishes to "take care of" someone. Thus the woman moves from her parents' home to her husband's home with the Child ego state being the most cathected. The husband, at least for a time, may be quite happy in such a relationship. It fulfills his need to be needed.

Often such marriages run rather smoothly until the woman decides that she doesn't wish to continue to be "daddy's little girl" any more. At that point she may have difficulty in asserting her independence, and the husband may be utterly confused about what is happening. The woman is trying to break the symbiotic relationship. The man may not be able to understand why. It can, of course, work the other way, whereby the man tires of being "big daddy."

The counselor can enable couples to look at the nature of their relationship in the present. If it is symbiotic in the premarital stages, it is certain to remain so after the marriage takes place. It may remain so throughout a long marriage. Difficulty develops when one or the other of the partners wishes to become a whole person. Either partner can play the role of Parent-Adult or either can play the Child in a symbiotic relationship.

Synergic marriage starts off with two whole persons with all three ego states functioning, as in Figure 6–4. It involves a greater amount of trust and flexibility, with more variation in role definition. You might say that the symbiotic couple are involved in a "hot" marriage and the synergic couple are involved in a "cool" marriage. The question for the premarital couple may then be: "Are you looking for a 'hot' or 'cool'

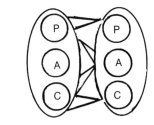

Figure 6–4.

marriage? Or if it starts out 'hot' is there a possibility that you could be comfortable if it changes to 'cool'?

A "hot" marriage is one in which each person has a highly defined role in terms of expectations and behavior. A "cool" marriage is much more flexible, and each person is much more independent. The "hot" marriage is goal-oriented. The "cool" marriage is person-oriented.

The Three "C's" of Marital Relationships

The key word in successful marriage relationships is communication. Three important kinds of communication are involved.

COMMUNICATION ABOUT EXPECTATIONS AND LIFE STYLES

One of the primary areas that it is essential for premarital couples to explore is that of expectations, desired ends, goals, and anticipated life style. Not the least of these is role expectations. Will it be a "hot" marriage in which roles are specifically spelled out? Will the roles be traditional ones that are commonly accepted in the surrounding culture, or will they be unique to this marriage? Will the female role be defined as homemaker, wife, and mother, and the male role be defined as breadwinner, husband, and father? Whatever the roles, if they are specific and inflexible, it will be a "hot" marriage. If the marriage is looked upon as "cool," then there will be much more flexibility and frequent interchanging of roles. For short or long periods of time the female may become the breadwinner while the male becomes the homemaker. Roles may change on a day-to-day basis, depending on skills, time available, preferences, resources, and so forth. A "cool" marriage is concerned with what is happening to each individual in terms of self-actualization, and adjustments are made accordingly. Obviously, if one partner is anticipating a "hot" marriage and the other a "cool" one, there is a built-in conflict even before the marriage begins.

Whether it is to be a "hot" marriage or a "cool" one will have a strong influence on the life style of the couple. But other factors also may enter in. The realities of time, money, and energy have a large effect on life style, but within those perimeters there is much room for differences of opinion:

"My husband's a night person. I'm a day person."
"I didn't want any children. My wife wanted three."
"I would like a big old house in the center of town. He wants a ranch house in the suburbs."
"I like the mountains. She likes the ocean."
"I want to save money so that we can buy a home and put our kids through college. He spends every penny."
"I like to go out on the town at least once a week. He only wants to stay home and watch the T.V."
"I'm interested in people. She is interested in things."
"I like to entertain. He likes to go out with the boys."
"I would like to live in a cooperative with other singles or families or in a commune. He wants a large amount of privacy."

The time to begin to communicate about life style is prior to marriage. Communication will continue after the ceremony. Obviously there are many life styles that various people choose to follow. No one life style is right. It is necessary, however, if a marriage is to survive and function with some degree of satisfaction, that there be some commonality of agreement about the life style that is to be followed.

COMMUNICATION ABOUT LIVING AT THE FEELING LEVEL

We in America pride ourselves on being intellectual, rational, and objective. Don't believe it! Our feelings and emotions have far more to do with the way we act and function than we are willing to admit. Unfortunately, in many situations in our early childhood we were, in all probability, encouraged not to feel. The first law of communication is to come on straight about feelings, for feelings are the bridge between people.

There is a great confusion in our verbal expression between *thinking* and *feeling*. Ask someone what he is feeling and more often than not you will be told what he is thinking. If the person is pushed by the counselor to identify what feelings are present, he may be unable to respond, and may say, "I don't have any feelings." Feelings are always present. What happens is that they are often pushed below the conscious level. When feelings are suppressed they come out in some disguised form. Fear may come out as anger. Anger may be expressed in tears and sadness.

In the transactional analysis model, the habitually expressed feeling that is a substitute for the more genuine feeling is referred to as a *racket*.

Typical rackets are sadness, anger, depression, withdrawal, sweetness, self-righteousness, self-depreciation, bragging, and so forth. The expressed feeling is a substitute for a feeling that the person does not feel comfortable in expressing. When the individual was a child the suppressed feeling was not considered acceptable by the family, parents, or parent figures. As an adult that feeling is still kept hidden.

Of late, a great deal more attention has been paid to understanding, accepting, and being aware of feelings. This certainly is supportive of mental health. It is therapeutic just to recognize and verbalize what our feelings are. In doing so we are more aware of the choices of behavior that we have. There is, obviously, a difference between verbalizing "I'm angry," and shoving your fist through a wall. One is acceptable behavior; the other is not.

In situations such as marriage in which one or both the spouses are unwilling to communicate openly about feelings, there is a high probability that the couple will spend much of their time in game-playing. Game-playing, by definition, is done below the level of consciousness and, according to Eric Berne, is played at first-, second-, and third-degree levels. Third-degree games are the most harmful and may result in "tissue damage."[2, 6, 7]

Much has been written about games, and there is no need to repeat that material here. What may be beneficial is to point out that, according to Taibi Kahler, all games begin with a discount, either a self-discount or a perceived discount from some other person or persons. The feeling that we get as a result of accepting the discount is an invitation to join in a game. Awareness of the discount is the first step in keeping out of a game. A straight-on expression of feelings and owning the feelings will be effective in avoiding most games.[7] The counselor can also become involved in game-playing, and the same rules apply for the counselor in avoiding games.

COMMUNICATION ABOUT THE SEXUAL DIMENSIONS OF THE MARITAL RELATIONSHIP

Sexual counseling should of course be a part of premarital counseling. And, again, the comfort of the counselor is of strategic importance. If the counselor is uncomfortable, the clients are going to be uncomfortable, and the tendency will be for the counselor to make unfounded assumptions about the clients. On the one hand, the counselor may assume that the couple is fully informed about sexual matters. On the other hand, the assumption may be that the couple is completely ignorant. The likelihood is that the couple has some knowledge but probably not as much as they think they have.

The fact that a couple has engaged in sexual intercourse prior to counseling is by no means a guarantee that they are sexually educated. It may rather mean that they are sexually miseducated.

Human sexuality is far broader than genital sex. We are sexual beings 24 hours a day, seven days a week, from the time of birth until death. On the average, a married couple will have sexual intercourse twice a week. It is unlikely that each such experience occupies more than 60 minutes. The actual time spent in copulation, then, is quite small; about four days out of the 365. Human sexuality is also important the other 361 days of the year. The fact is that if our sexuality is ignored or neglected during the 361 days, what happens during the "four days" probably won't be very satisfying.

Masters and Johnson and other sex counselors and researchers emphasize very strongly that people do not automatically know how to respond and function in their sexual relationships. A man does not automatically know what is sexually pleasurable and stimulating to his partner, and the same is true of women. Neither is a mind reader. Good sexual relations, then, demand good communication. The time to start such communication is during the courtship period.

In the past, and perhaps still in the present, a man was supposed to be knowledgeable about sex and therefore in a position to teach the woman. That may well have been a substantial myth. Many women have discovered that what men don't know about sex is much greater than what they do know. Wide experience in genital sex does not qualify either a man or a woman for a diploma in sexuality.

Knowledge, Attitudes, and Expectations.   The areas of concern for the counselor are (1) sexual knowledge, (2) sexual attitudes, and (3) sexual expectations. There are numerous books on the market that can provide sexual knowledge. Some examples of such books are those by Comfort, Kaplan, and McCary.[4, 8, 10] Another such book, now in paperback, is *The Fundamentals of Human Sexuality* by Katchadourian and Lunde.[9]

Attitudes are another matter. They have been shaped by many forces that have come to bear on each individual from birth onward. One way for the counselor to help the couple to an awareness of where they are in all three of these areas would be to use forms such as those shown here. Each person answers the questions on the form individually.

The knowledge questions are simply answered True or False. The attitude and expectation questions are answered in two ways. First, the individual writes his or her answer. Each then answers in the "partner's" column the way he or she thinks the other person would respond. After each person has answered the questions individually, both then compare and discuss their answers. The counselor can be a facilitator in this process and provide the correct information (see Key on page 73) on the knowledge section.

SEXUAL KNOWLEDGE, ATTITUDE, AND EXPECTATIONS — A FORM FOR USE IN COUNSELING*

Knowledge: T for True, F for False

1. (　) Men have a greater capacity for sexual response than women.
2. (　) For many men, the fondling of their breasts is sexually stimulating.
3. (　) Pregnancy cannot take place during menstruation.
4. (　) Pregnancy cannot take place unless the female has an orgasm.
5. (　) There are only two parts of the body, the breasts and the genitals, that can be erotically stimulated.
6. (　) Sexual intercourse is the only way that a woman can be stimulated to orgasm.
7. (　) Masturbation is injurious to one's health.
8. (　) The rhythm method is a safe way of avoiding pregnancy.
9. (　) Most men ejaculate within two minutes after vaginal penetration.
10. (　) In many marriages sex remains an important component after age 60.
11. (　) The size of sexual organs is an important factor in sexual satisfaction.
12. (　) If an approach to sexual activity is acceptable and satisfying to both members of the relationship, it cannot be considered perverse.
13. (　) More people who have not finished high school engage in oral-genital activity than do those who have gone to college.
14. (　) Women in their 20's are more inclined to be orgastic than women in their 30's.
15. (　) It is impossible for a woman to become pregnant while nursing a baby.
16. (　) Stimulation of the clitoris is essential for a woman to reach orgasm.
17. (　) Premature ejaculation on the part of the male will not continue if he has sex frequently.
18. (　) Most men experience impotence at some time during their lives.
19. (　) It takes less time for a woman to become sexually excited when stimulated than it does for a man.
20. (　) Only a very few women continue to masturbate after they are married.

---

*Permission to copy this form is hereby granted by the author and publisher.

ATTITUDES AND EXPECTATIONS

What I Think, Feel, or Believe

1. I think that having sex during menstruation is _____
   _____ .

2. My expectation is that we will have sex _____ times a week.

3. My feeling about oral-genital sex when I am the recipient is
   _____ .

4. My preferred method of contraception is _____
   _____ .

5. What I would like in the way of verbal communication during sex
   is _____ .

6. The time of the day when I am most ready for sexual play is
   _____ .

7. My feeling about being nude in my partner's presence is _____
   _____ .

8. My feelings about having sex during pregnancy are _____
   _____ .

9. If I were to masturbate, I would feel _____
   _____ .

10. If my partner had a close friend of the opposite sex, I would feel
    _____ .

What I Think My Partner Will Think, Feel, or Believe

1. I think my partner's feeling about sex during menstruation is

   _____.

2. I think my partner's expectation is to have sex _____ times
   a week.
3. My partner's feelings about oral-genital sex are _____

   _____.

4. My partner's preferred method of contraception is _____

   _____.

5. What I think my partner would like in the way of verbal communi-

   cation is _____.
6. The time when my partner is most ready for sexual play is _____

   _____.

7. I think my partner's feeling about my being nude is _____

   _____.

8. I think my partner's feelings about having sex during pregnancy

   are _____.
9. If I were to masturbate, I think my partner would feel _____

   _____.

10. If my partner had a close friend of the opposite sex, I think my

    partner would feel _____.

Any counselor can compose his own form, incorporating statements and questions that may seem appropriate. Such an instrument is valuable in opening up various areas of human sexuality for discussion by the premarital couple.

The sexual expectations, attitudes, and experiences of a couple will be heavily influenced by their chosen life style. A couple with a "hot" life style will probably engage in "hot" sex.

"Hot" and "cool" sex have certain characteristics that are carefully identified by the Francoeurs in their book *Hot and Cool Sex.*[5] Their summary is shown in Table 6–1.

TABLE 6–1. Hot vs. Cool Sex*

HOT SEX	COOL SEX
High definition	Low definition
Reduction to genital sex	Sexuality coextensive with personality
Genitally focused feelings	Diffused sensuality/sexuality
Time and place arrangements	Spontaneous
Highly structured with many games	Lightly structured with few games
Clear sex-role stereotypes	Little, if any, role stereotyping
Many strong imperatives from socially imposed roles	Few imperatives, self-actualization encouraged
Value Systems	
Patriarchal	Egalitarian
Male domination by aggression, female passivity	Equal partnership as friends
Double moral standard	Single moral standard
Behavioral Structures	
Property-oriented	Person-oriented
Closed possessiveness	Open inclusiveness
Casual, impersonal	Involved, intimate
Physical sex segregated from life, emotions, and responsibility	Sex integrated in whole framework of life
Nonhomogenous, grossly selective of playmate	Homogenous, finely selective in all relations
Screwing sex objects for conquest	"Knowing" sexual persons
Genital hedonism	Sex as communication
Concerns	
Orgasm-obsessed	Engaging, pleasuring communication
Performance pressures obligatory	Sexual relations not primary, truly optional
Fidelity = sexual exclusivity	Fidelity = commitment and responsibility
Extramarital relations an escape	Comarital relations a growth reinforcement
Fear of emotions and senses	Embracing of emotions and senses
Nudity a taboo	Group nudity optional
Sexuality feared, tenuously situated	Sexuality accepted, securely situated
Entropic, property can be used up	Synergistic, mutually reinforcing relations
Frequent alcohol and drug usage	Few drug-altered states
Territory, preservation of social distance	Grokking

*From Francoeur, K. Anna and Robert. *Hot and Cool Sex.* New York: Harcourt, Brace & Jovanovich, 1974, p. 86.

If Masters and Johnson are correct in their estimate that at least 50 per cent of married couples are contending with a significant degree of sexual dysfunction, then certainly counseling in the area of human sexuality is most appropriate with premarital couples.

It is not true, of course, that sex is the only thing in marriage. Many happily married couples do not have a very active sex life. Whatever amount of sexual activity is mutually satisfying and acceptable is fine, whether it be little or much. There is no problem for those whose sex life is mutually satisfying. The problem arises when one or both partners are not experiencing the kinds of sexual satisfaction that they would like to experience. In most cases, more than 99 per cent, there is no physical cause for the sexual dysfunction. The correction of the problem can only come, then, from counseling. Premarital sexual counseling, therefore, may be preventive sexual counseling. It may enable the couple to make the best of a very good thing.

ANSWERS TO TRUE–FALSE QUESTIONS

(1) F, (2) T, (3) F, (4) F, (5) F, (6) F, (7) F, (8) F, (9) T, (10) T, (11) F, (12) T, (13) F, (14) F, (15) F, (16) T, (17) F, (18) T, (19) F, (20) F.

REFERENCES

1. Anonymous. *Go Ask Alice*. New York: Avon Publishing Company, 1972.
2. Berne, Eric. *Games People Play*. New York, Grove Press, 1964.
3. Berne, Eric. *What Do You Say After You Say Hello?* New York: Grove Press, 1972.
4. Comfort, Alex. *The Joy of Sex*. New York: Crown Publishing, 1973.
5. Francoeur, K. Anna and Robert. *Hot and Cool Sex*. New York: Harcourt, Brace & Jovanovich, 1974.
6. James, Muriel and Dorothy Joungeward. *Born to Win*. Reading, Mass.: Addison-Wesley Publishing Co., 1971.
7. Kahler, Taibi. *Invitation to Okness*. To be published.
8. Kaplan, Helen Singer: *The New Sex Therapy*. New York: Brunner/Mazel, 1974.
9. Katchadourian, Herant A. and Donald T. Lunde. *Fundamentals of Human Sexuality*. New York: Holt, Rinehart and Winston, Inc., 1972.
10. McCary, James Leslie. *Human Sexuality* (2nd edition). New York: D. Van Nostrand Company, 1973.
11. Shain, Merle. *Some Men Are More Perfect Than Others*. New York: Bantam Books, 1974, p. 61.

CHAPTER
7

SEX EDUCATION: WHOSE RESPONSIBILITY IS IT?

Kathryn Christiansen, R.N., M.N.

HISTORICAL PERSPECTIVE

To understand where we have been and perhaps where our Western attitudes have come from, a brief description of the attitudes toward sex through history may be helpful. We are products of our history and our environment. Our early attitudes often arise not from something we've personally explored and found to be true, but from something our parents and significant others have told us or otherwise indicated to us was good or bad. Our parents, likewise, are products of their environment, and so on back through the ages. As one looks at our history of sexual behavior, two influences that have shaped present-day thinking keep reappearing: survival and religion. Another aspect, that of ignorance or lack of knowledge, also exists throughout our sexual history and is still present today.

Very probably, cave men and women utilized their sexuality for procreation purposes only. They were most likely far too busy struggling to exist from day to day to dwell on the pleasurable and intimate moments derived from their sexual experiences. No doubt sex was an instinctual behavior, like eating and sleeping, that was necessary to help the tribe survive by producing more members.

The most definitive and often quoted history of modern-day sexual attitudes comes from the Old Testament. In Genesis (1:27), God said to Adam and Eve, "Be fruitful and multiply and fill the earth and subdue it. . . ." In order to obey God's word, it was necessary for the ancient tribes of Israel to devote all of their sexual energies toward procreation. It is easy to imagine how their taboos and negative attitudes regarding masturbation, homosexuality, and any other sex act causing the sperm to be "spilled" (and thus wasted) would occur and be reinforced.

Authors[7, 11] have indicated that Jesus said very little on the subject of sex. He was himself chaste and celibate, yet he did not indicate that he was trying to be a role model for the society. It is interesting to consider the paradox that today, unless one is a priest or a nun, celibacy is not considered to occur from choice but out of rejection by others. Celibate persons are often categorized as being weird, uptight, neurotic, and fearful of "normal" sexual drives. In I Corinthians 6 and 7, Paul had much to say about sexual morality. He indicated that marriage was necessary if sexual acts were to be indulged in at all and concluded, "It is better to marry than burn in lust." Katchadourian states that St. Augustine also "severely condemned premarital and extramarital sexual outlets, including beastiality, homosexuality and especially masturbation."[7]

Although many others added to our current attitudes and beliefs regarding sexuality, the Puritans seem to be credited with formulating most of our existing laws, traditions, and attitudes on the subject of sex. The Puritan movement began in the 1600's and was committed to religious freedom from the political and persecuting Church of England. Large numbers migrated to America and settled in New England. The Puritan doctrine, like that of St. Augustine, indicated that man was sinful, weak, and in need of stringent rules governing his sexual behavior. Sexual relationships outside of marriage were dealt with harshly. It must be remembered, however, that this sect was fighting for its religious life; the major emphasis was again on "safety in numbers," with the family units being the most important factor in providing the necessary population. It can easily be seen, then, why the Puritans would set stringent norms for sexual behavior and would condemn relationships that would cause controversy and divide the group.

The Victorian Era, named for the reign of English Queen Victoria (1819–1901), was probably more directly responsible for our present-day attitudes regarding sexual behavior. There is some question about why Victorians imposed moral judgments on such sexual relationships even within marriage. According to Katchadourian, "Victorians were concerned with character, health, and how best to harness sex and rechallenge it to loftier ends."[8] It has been suggested that, in part, these attitudes stemmed from the erroneous opinions of the newly developing scientific and medical fields. To be sure, books written at this time were filled with medical myths, half-truths, and warnings of dire consequences if a person should explore his or her own body. Masturbation was deemed "the solitary vice," and mothers were admonished to look for certain telltale signs in their children such as hair and eyes losing their luster, confusion, premature sexual changes, interest in being alone, and acne. Insanity or loss of an appendage was believed to be the eventual outcome. What a horrifying concern for the normal adolescent who is undergoing normal hormonal changes with accompanying changes in behavior, complexion, and secondary sexual characteristics. Little wonder our parents, grandparents, and great-grandparents were so concerned about normal adolescent curiosity and steadfastly enforced rules regarding sexual behavior.

It was not until more information was obtained by means of travel and scientific investigation that our attitudes regarding sexuality were modified. During the two World Wars, the GI's were given the opportunity to explore the sexual practices of other countries. Although nothing is directly evident in the literature indicating an alteration in sexual thought, attitudes, and practices of the returning service people, it can be hypothesized that at least the exchange of stories while in service would be an eye-opening experience for many young people. The fact that the armed services were spending money to produce informational films about venereal disease indicates that the "boys" were doing a little sexual experimenting away from home.

Travel became more commonplace in the 1930's and 1940's, and individuals and families could move from coast to coast or even from state to state and encounter differences in sexual norms and attitudes. It was also during the 1940's that Alfred C. Kinsey (1894–1956) and his associates were gathering data about sexual behavior. Their sample consisted of 5940 female and 5300 male volunteers. The 11,240 individuals represented many ages, educational levels, occupations, geographical locations, religions, and marital statuses. It is stated by Brecher that Kinsey alone collected an average of two histories, each a detailed and extensive personal interview, every day for ten years.[1] Kinsey's published works, *Sexual Behavior in the Human Male* (1948) and *Sexual Behavior in the Human Female* (1953), were greeted with furor and outrage. According to one author, "Probably no other book published during the past several decades has elicited as widespread a response as has the first Kinsey report on sexual behavior of the human male." Although the data have been criticized for a multitude of reasons, varying from the invalid to the valid, the fact remains that it is still the most remarkable and industrious undertaking describing sexual behavior. Kinsey himself noted that "this is a study of sexual behavior in certain groups of the human species," but ". . . not a study of the sexual behavior of all cultures of all races of man."[8] Masters and Johnson have commended Kinsey by stating, "Possibly history will record Kinsey's greatest contribution, the fact that his incredible effort actually enabled him to put his foot firmly in this door [investigative objectivity] despite counter pressures that would have destroyed a lesser man."[10]

The 1960's produced several important contributions to our knowledge about and our attitudes toward sexuality. In May, 1964, the Sex Information and Education Council of the U.S. (commonly known as SIECUS) was chartered as a nonprofit educational organization. The purpose of SIECUS is as follows:

> *To establish human sexuality as health entity: to identify the special characteristics that distinguish it from, yet relate it to, human reproduction; to dignify it by openness of approach, study, and scientific research designed to lead towards its*

understanding and its freedom from exploitation; to give leadership to professionals and to society, to the end that human beings may be aided toward responsible use of the sexual faculty and toward assimilation of sex into their individual life patterns as a creative and re-creative force.[13]

The organizers of SIECUS were a family-life educator, a health educator, a lawyer, a physician, a Protestant clergyman, and a sociologist. Shortly after its formation, the membership was increased to include representatives of the Jewish and Catholic religions and additional professionals. Although there were hints of SIECUS being a communist-inspired plot, and the usual concerns about decline of morality that such an organization would incur, the reaction of those interested in furthering their knowledge of sexuality was encouraging. According to Calderone, in the first 18 months of SIECUS "4,000 direct requests for services, from schools, colleges, churches, professional and family centered organizations and representatives of all the family helping disciplines" were received.[2]

The second and perhaps most far-reaching occurrence in the 1960's was the publication of *Human Sexual Response* by William H. Masters and Virginia E. Johnson. It represented 11 years of a carefully designed research program. Data were gathered from 382 females ranging from 18 to 78 years of age and 312 male subjects aged 21 to 89 years. In the introduction, Masters and Johnson state their intent with the following statement:[10]

Although the Kinsey work has become a landmark of sociologic investigation, it was not designed to interpret physiologic or psychologic response to sexual stimulation. These fundamentals of human sexual behavior can not be established until two questions are answered: What physical reactions develop as the human male and female respond to effective sexual stimulation? Why do men and women behave as they do when responding to an effective sexual stimulation?

Masters and Johnson followed this publication with another, *Human Sexual Inadequacy,* in 1970. The research has clarified and enlightened today's attitudes toward sexuality and has opened the doors for other sex researchers and investigators. At the same time, "A variety of social ills has been ascribed to the sex research of Masters and Johnson—from spreading venereal disease to pushing the nation toward the brink of moral disaster."[11]

Obviously, to imply that all is now well and that we are at a pinnacle of knowledge and openness regarding sexuality would be misleading and far from the truth. We have, perhaps, made some progress in being able to accept the fact that we are all sexual beings and that sex is much more than physical expression. Today people are questioning, discussing, sharing experiences, and attempting to understand the sexual norms, practices, and preferences of others. Almost any bookstore has a section for sex education or sexuality. In addition, there are numerous seminars, classes, and rap sessions provided by schools, colleges, health agencies, churches, and volunteer agencies. It is not difficult to be informed about basic sexuality; as a matter of fact, it seems impossible to avoid being informed. Yet there is still opposition to school sex education programs, and people continue to predict doom if society persists in its degenerate trend toward immorality by overemphasizing sex.

Today there is no longer the urgent matter of survival to justify strict nonvarying sexual standards and laws, nor are religious institutions as dogmatic in their views of sexual behavior. We also have more knowledge available to everyone than ever before; therefore, theoretically, the excuse of ignorance can no longer be used. Why then is sex such a burning issue? Why are some individuals fighting against sex education in the schools? Why are parents reluctant to discuss sexual information with their children and with each other? Why are many professionals not initiating sexual counseling even when they suspect that problems may be present? Perhaps lack of knowledge is still sex education's greatest deterrent. Our current task, then, is to ascertain what people know about sex, determine who is qualified to teach about sexuality, and then look at who should take the responsibility for educating others.

EMOTIONAL FACTORS IN SEX EDUCATION

Because of their highly diverse emotions, attitudes and knowledge, parents are not in the best position to provide the total sexual education of their children. Some individuals have indicated that if parents would "do their job right," the school would no longer need to be concerned with the teaching of sex and sex-related information. At best, that statement is a half-truth. It assumes that parents have the necessary knowledge and ability to impart all necessary information about sex to their children. It also assumes that parents are best qualified to impart sexual information and that schools are merely a stopgap for what parents are not doing. In reality, most parents view sex education as reproductive information only. Parents seem to be most reluctant to answer the questions "How are babies made?" and "How does daddy help make the baby?" They gear up to teach their children about basic differences between boys and girls and between men and women, about the fertilization of the ovum by the sperm, about the growth of the baby in utero, and about the birth process. Some intermediary topics are menstruation, feminine hygiene, and penile functioning (with or without information on nocturnal emissions), and some word of warning may be given about heavy kissing, heavy breathing, and heavy petting. Unless the parents of today very suddenly become more open and communicative about sex and sexuality, it is doubtful that they will be comfortable discussing the variety of frank questions their children will ask.

Expecting parents to be totally responsible for and comfortable teaching sex education to their children is like expecting them to teach their children a language after taking an introductory course in it. Even those who are comfortable using words like penis and vagina may still need some assistance in discussing the pros and cons of premarital intercourse and whether preparation with contraceptive devices implies that the woman expects to have sexual relationships.

Parental efforts must not be slighted, however, and one must not overlook the firm foundation of sex education that they do provide. It must not be supposed that they are unwilling to teach their children about sexual matters. The problem, then, becomes how to discuss attitudes and values as well as factual information, at the same time conveying openness toward obtaining sexual information. Woody[18] has suggested that parents must:

1. Face the issue openly.
2. Examine objectively contemporary scientific knowledge of human sexuality.
3. Scrutinize their own sexual beliefs and behaviors.
4. Become consciously aware of the value they wish to convey to their children.
5. Attempt to integrate contemporary scientific knowledge into their value system.
6. Understand how sexual information, attitudes, and values get conveyed to children from infancy on.

The author would like to add two points to this list.

1. Strive for consistency between parents and with significant others in their ideas, values, attitudes, and demands, keeping in mind that inconsistency can only produce confusion and insecurity in the child.
2. Strive for consistency between home and societal expectations.

According to SIECUS, "Parents cannot choose whether or not they will give sex education; they can only choose whether they will do something positive or negative about it, whether they will accept or deny their responsibility."[15]

PARENTAL RESPONSIBILITY

The traditional and habitual response to the assertion that parents should be teaching their children about sex is, of course, that parents do teach children about sex from infancy on. The parent who himself learned that touching his own body was wrong is now being expected to regard a child's genital exploration as normal—a difficult task for the most enlightened parent. Even if parents have little anxiety about sexuality, the grandparents, neighbors, friends, or babysitters are likely to indicate to the young child their dislike and disapproval of sexual play. How many have seen a parent or grandparent remove a child's hand from penis or labia and, without saying a word, indicate that this is unacceptable behavior? Perhaps parents feel that the child will be so enthralled with masturbation that he will have no inhibitions in public places. Probably, parents fear this public display more than the acts of exploring sexuality in private. The unfortunate concern for what the neighbors or grandparent will think has caused many a child to grow up feeling guilty about normal sexual behavior.

What parents do or don't do, what they teach or don't teach, and how they act and don't act are highly individualized matters. Just because the Smith family is very comfortable with their own sexuality and with questions about sex is no indication that the Jones family next door has the same orientation. Also, while the Smith child has a healthy and comfortable attitude about sex, the Jones child is fearful and anxious about his normal fantasies and feelings. Some parents have been so concerned about transmitting "sexy" ideas to their children that they refrain from showing any overt affection toward one another: no sitting close, no hand holding, no kissing with passion, and no sexual play. What a sterile, emotionless environment in which to raise a child! Moreover, what a waste of an opportunity to demonstrate caring, affection, and play in a serious relationship.

A past sexuality workshop for health professionals discussed parental attitudes toward sex. All members were able to remember the behavior of their parents, and many attributed their comfort or lack of comfort with their own sexual feelings to their parents' actions toward one another and their children. Even though parents are not able to teach about reproduction, it does not mean that the children are not receiving sex education. Kirkendall states, "Sex education is giving the child help by what is said, by example, by the way people live, in fitting sex into his feelings and behavior so that he can live in a satisfying way with himself and others."[9] It is clearly indicated that parents, regardless of their intentions, do transmit their own attitudes of sexuality to their children. Coupled with this is the great lack of knowledge of basic anatomy, physiology, and psychology of sexuality of many parents. It has become apparent while interviewing women at family planning clinics that they have only a rudimentary knowledge of how their own bodies are built and how they work. Many are truly ignorant of what is happening during a pelvic examination and do not know where the cervix is or its relationship to the vagina.

Is it any wonder, then, that parents are often uncomfortable with the responsibility of teaching sexuality to their children? They themselves are in great need of the knowledge. In many cases it is like the old axiom: The blind lead the blind.

SCHOOL RESPONSIBILITY

The fact that parents and family need help with sex education is quickly identified by them and their children. The President's Commission on Obscenity and Pornography included information relating to sex education in their survey.[16] They found that although "Parents, especially mothers, are regarded as the best source of sex information for boys and girls," parents are often poorly informed about sex and have difficulty communicating with their children.

This study also indicated that the "trend toward delegating the responsibility for sex education to the schools is approved by a substantial majority of adults in our country."[14] Sex education in the schools has evolved largely owing to expressed dissatisfaction on the part of adults and young people with the previously existing alternatives for communicating information relating to human sexuality.

For some it may be taken for granted that sex education classes have always been a part of the school curriculum. Almost everyone was required to take a health course; this was often the mechanism for teaching masculine and feminine hygiene and showing films on menstruation to the girls and films such as *Boy to Man* to boys. Reproduction was saved for biology class, and as often as not, human reproduction was not discussed.

As one might suspect, the actual teaching of sex education (and calling it such) has been the cause of great debate among teachers, school administrators, school boards, and parents. Issues of contention include what should be the school's responsibility, what should be the content of such courses, and who should teach them.

In April 1966, at Princeton, New Jersey, a meeting sponsored by the Committee on Education Practices of the National Association of Independent Schools was held. Questions such as the above were considered and expanded upon. The group "came to realize that as educators, and as parents too, they had failed to provide children not only with essential knowledge about sex as a natural body function, but also with an understanding of sex as a basic and vital life force."[6] In addition, they were in full agreement that the responsibility for sex education must be shared by the schools and the family. This may have been the impetus needed to begin formal sex education in the schools, although the influence of SIECUS, formed several years before this meeting, was also being felt by the education circles.

School authorities have made some progress since the time of that meeting, but not very much in some cases. In an attempt to include content on human sexuality yet not call the course "Sex Education," schools have designed courses entitled "Marriage and Family," Family-Life Education," "Child Development," or "Health." Alternatively, they have attempted to integrate concepts of sex education into pre-existing courses. The results have been as diverse as the course titles. Many schools have excellent programs from kindergarten through senior high that stress knowledge as well as value appraisal. Other schools have chosen to teach only junior high and high school students. The extent to which issues such as contraception, abortion, homosexuality, masturbation, and premarital sex are discussed is largely dependent upon the principal, the superintendent, the school board, and, of course, the community. There are teachers who are committed to providing as much information as the students can absorb, including information about a range of alternative choices, but without the support of the school authorities, these teachers are at risk of losing their jobs.

One must look at the motivation for sex education programs in various schools to determine what the outcome will be. For example, the school nurse in one small Midwest town suggested the introduction of a sex education program in the upper grades of the school. The school superintendent and principal agreed that it was needed, since several of the young women in high school were pregnant and had dropped out of school. The program was well received by students and parents alike. After the second year, the course was discontinued because the pregnancy rate had not declined over the period of time that the class had been taught. Obviously, the school authorities were concerned only with the outcome of a situation that they thought was brought on by a lack of knowledge. They had little commitment to the program when their own personal goal was not realized.

One must also look at the qualifications of the teachers who are providing the guidance and knowledge for sex education courses. Several surveys[3, 4, 12] have indicated that a qualified teacher is imperative for a successful program on human sexuality. Reed indicates that lack of a qualified teacher is the main reason used by schools having no sex education program to rationalize its absence.[12] Kirkendall also states that "the burden of good sex education rests on the individual classroom teacher."[9] Students, when asked, have indicated that the most important personality characteristic of the sex education instructor is the ability to talk freely and maturely without embarrassment.

How, then, does the teacher become qualified in this area and gain the necessary degree of comfort and maturity with the subject of sex? At the time of the Commission's report on obscenity and pornography, classes for teachers of sex education were offered at "less than 15% of our colleges and summer workshops." Even this was an increase over what had been available two years previously. As she surveyed the status and further directions of graduate programs in health education in the United States, Dunn found that 71 institutions offered an advanced degree in health education.[5] Of these, however, most indicated that they were emphasizing only drug and sex education, the two areas most prominent in the news and for which there is the most demand for knowledge.

As often as not, however, the sex education teacher is either the physical education teacher, who may or may not hold a minor in health, or the biology teacher, because of his "expertise in reproduction." The school nurse is, at times, called upon to discuss menstruation or other specific topics but is rarely given the opportunity to plan or present a unit on sex. Films are utilized, as well as guest lecturers. All in all, most sex education programs in the schools are haphazard, fragmented, and planned with the main purpose of offending no one.

Another aspect of sex education programs that is, at times, underemphasized is that of morality and examination of values. In one survey, the teaching of morals and values gained overwhelming support from both teachers and students.[3] According to Reed, "Principals as well indicated that morality education has a place in these programs."[12] Certainly, with the current emphasis on values clarification as a teaching technique, this is something that can and must be utilized as students examine attitudes and feelings about sexuality. Part of a healthy sexual experience should be a consideration of the feelings, values, and beliefs of others, as well as the examination of one's own feelings. Values clarification, while not the only method, is one means of helping the student consider all aspects of his own sexuality and respect and understand the sexuality of others.

Because of both the recent cutbacks in federal aid to education and the declining enrollment rate, many schools have seen fit to cut back on the "frills." Often, this means that everything other than the basic reading, writing, and arithmetic must go. It will not be surprising if sex education programs are cut back because they are not basic to the traditional educational approach.

PROFESSIONALS IN SEX EDUCATION

According to Ann Landers, whenever you have a sexual problem that you cannot solve, or when you need advice, your doctor is a ready resource. The implication is that physicians know all the answers to sexual problems and that they are willing to assist you with these troubles. The fact is that it is only recently that medical schools and some nursing schools have included presentations and discussions on human sexuality in their curricula. Physicians have had courses in anatomy and physiology, but this in no way prepares them to discuss the intimate and candid aspects of sexuality. It may, in fact, inhibit discussion if the physician approaches the subject as a technical and unemotional issue, much the same as the textbook would. Certainly some physicians, some nurses, and some social workers are very adept at exploring sexual problems, but it cannot be taken for granted that this is true for the majority. The woman or man who gathers enough courage to present problems or questions of a sexual nature to a professional, only to be told not to worry about it, will think twice before bringing up the subject again.

Several important findings regarding the impact of professionals, especially physicians, were found in three separate studies. Volume VI of the *Technical Report of the Commission on Obscenity and Pornography* indicates that although doctors are listed third, after mother and father, as the best place for the average adolescent to get *most* of his information about sex, in actuality only 3 per cent of boys and 5 per cent of girls do receive most of their sex education from doctors.[16] Of the adult group, 4 per cent of men and 5 per cent of women received most of their sex education from their doctor Although schools as a source of sex information were not rated much higher for the adult group (8 per cent of men and 9 per cent of women), they were rated considerably higher (38 per cent) for both boys and girls. The church as a source of information was rated low in both the adult and adolescent groups. The results of this study indicate that "actual sources of information are somewhat different from the preferred sources."[16] It is interesting to note that adolescents listed adults as the best source of sex information; doctors, school, and church were second, third, and fourth on the list, rating above books, siblings, and friends. In other words, the expectation is that the professionals are second only to parents as the best potential sources of information about sex.

Another study compared initial sources of sex information.[14] Of 4191 college students from Arizona and Oklahoma, 37.9 per cent received their sex information from peers. Twenty and six tenths per cent of their information came from literature, 19.3 per cent from mother, 14.8 per cent from schools, 0.8 per cent from ministers, and 0.59 per cent from physicians. As the subject matter was categorized, it was interesting to note that most of the information that ministers did provide was on petting, and the greatest amount of information from physicians was on contraception, seminal emission, and masturbation.

A final survey dealt with sources and accuracy of college students' sex knowledge. Of 266 students who were asked to list their sources of sex information, not one listed a health professional. School courses were listed by 48 of the students; 89 named friends; and 71 cited books.

Two conclusions could be drawn from these data: (1) It is unrealistic to expect that the professional should be the initial or even the best source of sexual information, and (2) professionals, especially physicians, are not meeting the public's expectation of them as one of the best resources of sex information — second only to parents. Regardless of which stand one would take, it is obvious that there is a gap between what the public expects from a professional and what is actually happening. That nurses, social workers, counselors, and other professionals were not even mentioned by respondents in the first two studies, and not even listed by the investigator in the last study, indicates that they have not been acknowledged as possible sources of sex education.

THE NURSE AS A SEX EDUCATOR

Today, more than at any other time, nurses are actively involved in health education. Not only public health nurses but also nurses in hospitals, outpatient departments, offices, industry, and home care are concerned about the health of the individual. Nurses traditionally spend more time with patients than any other health care worker, and because of this, the opportunity to discuss sex-related topics is far greater. Medical-surgical nurses are incorporating sexuality into care plans for patients who have suffered a cerebrovascular accident, have had a myocardial infarction, or have chronic illness or any other condition that interferes with normal functioning. Obstetrical nurses have led the way in discussing birth control, timing of return to sexual activity after delivery, and other topics about which mothers and fathers have questions. Public health nurses are actively involved in family planning clinics — not only teaching but actually doing the examinations and dispensing some methods of birth control. Clients who have been surveyed indicate that they prefer the nurse to do the examination and teach because she takes more time, explains what she is doing, and provides more information so that clients can make their own decisions.

Schools of nursing and continuing education programs for nurses have begun to include more and more information on sexuality in their curricula. Nurses are just beginning to demonstrate their ability to provide sex education on an ongoing basis. As with any other "new" approach, incorporating sex information into the plan as a routine part of patient care will be slow to gain acceptance. Until then, concerned nurses must work hard to provide the atmosphere to facilitate patients' comfort in asking questions and to provide the information needed to attain their optimal level of sexual functioning.

One can only hope that nurses will continue this trend. What the future holds for nurses as a source of sex information is dependent on how the public views the nurse in this role and the impact the nurse makes as a sex educator.

CONCLUSION

All professional programs must include more information about human sexuality through the didactic method, discussion, and sharing of attitudes, beliefs, and concerns. The importance of sex information for professionals is paramount. This information must be incorporated into undergraduate curricula and must become a part of continuing education for professionals. The public expects professionals to provide sex information and, theoretically, most professionals feel that they can provide this information.

Where are we now? We've come from an age of almost total repression of sexual expression, for reasons of protection, religion, or ignorance, to an age of sexual openness. Yet there are still discrepancies between what is expressed and what is internalized. How do we bridge the gap? Here are a few closing thoughts on the subject:

1. Sex education by adequately prepared professionals is limited to some students, some professionals, and very few adults. Therefore, education for human sexuality must be provided for all ages and all levels.

2. Didactic presentation of human sexuality information is not enough. Discussion and time for personal exploration of attitudes and values is essential.

3. Sexuality is as normal and natural as eating and sleeping. But to arrive at that level of acceptance it may be necessary to teach it separately to groups divided by age or sex until the total populace is able to discuss it openly and without fear.

4. There must be a personal and community commitment to the presence of sex information in everyday life: at home, in school, in church, at work, and in professional agencies.

5. To thoroughly enjoy and understand our own sexuality, we must respect the sexuality of all individuals, from infants to the elderly. Thus, respect and concern for one another is an absolute necessity if one person or group is not to dominate another by using sexuality as a weapon or a defense.

6. With adequate knowledge and open exploration of sexual values come tolerance, openness, and individuality. What more could we want!

REFERENCES

1. Brecher, E. M. *The Sex Researchers*. Boston: Little, Brown & Company, 1969.
2. Calderone, Mary S. and Sally Fox. SIECUS as a Voluntary Health Organization. *California School Health*, 3:7–9, January, 1967.
3. Conley, John A. and Robert S. Haff. The Generation Gap in Sex Education: Is There One? *The Journal of School Health*, 44:428–437, October, 1974.
4. Dearth, Paul B. Viable Sex Education in the Schools: Expectations of Students, Parents, and Experts. *The Journal of School Health*, 44:190–193, April, 1974.
5. Dunn, Patricia C. An Exploration of the Status and Future Directions of Graduate Programs in Health Education in the United States. *The Journal of School Health*, 44:493–500, November, 1974.
6. Hilu, Virginia (ed.). *Sex Education and The Schools*. New York: Harper and Row, 1967.
7. Katchadourian, Herant A., and Donald T. Lunde. *Fundamentals of Human Sexuality*, New York: Holt, Rinehart and Winston, Inc., 1972.
8. Kinsey, A. C., W. B. Pomeroy, and C. E. Martin. *Sexual Behavior in the Human Male*. Philadelphia: W. B. Saunders Co., 1948.
9. Kirkendall, L. A. *Kirkendall on Sex Education*. Eugene, Oregon: E. C. Brown Center for Family Studies, 1970.
10. Masters, William H. and Virginia Johnson. *Human Sexual Response*. Boston: Little, Brown & Company, 1966.
11. McCary, James Leslie. *Human Sexuality* (2nd edition). New York: D. Van Nostrand Company, 1973.
12. Reed, Charles E. An Analysis of the Perceptions of High School Principals in Public and Catholic Schools Relative to the Importance of Sex Education in the Curriculum. *The Journal of School Health*, 43:198–200, March 1973.
13. Reiss, Ira L. *Premarital Sexual Standards* (Study Guide No. 5). Sex Information and Education Council of the U.S., 1967.
14. *Report of The Commission on Obscenity and Pornography*. Washington, D.C.: U.S. Government Printing Office. September, 1970.
15. SIECUS. *Sexuality and Man*. New York: Charles Scribner's Sons, 1970.
16. *Technical Report of The Commission on Obscenity and Pornography*. Vol. II, V, & VI. Washington D.C.: U.S. Government Printing Office, 1971.
17. Vincent, Clark E. (ed.). *Human Sexuality in Medical Education and Practice*. Springfield, Illinois: Charles C Thomas, 1968.
18. Woody, Jane Divita. Contemporary Sex Education: Attitudes and Implications for Childrearing. *The Journal of School Health*, 43:241–246, April, 1973.

CHAPTER
8

CULTURAL ASPECTS OF HUMAN SEXUALITY

Carol Taylor

ORIENTAL BELIEFS

Many years ago I was hired by a Chinese warlord to teach his three top wives correct American social behavior. This particular warlord wished to father 100 sons, a traditional Chinese ambition, and in order to do so he had acquired many more wives than my three students. He had one set of wives for whom bearing children and exchanging sexual attentions was optional. These wives were professional women — teachers, nurses, doctors, and the like — and the warlord had married them to add prestige to new roles of this sort for Chinese women. At that time this seemed to me to be a creative use of polygyny, and I thought of this set of wives as the "token wives." My three students were the top three wives of the warlord's "traditional" set of wives, and he wanted them taught correct American social behavior, so that he could take a wife with him when he went to dinner parties in the homes of his American, Canadian, and English friends. Each Saturday morning the three wives would come for me in one of the warlord's cars, and we would ride from the university where my father taught to the center of the city, where the warlord, his wives, and their children lived. Each week I would spend a day, or a weekend, teaching the American way of life and observing the life style of a polygynous family.

According to his wives, this warlord discouraged jealousies by treating each of his wives fairly according to which set of wives she belonged to and according to her hierarchical position in that particular set of wives. Wives in both the traditional and token sets explained this sort of fairness to me in considerable detail. Position in each hierarchy was determined by a combination of factors. For the traditional wives such things as bearing a son, sexual and culinary skills, the size of the dowry, artistic accomplishments, size of feet, and other physical characteristics combined to determine position in the hierarchy. For the token wives, position in their hierarchy was established by a mixture of factors, which included such things as length of schooling and professional accomplishments. When Western experts praised the work of a token wife, her position in the hierarchy changed in the same way as a traditional wife's position was changed when she bore a son. Position in both hierarchies, traditional and token, was visible in such things as size and location of the wife's apartment, its furnishings, her clothing, jewelry, servants, and so forth.

When some months had passed, the warlord's wives began to ask me about monogamy. Why did Westerners who were wealthy enough to maintain many wives restrict themselves to a single wife? Were these single wives lonely? Were they overburdened by their responsibilities? (For them, these responsibilities included seeing to it that there were a sufficient number of male descendants to worship ancestors.) Who did these single wives confide in? When I replied, "Their husbands and their friends," they said, "Husbands should not be burdened in this fashion by their wives, and talking about family affairs outside the family is dangerous." I had assumed that these wives would be competitive; instead, I found them cooperative. One wife said, "From time to time one or another of us gets out of hand and the others work together to restore harmony."

They also asked me how Western wives learned the art of pleasuring their husbands. Their pleasuring arts included playing the flute and preparing culinary delicacies. When I explained that in the West we learned musical and culinary skills in our schools and became proficient at them not for the sake of our husbands but because it gave us pleasure as individuals to do so, one of them said, "Our pleasure comes from giving pleasure to our husband, to each other, and to our children. With us it is the group, with you the individual." The wife who made this comment had a high position in the hierarchy of the traditional set of wives despite her failure to produce a son and a rather plain appearance. She was well read and had written some elegant verse, rare accomplishments among Chinese women at that time. About sexuality they were less inhibited than I was. They learned from the most knowledgeable among them; we learned from peers as ignorant as ourselves. While they accepted human sexuality as being natural and a source of pleasure, we rated sex on a scale of best to worst.

One night as I was drifting off to sleep, I overheard my three students discussing me and monogamy. About monogamy they said, "Those unfortunate women. In the West the wives of the rich and powerful endure many of the hardships of the wives of poor men in our country. They do not lack for food, servants, and other comforts, but, as sole wives, they have no one to share their family responsibilities with. How could Western women have let this sort of thing happen to them?" They thought me strange but nonetheless liked me. One of them said, "She's like bird's nest soup: it gets better each time you taste it." They thought it unfortunate that my parents had not had my feet bound. As one wife put it, "Even with a large dowry, who is going to marry someone with feet that size?" On the whole they concluded that it would be better for me not to marry. They considered it a hardship to be a sole wife, and they did not consider me sexually adept. One of them said, "Even with bound feet she'd be too clumsy for it."

They also discussed my future as a nonwife. One wife said, "She could go into a nunnery." After discussing this possibility, they concluded that I was not sufficiently submissive. Finally, they decided that I would be well advised to follow in the footsteps of one or another of the token wives. They thought me too clumsy to be trusted with the task of "sewing people up" which, in their opinion, ruled out medicine, but felt that my loud voice would be an asset if I were to become a teacher.

FRENCH BELIEFS

My next encounter with sexuality in an alien culture was in France. During my first days as a student in Paris, male strangers accosted me on the streets. Some of them touched and patted me; all of them wanted a rendezvous; and most of them made comments about various parts of my anatomy. Thinking my accosters had mistaken the sort of woman I was, I ignored most of these advances. On several occasions, however, the accosting males were persistent, and I threatened to call a policeman. This threat did not seem to be an effective deterrent. Once a policeman was close enough to be called, and I called him. He listened to my complaint, then laughed and told me that these attentions were intended as compliments. In due course I learned how to accept encounters of this sort as compliments.

During my sojourn in France I became aware of two other aspects of human sexuality that surprised me. The sister of my best friend was preparing to get married and I discovered that she was being instructed in the techniques of love play by a prostitute, who was considered an artist in that sort of activity. When I expressed surprise my friend said, "Would you consider it sensible to learn how to cook as a preparation for marriage?" I agreed, and she said, "We consider it equally important to learn the art of the other way to a man's heart." At a later date I came to the conclusion that this approach to human sexuality had much to recommend it. Several summers later I was talking with two prostitutes in Avignon. Both of them were supported as mistresses and "freelanced" on the side. They told me that they were engaged to be married and would return to their villages to get married when they had saved adequate dowries. Apparently the industrialists who kept them as mistresses did not object to their increasing their savings by freelancing in their spare time; and their fiances knew about, and did not object to, the way in which they were earning their dowries. In our society dowries are not mandatory, but if they were, I suspect that this sensible way of earning one would not be acceptable. Both young women had explained to me that accumulating a dowry in other ways—farmwork, domestic service, and so forth—would lower their social status as well as take many years longer than this easier way.

AMERICAN BELIEFS

When I began to examine human sexuality in American culture I used these glimpses of sexuality in traditional China and in pre-World War II France to increase my objectivity. Instead of accepting what I saw, read, and heard as being "only natural," I asked myself what the reaction of the French and the prerevolutionary Chinese would be to the data I was collecting. The French cultivate the art of human sexuality. To the sophisticated American, sexuality has become a technologic feat measured in orgasms. The French seek advice from skilled courtesans; Americans learn about sexuality from a book. When the recipe fails, they seek help from sex therapists. The Chinese wives I knew would have found the French approach to human sexuality less alien than the American approach. My Chinese informants learned from expert practitioners and took pleasure in giving pleasure; when I translated pages out of a sex manual to them, one of them said, "It [sexuality] is an art, not a science."

How did human sexuality in its American cultural setting become a science, something couples work hard at and undergo therapy for? Societies organize sexuality into their life styles in many different ways. In some societies sexuality is reserved for procreation; at the other end of the sexuality continuum this source of abstinence is considered a crime against nature. In our own case, we have inherited a Puritan tradition that attempted to limit sex to procreation. Well into the present century, sex in America was supposed to be used only for procreation, and talk about sex was taboo. "Good" women endured sex but did not enjoy it; when they weren't using their sexuality to father children, men had "it" for their health as much as, if not more than, for the pleasure it gave them. In those days men were thought to need premarital sex in order to sow their wild oats and extramarital sex for the sake of their health. "Fallen" women and the victims of the white slave traffic populated the "houses" and "red light" districts that catered to these extramarital needs.

HISTORICAL ASPECTS

The history of concepts about masturbation in American society suggests how rapidly and in what directions our notions about sexuality have changed. Until the early part of the present century masturbation was credited with causing insanity and criminality. During most of the nineteenth century scientists apologized for using the word masturbation in scholarly papers rather than substituting a euphemism for it. During recent years the taboos against masturbation have weakened. Masturbation was realized to be harmless at the end of the first quarter of the twentieth century, and in recent years it has become a therapeutic technique.

In the early part of the nineteenth century, a study was done that proved that masturbation caused insanity and criminality. A sample of subjects from the general population could not be questioned at that time because people did not talk about that sort of thing in those days. Consequently the researchers were forced to question and observe the inmates of prisons and insane asylums. The researchers were attempting to discover if masturbation, a sin, endangered the body as well as the soul. Their hypothesis was that it did. The high frequency of masturbation in prisons and insane asylums supported this hypothesis and led the researchers to conclude that masturbation did indeed cause criminality and insanity. As a consequence, instillation of antimasturbation values became standard American child-rearing practice until after World War I. One of the methods advocated by the experts was to tether the infant's hands and feet to the four corners of the cot. After World War I child-rearing experts discovered that masturbation was not as dangerous as it once was thought to be. The experts explained that infants masturbated because they needed to explore the world around them, including their own bodies. Parents who worried about masturbating offspring were advised to give their infants more attractive toys to play with. The most recent shift in expert opinion about masturbation in our society is toward its becoming a therapeutic technique. Today masturbation is used by the male in the treatment of premature ejaculation, and masturbation therapy is used to "introduce" female patients to their orgasms. Although the status of masturbation has changed, the lay public continue to attach a stigma to its practice. Sex therapists have stated that the taboo against masturbation and superstitions about its harmful effects make many of their patients reluctant to use masturbation as a therapeutic modality. For example, a wife reported being unable to talk to her young son about masturbation and asked her husband to do so. When he returned, she asked him what he had said. He answered, "I didn't know what to say so I told him next time he wanted to do it to wash his hands first."

KINSEY REPORT

In our society masturbation and sexuality did not become acceptable topics of conversation until the 1950's, after the Kinsey report disclosed considerably more sexual activity in the American life style than most Americans were willing to admit. This report startled a population that apparently had presumed itself to be more sexually inhibited than it was, and the consequences were interesting. Some members of our society predicted that the Kinsey report would incite rampant sexuality and that the promiscuity rate would rapidly become astronomical. Others began to behave as if they had been presented with a yardstick for measuring their sexual prowess. "I must have been underindulging for years." "I'm above average in that respect [intercourse frequency]." "She's a ninety-plus percenter [his partner's orgasm — intercourse ratio]." "We're losers; on all counts, we're in the bottom twenty-five percentile." "We're working on it and our rating is going up, up, and up." Comments of this sort were typical and suggested that the Kinsey report not only had brought American sexuality into the open but was also turning American sexual behavior into a competition.

CHANGING SEXUAL BEHAVIOR

A number of factors combined to modify the patterns of sexual behavior in American society. Originally American sexuality was expressed within the limits imposed by the Judao–Christian value system. Enjoying sexual activity was against our religion, and any sexual behavior that did not contribute to procreation threatened the integrity of body and soul. Science began to replace religion as arbiter of our social and sexual behavior. After all, God was against masturbation, and the first research done about masturbation by American scientists seemed to prove that masturbation was extremely dangerous. These scientists may have doubted God's existence, but they knew He was right about masturbation! Subsequent research proved the experts wrong, and masturbation became a harmless way of passing time — unless too much time was consumed by it.

Traditional male and female roles also helped to pattern sexuality in the American culture. Traditionally, the American female was not encouraged to be sexual. She was, and in many cases still is, trained from early childhood to evaluate the males she encountered as possible mates. Before she entered school she was told by her mother, her mother's friends, and older girls that she and this or that male made a "cute" couple. During the years spent in school, teachers and peers frequently made comments about what kind of couple she and various males would make. In our society the female is expected to be passive, to defer to males, and to be flexible. When she married she was expected to pattern her life style on her husband's. In our society marriage is not arranged; the female is prepared for it by the educational system in much the same way males are prepared to earn a living. In short, society makes the American female's role a dependent, mate-seeking one; however, built into it is the ability to assume the independent role of breadwinner should it become necessary to do so.

The traditional American male is expected to be aggressive and competitive. From birth he is encouraged to behave "like a man." Boys are taught to fight with each other; not to cry when they are hurt; to play with manly toys—guns and soldiers rather than houses and dolls; to excel in manly sports (football and hunting, for example); and to come out on top. They are expected to work when they are adults even if there is no economic necessity to do so, and they are trained in mate seeking. As one young man put it, "Its O.K. to screw around but you gotta avoid getting trapped into marriage. You don't marry the ones that screw around." When the male marries he is expected to be a good provider and to see to it that his children have a better chance to get ahead than he did. America is an upwardly mobile society. American families share the responsibility with the educational system of making upward mobility work, and the American father is expected to see to it that his children, particularly his sons, surpass him. Although women's liberation, humanistic psychology, and other influences have done much to modify the American male and female roles, many males and females in our society retain more of the traditional characteristics of their sex roles than they sometimes realize.

American sexuality has been secularized, and the scientist has replaced the priest as the expert on acceptable sexual behavior. When sexuality was taboo as a topic of conversation in mixed company, males could, and frequently did, boast about their sexual prowess to other males. This sort of boasting is one way in which males in many societies, including America, display their manliness. The American female boasted to other females about her prowess in what society had trained her to do—to attract and evaluate potential mates—and she tended to be reticent about and to understate the sexuality she exuded in doing so.

The Kinsey report brought American sexuality into public view, and it provided the American male with an impartial yardstick with which to measure his sexuality. Because males in our society are supposed to succeed, American males began to measure their sexuality and manliness in terms of frequency of intercourse and their partner's orgasm–intercourse ratio. The female response to the changing sexual scene was more complex. Some females became competitive not only with the Kinsey statistics but also with their partners. One victim of this phenomenon said, "She [his wife] has become insatiable, she's wearing me out." Females with a low orgasm–intercourse ratio were placed in an awkward position. Although they knew that many other women had equally low ratios and that some women claimed never to have experienced an orgasm, most females with low orgasm–intercourse ratios felt that something was wrong either with themselves or with their partners. The experts have placed the responsibility for bringing the female to orgasm on the male: In usual cases, inadequate foreplay or premature ejaculation or both are supposed to cause the female's failure to reach orgasm. As one woman said, "What is a poor couple to do? The man can wear himself out trying. The woman can boost his ego by lying about it [having an orgasm] or she can really cut him down to size." And a man said, "There must be more to it [intercourse] than keeping score." An Italian friend of mine said, "I knew Americans counted calories which, in my opinion, takes the pleasure out of eating, but I did not know that they were taking the pleasure out of sex in your country by counting orgasms." And his wife said, "It is so American to make work out of love play." It seems to be equally American to seek treatment from a therapist when one suspects sexual deficiencies rather than to conclude that a lack of skill is causing the problem and consult an artist in sexuality.

The emergence of sex therapy is an excellent example of culture-patterning sexuality. America is a scientifically oriented society that values individual achievement and is proud of its technology. As soon as the Kinsey report came out, one could have predicted that sex therapy rather than rampant promiscuity would be its most striking product. In a society where individual achievement is valued, impartial yardsticks lead to competitiveness. Most Americans want to be as above average as they possibly can. One man put it this way: "Bigger and better is the American way of life. As a country we've made it: we're the richest, most advanced country in the world, and we got there because most Americans are determined to make it to the top as individuals. In America there is more get-up-and-go per capita than there is in any other country in the world." The Kinsey report provided a score board for recording American sexuality. It could have been predicted that many couples would be dissatisfied with their sexuality scores and would work hard at improving their performances. In a success-oriented society, even those with high scores wish for higher scores. If these improvements did not meet expectations, couples would tend to blame each other—scapegoating is common practice in our culture. The next step would be to seek help, and before sex therapy emerged as a specialty, couples seeking help would be most likely to consult marriage counselors (lay and religious), physicians, and psychologists. They would seek help from therapists of one sort or another because they would assume that they needed a cure for whatever was wrong with them. An American would not be likely to conclude that what he or she needed was instruction in the art of sexuality. The French, the Japanese, and a number of other cultures recognize the need for this sort of instruction. In their societies sexuality is an art; in our society sexuality has been sanctioned for pleasure as well as procreation but is more of a science than an art.

Overpopulation and reliable contraceptives have shifted the

emphasis from procreation to human sexuality as an end in itself. Residual Puritan hang-ups are becoming weaker. The male and female roles in our society are becoming less polarized and more flexible. Communes, open-ended marriages, and other innovations are changing American mating patterns. There is an increasing emphasis on being open with and sensitive to others. Life styles in which satisfaction comes from what one is doing rather than how much one is being paid are emerging. These and other changes in our cultural climate suggest that the sexual inhibitions invented by our forefathers and their gods are eroding rapidly. American sexuality was a sin in the past, became a technology measured in orgasms, and in the future will become a pleasure and an art.

An expansion of the notions touched on in this chapter is to be found in: Taylor, Carol. *America and Us: The Two Hundred Year Old Invention.* New York: Holt, Rinehart and Winston, 1977.

REFERENCES

1. Goodman, P. *Growing Up Absurd.* New York: Random House, 1960.
2. Masters, William H. and Virginia Johnson. *Human Sexual Response.* Boston: Little, Brown & Company, 1966.
3. McBride, A. *The Growth and Development of Mothers.* New York: Harper & Row, 1973.

COUNSELING REGARDING BIRTH CONTROL METHODS

*Linda Huxall, R.N., M.N.,
and Suzanne Sawyer, B.S.N.*

The purpose of this chapter is twofold: (1) to increase the health professional's knowledge by presenting the latest information on the normal physiology of the menstrual cycle and how methods of contraception relate to it; and (2) to offer some practical and, it is hoped, helpful suggestions regarding patient counseling and teaching. Knowledge of the physiology of the normal menstrual cycle will better equip a person to understand how the various methods of contraception work.

THE NORMAL MENSTRUAL CYCLE

The menstrual cycle affects the reproductive system for approximately 30 to 40 years of a woman's life. Continuous activity, largely unseen and unfelt, occurs in widely separated organs that normally interact in a unified and predictable manner via the actions of specific hormones.

The action of the hypothalamus, anterior pituitary, and ovaries cannot be directly observed. However, changes in the many "end organs" can be studied that reflect the activity of ovarian hormones. In this chapter, the term reproductive "end organ" is used to denote one that is affected by the ovaries but does not, in turn, exert any effect upon them. The endometrium of the uterus is one of the most important of these "end organs."

The relationships between the hypothalamus, anterior pituitary, and ovaries can be explained in simple terms.

1. The hypothalamus secretes gonadotropin-releasing factor,* which affects the anterior pituitary.
2. Via this releasing factor, the anterior pituitary secretes hormones—follicle-stimulating hormone (FSH) and luteinizing hormone (LH)—that stimulate the ovaries.

---

*There is considerable debate whether a separate releasing factor exists for each of the pituitary hormones, FSH and LH, or whether a single releasing factor controls both.[6]

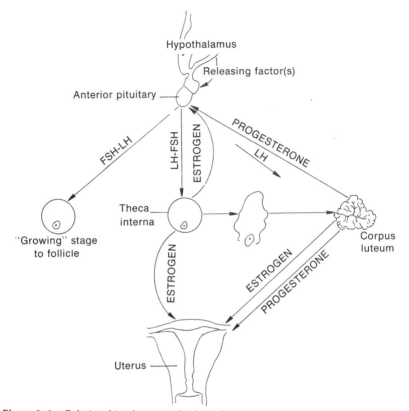

Figure 9–1. Relationships between the hypothalamus, anterior pituitary, and ovaries.

3. Under the influence of FSH and LH, the ovaries secrete hormones that
    a. stimulate or inhibit the releasing factor and pituitary hormones;
    b. affect a group of end organs within the reproductive system; and
    c. affect end organs and structures in other systems.[10]

Hypothalamus

The hypothalamus, centrally located at the base of the brain, is a complex collection of nerve centers called "nuclei" connecting to many portions of the brain. Each nucleus is a collection of many individual nerve cells. The interrelationships of the hypothalamic nuclei to each other and to adjacent brain centers have not yet been precisely defined. However, it is well documented that the hypothalamus is involved in numerous important physiological control mechanisms other than reproductive hormone secretion. These include temperature regulation, appetite, thirst, some elements of cardiovascular interrelations, and many aspects of emotional display.[2]

Hypothalamic function can be altered by external stimuli such as emotion, stress, and major time-zone changes. These stimuli can affect the output of hypothalamic releasing factors and, therefore, ultimately affect the function of the pituitary and the ovaries. An example of this effect is frequently seen when young women cease menstruating or menstruate irregularly while away from home for the first time. Another example is demonstrated when a woman who is fearful or extremely desirous of pregnancy has a delayed menstrual period.

The Pituitary Gland

The pituitary gland is a rounded body formed of two distinct portions: the anterior lobe and the posterior lobe. This gland rests in the bony portion of the skull known as the sella turcica (little saddle). The pituitary gland is attached to the base of the hypothalamus by a stalk of nervous tissue continuous with the posterior lobe. The posterior lobe secretes antidiuretic hormone (ADH) and oxytocin.

The anterior lobe is not directly connected to the hypothalamus; central nervous system control of this lobe's secretion is exerted via an unusual vascular blood supply. All the blood supplying the anterior lobe is derived from vessels that begin as a capillary bed in the hypothalamus. These capillaries progressively coalesce to form the long portal vessels that course down the pituitary stalk into the anterior lobe and once again break into capillaries. Thus, hypothalamic secretions reach the anterior pituitary through a neurohumoral route. The anterior lobe secretes growth hormone (GH), thyroid-stimulating hormone (TSH), and adrenocorticotropin (ACTH) in addition to the two gonadotropic hormones, follicle-stimulating hormone (FSH) and luteinizing hormone (LH). There are also inhibiting factors for melanocyte-stimulating hormone (MSH), growth hormone (GH), and prolactin (HPr or LTH).*

FOLLICLE-STIMULATING HORMONE

Follicle-stimulating hormone (FSH) stimulates the development of ovarian follicles. In combination with LH (luteinizing hormone), FSH contributes to the secretion of estrogens and the release of the ovum from the mature follicle.

---

*HPr (human prolactin) is now the preferred abbreviation. Prolactin was originally thought to be essential for maintenance of the corpus luteum—hence the abbreviation LTH (luteotropic hormone).[8]

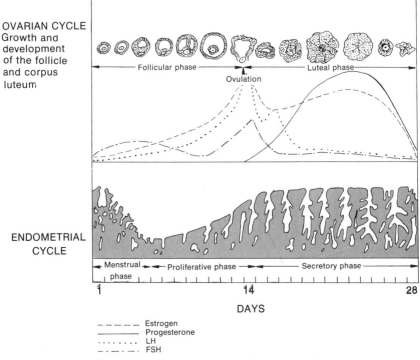

OVARIAN CYCLE
Growth and
development
of the follicle
and corpus
luteum

ENDOMETRIAL
CYCLE

DAYS

– – – – – Estrogen
———————— Progesterone
. . . . LH
– . — . — . FSH

Figure 9–2.   The ovarian and endometrial cycles.

The release of FSH (and LH) is inversely related to estrogen levels. When estrogen levels are *low,* the hypothalamic releasing factor increases, causing increased secretion of FSH. This signals the ovaries to produce more estrogens. Conversely, when estrogen levels are *high,* the hypothalamic releasing factor decreases, causing decreased secretion of FSH. This signals the ovaries to decrease production of estrogens.[10]

The level of FSH spikes significantly just before ovulation and then returns to lower levels until shortly before the onset of menses. The exact stimulus for this preovulatory spike is not yet completely understood. Rising levels of estrogens probably trigger the hypothalamus. Recent experiments suggest that the ovarian hormone 17-hydroxyprogesterone may also play a role. The less dramatic rise in FSH before the onset of menses may initiate the growth and development of a new set of follicles.

LUTEINIZING HORMONE

Luteinizing hormone (LH) acts with FSH to effect the release of the ovum from the mature ovarian follicle. A small amount (basal level) of

LH is necessary to maintain the corpus luteum after ovulation. Luteinizing hormone is also necessary for steroidogenesis, the process by which ovarian, testicular, and adrenal hormones are manufactured.

Levels of LH are low early in the ovarian cycle, increase gradually, surge sharply approximately 24 hours before ovulation, and then fall to low and fairly constant levels until just before the next menses. The preovulatory surge of LH is also believed to be caused by rising levels of estrogens or, possibly, the ovarian hormone 17-hydroxyprogesterone. The rise in LH before the next menses may serve to augment the actions of FSH on follicular growth for the next cycle.

The Ovarian Cycle

The ovary is a dynamic structure in which vesicular follicles are constantly developing from those of the prenatal type. The very first "growing" (primary) follicles appear in the fetus during the second month of gestation and reach a peak level of about seven million by the fifth month. From this time onward, the oocytes rapidly begin degenerating by a process known as atresia. Approximately one million remain at birth to provide the stock for the 300 to 400 oocytes that will undergo varying stages of maturation during the average reproductive life span of any given woman.[2]

FOLLICULAR PHASE

The factors that *initiate* follicular growth in the primordial follicle are unknown at present. This early stage of development is independent of cyclic pituitary hormone stimulation.[*] It is known, however, that the FSH and LH present during the reproductive life cycle stimulate "growing" follicles to undergo further growth and maturation. During each ovarian cycle, about 20 antral follicles have matured enough theoretically to respond to the LH surge--FSH spike that produces ovulation. Of course, usually only one follicle develops into a fully mature graafian follicle and undergoes ovulation. The remainder degenerate. The mechanism that selects the follicle for ovulation from among the 20 or so seemingly identical neighboring follicles remains a mystery at this time.

---

[*]Many diagrams of the ovarian cycle misleadingly show a primordial follicle developing to full maturity in one cycle.

OVULATION

As the follicle destined for ovulation is developing, specialized cells known as the theca interna are secreting estrogens. The graafian follicle enlarges, gradually reaches the surface of the ovary, and finally protrudes above it. The cells in the exposed tip of the follicle float away so that the region becomes transparent and quite thin. The actual rupture of the follicle (ovulation) takes several minutes.

LUTEAL PHASE

After ovulation, the graafian follicle undergoes dramatic changes, during which it is rapidly converted into another endocrine gland, the corpus luteum (yellow body). The main function of the corpus luteum is to produce the hormone progesterone, which is essential to the maintenance of pregnancy. Estrogens and other steroids are also produced in large amounts.

If fertilization does not occur, the corpus luteum is maintained via the action of LH for 14 ($\pm$2) days. Thereafter, degeneration and eventual scarring convert the structure into a fibrous mass, the corpus albicans (white body).

If fertilization takes place, the corpus luteum is maintained via LH and later by human chorionic gonadotropin (HCG), a product of the placenta. The corpus luteum is essential for implantation and for hormone production up to about seven weeks of gestation. By this time, the placenta is capable of assuming the responsibility for hormone production.

The portion of the ovarian cycle during which the corpus luteum develops and regresses is known as the luteal phase. This phase begins immediately after ovulation and ends with the onset of development of a new crop of follicles, approximately the first day of menses.

The Endometrial Cycle

The endometrium, the layer of tissue lining the uterus, plays a vital role in reproduction. As sperm pass through the intrauterine cavity to the oviducts, they are bathed in endometrial secretions. As the fertilized ovum is transported to the uterine cavity, it receives nutrients from these secretions during the days before implantation. Following implantation, the embryo is dependent upon an adequate vascular supply within the endometrium.

The endometrium is selectively responsive to the ovarian hormones, estrogens and progesterone.* These hormones must be secreted cyclically and with an optimal quantitative ratio of each in order to produce maximal growth and maturation of the endometrial tissue.

PROLIFERATIVE PHASE

The proliferative phase of the endometrial cycle begins the last day of menses and ends just after ovulation. During this phase, under the influence of estrogens, proliferation (growth) occurs in the glands, stroma (connective tissue elements), blood vessels, and superficial epithelium of the endometrium. The proliferative phase varies from one woman to another; this accounts for the difference in menstrual intervals (the first day of one menses to the first day of the next menses). Only about 15 per cent of all women actually have a 28-day menstrual interval. Approximately 77 per cent have menstrual intervals that fall within the range of 25 to 31 days, however.[4]

SECRETORY PHASE

Estrogens continue to be secreted following ovulation as the graafian follicle is incorporated into the corpus luteum. In addition, progesterone converts the proliferative endometrium into a secretory endometrium. The stroma and supporting tissue of the endometrium become edematous in appearance. This "succulent" tissue is rich with glycogen-containing vacuoles.

If implantation does not occur, white blood cells (polymorphonuclear leukocytes) migrate into the tissue about 14 days post ovulation, and the endometrial tissue prepares for menstruation. The secretory phase is fairly constant from woman to woman, averaging 14 ($\pm$2) days.

Estrogens: Estrogen is the collective term for all substances capable of producing the following changes in the reproductive tract: proliferation of the endometrium; growth of the cells of the uterus; increase in amount of cervical mucus and increased permeability by sperm; growth of the duct system in breasts; and cornification of the vagina with an acidic pH. Estrogens also increase cardiovascular blood flow and factor V and prothrombin levels, diminish sebaceous activity and increase water content of the skin, and stimulate epiphyseal closure of long bones.

Progestogens: A group of compounds capable of inducing a secretory change in the endometrium, which has been prepared or "primed" by estrogens; decreasing the amount of cervical mucus and also making it hostile to sperm; and developing the glandular portion of the breasts. Progestogens increase the basal body temperature by 0.4 to 0.6° C after ovulation. Progesterone is the major progestogen produced by the corpus luteum.[4]

TABLE 9–1.   Comparison of Ovarian Cycle and Endometrial Cycle

OVARIAN CYCLE		*ENDOMETRIAL CYCLE*
Follicular phase	=	Menstrual phase plus proliferative phase
Ovulation		
Luteal phase	=	Secretory phase

MENSTRUAL PHASE

When the corpus luteum ceases to function, the levels of estrogens and progesterone fall. Menstruation is estrogen-progesterone withdrawal bleeding, since both hormones have been withdrawn from the endometrium. The menstrual phase averages four to six days, but lengths from two to eight days may be considered normal. The duration of menses is, however, usually fairly constant in each woman.[4]

Comparison of Ovarian Cycle and Endometrial Cycle

The menstrual plus the proliferative phases of the endometrial cycle correspond to the follicular phase of the ovarian cycle. The secretory phase of the endometrial cycle corresponds to the luteal phase of the ovarian cycle.

HORMONAL CONTRACEPTION

Oral Contraceptives

Two types of oral contraceptives are currently in common use in the United States.

1. *Combination* pills, containing both an estrogen and a progestogen, are taken in the same dosage each day for 20 to 21 days. This is followed by no more than seven days without medication to allow for withdrawal bleeding. Many companies have added seven placebo pills of a different color to the 21-pill cycle. These 28-day pills are taken continuously, since menses will occur while the placebos are taken.

2. *Progestogen-only* tablets, containing a low dosage of progestogen, are taken continuously whether or not bleeding occurs. These pills are commonly known as the "mini-pill."

Table 9–2 lists all the oral contraceptives available in the United States as of September, 1977. The pills are listed in order from the most estrogenic to the least estrogenic. Any attempt at producing such a chart has several shortcomings. Different estrogens and different proges-

TABLE 9–2.   Oral Contraceptives Available in the United States

Trade Name and Number of Pills	Progestogen	mg./tab.	Estrogen	mcg./tab.
Enovid-E (20, 21)	norethynodrel	2.5	mestranol	100
Enovid 5 (20)	norethynodrel	5.0	mestranol	75
Enovid 10 (20)	norethynodrel	10	mestranol	150
Ovulen (21, 28)	ethynodiol diacetate	1.0	mestranol	100
Norinyl 2 (20) Ortho–Novum 2 (20)	norethindrone	2.0	mestranol	100
Demulen (21, 28)	ethynodiol diacetate	1.0	ethinyl estradiol	50
Norinyl 1 + 80 (21, 28) Ortho–Novum 1/80 (21, 28)	norethindrone	1.0	mestranol	80
Ovcon-50 (28)	norethindrone	1.0	ethinyl estradiol	50
Zorane 1/50 (28) Norlestrin 1 (21, 28, Fe)	norethindrone acetate	1.0	ethinyl estradiol	50
Norinyl 1 + 50 (21, 28) Ortho-Novum 1/50 (21, 28)	norethindrone	1.0	mestranol	50
Ovral (21, 28)	norgestrel	0.5	ethinyl estradiol	50
Norlestrin 2.5 (21, 28, Fe)	norethindrone acetate	2.5	ethinyl estradiol	50
Ortho–Novum 10 (20)	norethindrone	10	mestranol	60
Zorane 1.5/30 (28) Loestrin 1.5/30 (28, Fe)	norethindrone acetate	1.5	ethinyl estradiol	30
Brevicon (21, 28) Modicon (21, 28)	norethindrone	0.5	ethinyl estradiol	35
Ovcon-35 (28)	norethindrone	0.4	ethinyl estradiol	35
Neocon (21)	norethindrone	1.0	ethinyl estradiol	35
Lo/Ovral (21)	norgestrel	0.3	ethinyl estradiol	30
Zorane 1/20 (28) Loestrin 1/20 (28, Fe)	norethindrone acetate	1.0	ethinyl estradiol	20

MICRODOSE ORAL CONTRACEPTIVES

Nor–Q.D. (42)	norethindrone	0.35	none	
Micronor (35)	norethindrone	0.35	none	
Ovrette (28)	norgestrel	0.075	none	

Fe = last seven pills contain iron.

togens do not have the same potency even though the dosage is the same. Also, the balance between the estrogen and the progestogen is very important; one compound may tend to overshadow the other. Finally, any pill ingested falls prey to each woman's individual chemistry; do not forget that the adrenal glands also produce hormones. This chart is intended to be used only as a guide for initial selection of or necessary adjustments in oral contraceptives.

MODE OF ACTION AND EFFECTIVENESS

Basically, the combination oral contraceptives suppress the hypo-thalamic–anterior pituitary–ovarian system, thus preventing normal cyclic ovarian production of hormones. Ovulation is therefore suppressed.

Combination pills also provide secondary contraceptive effects. The constant presence of the progestogen produces a cervical mucus that is thick, scanty, and hostile to sperm throughout the cycle. Also, the endometrium is an artificially induced mixed proliferative secretory type that does not easily support implantation. Taken correctly, this type of oral contraceptive is essentially 100 per cent effective.[11]

The progestogen-only pills, because of their low dosage, usually do not suppress ovulation. The constant administration of a progestogen produces a hostile cervical mucus and an endometrium that inhibits implantation. In well controlled studies in which these "mini-pills" were taken at the same time each day every day of the month, they were 97 per cent effective.[11]

In determining the effectiveness of any contraceptive, a distinction must be made between theoretical effectiveness (perfect usage without error or omission) and use-effectiveness (protection actually achieved under real-life situations, including errors and omission). There is frequently a higher failure rate than the stated percentages. Many women take their pills erratically, do not remember missing pill(s), or may believe that they are taking them correctly. Many women are reluctant to admit that they took the pills incorrectly until they have been assured that they are not pregnant!

SIDE EFFECTS AND CONTRAINDICATIONS

The side effects of oral contraceptives can roughly be divided into symptoms that mimic pregnancy and symptoms that are related to the menstrual cycle. Some of the most common "pseudopregnancy" symptoms include nausea, vomiting, fluid retention with cyclic weight gain, headaches, vertigo, breast enlargement and tenderness, chloasma, and leukorrhea. These symptoms are related to the estrogen content of the pills. Additional symptoms such as fatigue, depression, oily scalp, acne, and increased appetite with steady weight gain are related to the progestogen.[13]

Most women taking combination oral contraceptives experience some changes in their menstrual cycle. For the most part, these changes are physically and emotionally positive. The menstrual cycle is very regular. (Please note: the pills *suppress* the reproductive hormonal system, they do not "regulate" it. Bleeding is "regular.") The pills shorten the duration of the menstrual period for most women, a situation that is welcomed by most. In addition, most pills usually reduce or completely relieve spastic dysmenorrhea and the distressing symptoms of premenstrual tension. Endometriosis and menorrhagia are two other conditions that are usually relieved by combination pills.[11]

We are finding an increasing number of women who complain of too little bleeding (hypomenorrhea) while on the pill. Many want their pill switched for this reason alone; they may also simply stop taking them. There is a very strong conviction held by some women that a certain amount of bleeding is necessary for good health. In addition, if a woman is not told to expect a light menses, she very often fears that she is pregnant and will stop taking her pills.

Breakthrough bleeding ("spotting") is another frequent problem. Women should always be questioned carefully regarding their pill-taking schedules. When the spotting is caused by missed pills, as is often the case, these women need counseling and teaching rather than a change in pills. If a woman is taking her pills correctly and breakthrough bleeding occurs for two cycles, the pill should be changed. We do not recommend doubling up on the pills. This practice only confuses the woman's schedule.

The "mini-pills" almost always produce changes in a woman's menstrual cycle, but these changes are not as desirable as the aforementioned. Bleeding is very unpredictable. The main reason for women's discontinuing this type of pill is irregular bleeding and lack of cycle control. The "mini-pill" may, nevertheless, be a good choice for those women who cannot take estrogen or cannot tolerate an intrauterine device.[13]

Absolute contraindications for taking oral contraceptives include a history of thrombophlebitis or embolism, moderate to severe hypertension, pill-related migraine, undiagnosed breast masses, known or suspected estrogen-dependent neoplasms, undiagnosed abnormal genital bleeding, congestive heart failure, and severe liver disease. Women with cervical polyposis, a history of severe depression, deep vein varicosities, epilepsy, diabetes, gallbladder disease, or frequent monilial vaginal infections should be monitored closely.[6]

PATIENT TEACHING

Because there are such a large number of oral contraceptives, each with different packaging and schedules, patient teaching is of prime importance. One should never assume that a woman will understand how to take the pills correctly. Many women have been on several different pills and have utilized various schedules. For example, if the woman is not told that the last seven pills in a 28-pill package are placebos, she may very well take all of them and then stop for seven days.

Since so many birth control pills are now designed to be started on a Sunday, we almost exclusively teach the "Sunday schedule" to all women taking 21- or 28-day pills. The initial cycle of pills is started the first Sunday after menses or therapeutic abortion. We usually wait until the second Sunday after delivery to begin pills for postpartum patients who are not breast feeding, owing to their greater amount of bleeding. The "Sunday schedule" not only is easy to remember but also has an extra bonus: there is never bleeding on a weekend.

Although it still remains an all too common practice, women who have been on the pill two or three years do not routinely need to be taken off oral contraceptives for a few months. The reasoning behind this practice is now rather obscure but appears to be related to the belief that long-term usage would (1) "oversuppress" the system, making future pregnancy difficult and (2) lead to hypertension. Current large-scale retrospective and prospective studies have discredited both these concerns.[11] We do not, however, mean to imply that careful screening and follow-up of patients should be minimized. If the medical advisor recommends a "rest" from the pills, an alternate method of contraception must be used if pregnancy is to be avoided. Far too many therapeutic abortions are performed because women are taken off the pill, led to believe that they cannot get pregnant easily, and offered no other form of contraception.

Postcoital Contraceptives

Postcoital contraceptives, better known as "the morning-after pill," consist of high oral doses or injection(s) of estrogens. They are given within 72 hours after *one* episode of unprotected intercourse during a single menstrual cycle. These contraceptives are most often used for rape victims. Their mode of action is thought to be multiple. They appear to be effective by one or more of the following mechanisms: (1) interfering with ovum transport, (2) decreasing progesterone secretion by the corpus luteum, or (3) interfering with the implantation process. The estrogen diethylstilbestrol (DES) is no longer used for postcoital contraception because there is a danger of producing a rare form of vaginal cancer in the offspring.[12]

Injectable Progestogens

Depo-Provera (medroxyprogesterone acetate), a product of the Upjohn Company, is currently the only injectable progestogen in common use for contraception. Noristerat (norethisterone enanthate) by Schering AG will soon be available for family planning organizations. Injectable progestogens are highly effective in preventing pregnancy. They also have the advantage of being administered only two or four times a year and do not suppress lactation, as do the oral contraceptives. However, the injectable long-acting progestogens are not without problems. Their chief disadvantage is that they seriously disrupt the menstrual cycle. These progestogens are quite strong and suppress the hypothalamic-pituitary-ovarian pathways. Amenorrhea is common. In addition, the return of fertility after discontinuation may be delayed. Weight gain can also be a problem.[12] Injectable progestogens may be the contraceptive of choice for certain very unreliable patients and for women for whom sterilization is contraindicated.

Newer Approaches to Steroidal Contraceptives

Many of the future hormonal methods of contraception for women are now being field tested and may be available soon. Subcutaneous slow-releasing progestogen implants are being researched extensively and appear to show much promise. The one-pill-a-month contraceptive will no doubt be modified to decrease side effects.[2] One of the more thought-provoking ideas involves the use of the rhythm method together with pituitary gonadotropins. Testing is being done to determine whether a single pill of LH-FSH given orally near the calculated time of ovulation would induce predictable ovulation. Other researchers are working on finding a safe, inexpensive medication to be taken orally when the menstrual period is due that could render the corpus luteum inactive. In this way, pregnancy could not occur or continue.[6]

SURGICAL METHODS OF CONTRACEPTION

Endometrial aspiration is also known as menstrual extraction, menstrual planning, menstrual induction, and menstrual regulation. The actual technique is essentially the same as that used in performing an early therapeutic suction abortion. A local cervical block is usually given, after which a small uterine suction catheter is inserted. Suction of the endometrium is done by use of a special hand syringe or a standard vacuum pump.[5]

The major difference between endometrial aspiration and therapeutic abortion is the timing of the procedure. An "E.A." is done up to 10 or 12 days after the expected date of menses. This time period has been set because the majority of pregnancy tests are considered by many not to be accurate until after this time.

The entire procedure is, in fact, a matter of much controversy. Many feel that "an abortion is an abortion." They also do not believe that this procedure should be done "just for the convenience of the woman," citing the risks of unnecessary procedures and the complication of incomplete evacuation of the uterus, which occurs with use of small catheters and a syringe.

Proponents of endometrial aspirations believe that a woman should have the option of having this procedure before a pregnancy is confirmed, in order to reduce considerable anxiety. In addition, the cost of an endometrial aspiration ranges from approximately $25 to $60, whereas the most inexpensive therapeutic suction abortion averages about $150.

OTHER METHODS OF CONTRACEPTION

Nonsurgical methods of contraception include rhythm, the cervical mucus method, diaphragms and caps, spermicides, condoms, intrauterine devices, and hormonal control.

Mechanical Barriers and Spermicides

Mechanical barriers and spermicides are used by many couples who are concerned with possible alterations in body chemistry that can occur with oral contraceptives, and by women who do not feel that they need complete day-to-day protection from conception. They are also used as interim protection in the period before the contraceptive pill becomes effective.

CONDOM

Perhaps the most commonly used mechanical barrier is the condom, which is also known as a "sheath," "skin," "safe," "rubber," or "prophylactic." At present the condom represents the only reliable contraceptive short of vasectomy in which the male has the responsibility for prevention of pregnancy. A properly used high-quality condom can be as much as 80 per cent effective. In instructing patients in use of the condom, one must caution them that it should be applied to the erect penis carefully prior to penile-vaginal contact. Many of the more sophisticated condoms have "safety reservoirs" at the tip. In styles that lack this, a small space should be left at the end of the condom. For many couples, condom application can be made a part of the sexual foreplay. This aspect of sexual pleasure should be stressed, since many couples feel that this method of contraception may detract from rather than enhance intercourse. The pleasure attained from touching and stroking the genitals should be explained to couples.

A major advantage of the condom is that it also provides some venereal disease (gonorrhea) prophylaxis. The condom would probably be an unacceptable type of contraception for couples who enjoy complete sexual spontaneity. The most common complaint is of decreased sensation in the male, but many of the newer condoms are of finer material that is very thin, yet strong.

SPERMICIDES

For more certain contraception, spermicides in the form of creams, foams, or jellies may be used with the condom. This combination provides about 90 per cent effectiveness, while the spermicide alone is about 60 per cent effective. Foams have also proven to be gonococcidal in in vitro tests. Complaints about foam concern mainly the "messiness" involved. A few women may also have hypersensitivity reactions to them or may develop a vulvovaginitis associated with their use. Men may also have an allergic reaction.

Spermicides must be inserted vaginally near the time of intercourse and prior to each sexual act, which requires conscious effort. Patients should be cautioned not to douche for six hours after intercourse, since this removes the spermicide. Spermicides may be suggested as an interim method in women who desire an IUD or who are waiting to begin taking oral contraceptives, or as a back-up protection when pills are forgotten.

DIAPHRAGM

The diaphragm can be obtained by prescription only, since it must be fitted by an experienced person. The woman desiring a diaphragm must be comfortable enough with her own body to be able to insert and remove the device. In fitting diaphragms, care should be taken to insure that the diaphragm covers the cervix and fits snugly. The patient should be instructed in its insertion and removal while in the office. She should attempt it herself, with a check by the practitioner, before leaving the office. It is a good idea to have the patient sit up, move around the room, and do several deep knee bends. She should be unaware of the diaphragm's presence during these maneuvers. If it remains in place, it is the correct size.

The diaphragm should be used with contraceptive jelly or cream made especially for use with diaphragms. These agents are spread liberally on both sides of the barrier. Foams should not be used; they may damage the diaphragm material. The device should be cleansed thoroughly with a mild soap after each use, dusted with plain (not perfumed) talc powder, and placed in its container. After a pregnancy or drastic weight change, a diaphragm should be refitted. The diaphragm may be inserted up to two hours prior to intercourse and should not be removed for at least six hours afterward. A good candidate for the diaphragm must be willing to use it faithfully as well as willing to put up with the inconvenience it presents.

INTRAUTERINE DEVICES

The most effective mechanical method of contraception available today is the intrauterine device (IUD). Out of sight and not readily accessible, this small piece of plastic or metal may seem mysterious; this image is enhanced by the fact that the professional cannot tell the patient exactly how or why it works. It is effective, however, in 95 to 98 per cent of all women who use it.

The most current and widely accepted theory about the mode of action of the IUD is that of a foreign-body reaction of the endometrium, which makes it hostile to sperm and makes implantation impossible. The speeding up of sperm-ova transport was an early theory that has since been discarded.

As of September, 1977, the four types of IUD's available for general unrestricted use in the United States were: Lippes Loop (Ortho), Saf-T-coil (Schmid), Cu-7 (Searle), and the Progestasert (Alza). The Dalcon shield (A. H. Robins) has been suspended pending modification of the tail and establishment of a patient registry system. The Copper T (TCu-200) has F.D.A. approval but is not being produced to any extent at present.

The Cu-7 and Copper T have a tiny copper coil on their transverse component. Low doses of copper have been shown to be spermicidal. Copper also brings about changes in the cellular metabolism of the endometrium that somehow contribute to contraceptive efficacy.[9]

With all devices, it is desirable for insertion to take place near the end of a normal menstrual period. This assures that the patient is not pregnant, and any bleeding associated with insertion will be masked. At this time also, the cervical canal is more patent. Postpartum insertion is desirable as well. Studies indicate that the later the postpartum insertion, the better the retention results. The uterine contractions in the early postpartum period may be of a strength to cause expulsion of the device. Insertion should be accomplished carefully and slowly by a trained professional. Sounding of the uterine cavity gives an estimation of the uterine depth, which is prognostic of patient tolerance to the device. Parous patients experience less discomfort. There have been cases of insertion syncope—cervical shock—which have been treated symptomatically. This complication is very transient but may require immediate removal of the device.[7]

Pregnancy may occur in 1 to 3 per cent of patients with an IUD. If the patient does not wish the pregnancy to be aborted, she may be reassured that there will be no increase in chances of a congenitally deformed child being born with one of the inert plastic IUD's. The copper IUD's and the Progestasert *must* be removed. With tailed devices that are left in place, 53 per cent of the pregnancies are spontaneously aborted; upon their removal, the rate of abortion becomes 48.7 per cent. With tail-less devices left in place, the abortion rate is 42.6 per cent; when attempts at removal or actual removal are performed, the rate rises to 82.4 per cent.[14]

Women considering an IUD should be informed of the probability of increased menstrual bleeding and cramping and also the possibility of intermenstrual spotting. The patient should be instructed how to feel the device's strings. This may be done in the office before she leaves. The patient should be told to call for an appointment if she is unable to detect the strings, if the strings suddenly feel much longer, or if the device itself begins to protrude through the cervix. In the last case, complete removal should follow, with reinsertion if the patient desires. Because most problems occur during the first cycle after insertion, it is desirable to schedule a revisit after this cycle to answer any questions that the patient may have and to determine if the device is still in place. The Cu-7 and Copper T should be replaced every three years, and the Progestasert every year. The inert plastic devices may remain in place indefinitely.

Rhythm

A contraceptive method requiring no mechanical or chemical aids is rhythm. Rhythm may be suitable for the woman with very regular menses who does not desire pregnancy but would not find it devastating. Rhythm is based on two facts: (1) ovulation occurs 14 days prior to the onset of menses, and (2) the length of viability of sperm is 48 hours, and the length of viability of ova is 48 hours. Taking basal body temperature over a period of time can increase the efficiency of the method, but even under the most ideal circumstances the pregnancy rate is about 14 per cent. Both parties must be sufficiently motivated to make rhythm effective. The couple should abstain from intercourse three days prior to expected ovulation and three days after ovulation, or a total of seven and possibly eight days. For some couples this may be no problem; however, for those who find abstinence difficult, other

THE THEORY OF RHYTHM:

28 DAY CYCLE

1 MENSTRUATION BEGINS	**2**	**3**	**4**	**5**	**6**	**7**
8	**9**	**10**	**11** INTERCOURSE ON THESE DAYS LEAVES LIVE SPERM TO FERTILIZE EGG	**12**	**13** RIPE EGG MAY BE RELEASED ON ANY OF THESE DAYS	**14**
15	**16** RIPE EGG MAY ALSO BE RELEASED ON THESE DAYS	**17** EGG MAY STILL BE PRESENT	**18**	**19**	**20**	**21**
22	**23**	**24**	**25**	**26**	**27**	**28**
1 MENSTRUATION BEGINS AGAIN						

BLACK NUMBER—"Safe days" when conception is unlikely.
RED NUMBER—"Unsafe days" when pregnancy may occur.

Figure 9–3.   The theory of rhythm. (From Havemann, E.: Birth Control. New York: Time, Incorporated, 1967.)

forms of sexual expression not including penile-vaginal contact should be utilized.

A more sophisticated rhythm method is the ovulation method of contraception described in detail by Billings, Billings, and Catarinich in *Atlas of the Ovulation Method*. In brief, this method is based on the premise that women can detect changes in cervical mucus during ovulation and should practice abstinence during these times. In many cities, courses are held to educate couples in this method. The training course requires extensive record-keeping and a rather extended period of abstinence initially. Women who douche or have frequent vaginal infections are not good candidates. This method also requires a great deal of self-control.[1]

THE RHYTHM METHOD

HOW TO FIGURE THE "SAFE" AND "UNSAFE" DAYS

LENGTH OF SHORTEST PERIOD	FIRST UNSAFE DAY AFTER START OF ANY PERIOD	LENGTH OF LONGEST PERIOD	LAST UNSAFE DAY AFTER START OF ANY PERIOD
21 DAYS	3RD DAY	21 DAYS	10TH DAY
22 DAYS	4TH DAY	22 DAYS	11TH DAY
23 DAYS	5TH DAY	23 DAYS	12TH DAY
24 DAYS	6TH DAY	24 DAYS	13TH DAY
25 DAYS	7TH DAY	25 DAYS	14TH DAY
26 DAYS	8TH DAY	26 DAYS	15TH DAY
27 DAYS	9TH DAY	27 DAYS	16TH DAY
28 DAYS	10TH DAY	28 DAYS	17TH DAY
29 DAYS	11TH DAY	29 DAYS	18TH DAY
30 DAYS	12TH DAY	30 DAYS	19TH DAY
31 DAYS	13TH DAY	31 DAYS	20TH DAY
32 DAYS	14TH DAY	32 DAYS	21ST DAY
33 DAYS	15TH DAY	33 DAYS	22ND DAY
34 DAYS	16TH DAY	34 DAYS	23RD DAY
35 DAYS	17TH DAY	35 DAYS	24TH DAY
36 DAYS	18TH DAY	36 DAYS	25TH DAY
37 DAYS	19TH DAY	37 DAYS	26TH DAY
38 DAYS	20TH DAY	38 DAYS	27TH DAY

Figure 9–4.   The rhythm method. (From Havemann, E.: Birth Control. New York: Time, Incorporated, 1967.)

STERILIZATION

For the woman who is certain that she desires no more children, permanent sterilization is an alternative. This is accomplished by tubal ligation, which can be performed a variety of ways, depending on her physician's preference. Tubal ligation will not alter the woman's menstrual cycle, is virtually 100 per cent effective, and is a permanent means of contraception. Many women believe that hormone secretion may be altered by a tubal ligation. It is necessary to educate couples by means of literature, diagrams, and verbal information to insure that they understand the different surgical procedures and outcomes for tubal ligation and for hysterectomy with and without an oophorectomy.

For the male, surgical sterilization is accomplished by vasectomy, in which the ductus (vas) deferens is severed. This, too, is a permanent procedure, and is usually done in the office under local anesthesia. Because live sperm may continue to be present in the ejaculate for as long as six weeks after vasectomy, the couple should use an alternative method of birth control until the male has had several negative semen specimens.

The permanence of these methods makes them undesirable for many couples, especially for persons who maintain a large part of their identity through the fact that they know that they are capable of reproducing. Depressions following either type of surgery are not uncommon. It is important that the emotional stability of the persons requesting permanent sterilization be evaluated so that the possibility of the development of untoward effects can be diminished. It is also imperative that these individuals understand that present sterilization procedures are irreversible.

NONRELIABLE METHODS OF CONTRACEPTION

There are a number of techniques employed to prevent conception that are not considered reliable. Included among these are douching, coitus interruptus, different positions during intercourse, and homemade preparations or solutions.

Coitus interruptus, or withdrawal, fails because the pre-ejaculate of the male contains sperm. It is also less than satisfying to both parties involved. Although the male may intend to remove the penis before ejaculation, this is often physically and emotionally impossible, as well as dissatisfying.

Douching immediately after intercourse is a losing race for the woman. The sperm will be inside the uterus before she reaches the bathroom, since they travel their course in about 90 seconds. In addition, the flow of the fluid toward the cervix may hasten the transport of the sperm toward the uterus.

Tampons or sponges used to absorb the sperm are relatively ineffective, as well as uncomfortable for both partners.

The position of the male and female during intercourse likewise has no real bearing on the potential for conception. The female who does not reach orgasm is just as likely to conceive as her orgasmic counterpart. Much education needs to be done regarding this idea, for many women try to refrain from attaining orgasm because they think this protects them from conception. This not only is false, but also does not enhance the sexual relationship.

Vaginal deodorant suppositories are also ineffective, as are lubricating jellies. They may be mistaken for contraceptives, since they are often located near contraceptive foams, creams, and jellies in the drugstore. In addition, many "popular" women's magazines advertise deodorant suppositories for "keeping you safe"; persons misinterpret this information as meaning "safe" from pregnancy, not body odor.

Breast-feeding, if it is the only means of nutrition for the infant, may result in a period of infertility. However, many women supplement their infants' diets, and the amenorrhea they experience during breast-feeding may be an undetected pregnancy. Since a woman ovulates before she resumes menstruation, it is most difficult for her to ascertain when ovulation might occur unless she has experienced at least one and possibly two normal menstrual cycles. There are many advantages of breast-feeding, but reliable contraception is not one of them.

Patients may be unwilling to relate that they use any of these methods of contraception, but one should keep in mind that they are used by many people.

SUMMARY

The decision by an individual to delay or limit childbearing is based on a very complex interaction of social and economic conditions and pressures, myths and folklore, conscious and unconscious motivational factors, and emotional attitudes toward sex and childbearing. With the introduction of highly effective, inexpensive contraceptive methods such as "the pill" and intrauterine devices; with more liberal laws, which have increased the number of birth control facilities; and with an increasingly permissive society, many of the former barriers against contraception have been reduced or removed.

Health professionals, more than ever before, are finding it necessary to be well informed about this subject. This is true for those working as primary care providers of family planning, as well as for professionals in hospitals and offices, and those acting as the "neighborhood consultant." We firmly believe that every health professional has the responsibility to be the consumers' advocate on contraception, via counseling and teaching.

REFERENCES

1. Billings, Evelyn L., John J. Billings and Maurice Catarinich. *Atlas of the Ovulation Method.* Melbourne: Advocate Press Pty. Ltd., 1973.
2. Hafez, E. S. E. and T. N. Evans (eds.). *Human Reproduction: Conception and Contraception.* New York: Harper & Row, 1973.
3. Havemann, E. *Birth Control.* New York: Time Incorporated 1967.
4. Hellman, L. M. and J. A. Pritchard (eds.). *Williams Obstetrics* (14th edition). New York: Appleton-Century-Crofts, 1971.
5. Hodgson, J. E., R. Smith and D. Milstein. Menstrual Extraction. *Journal of the American Medical Association,* 228:849–850, May 13, 1974.
6. Kistner, R. W. (ed.), *Reproductive Endocrinology.* New York: Medcom, Inc., 1973.
7. Lesinski, John, H. J. Davis and H. G. Kummell. Consideration of the Relationship Between the Compliance of Some Intrauterine Contraceptive Devices and the Expulsion Rates (First). *The Journal of Reproductive Medicine,* 11:5, Nov. 1973.
8. Mastroianni, L., Jr. (ed.). *Clinician — Male and Female: An Endocrine Update.* New York: Medcom, Inc., 1974.
9. Newton, John, Julian Elias and John McEwan. Intrauterine Contraception Using the Copper-Seven Device. *Lancet,* 2:951–954, Nov. 4, 1972.
10. OMNI. *Reproductive Physiology of the Female.* Raritan, New Jersey: Ortho Pharmaceutical Corporation, 1974.
11. Potts, M. et al. (eds.). Oral Contraceptives. (Series A #2) *Population Reports.* Washington, D.C.: The George Washington University Medical Center, March, 1975.
12. Rinehart, W. and J. Winter (eds.). Injectables and Implants. (Series K #1) *Population Reports.* Washington, D.C.: The George Washington University Medical Center, March, 1975.
13. Robinson, D. B. Updating Usage of Contraceptive Pills and Mini-Pills: Patient Profiles. Unpublished paper presented at Ob/Gyn Resident Education Series, University of Kansas Medical Center, Kansas City, Kansas, December 2, 1973.
14. Sobrero, Aguiles. Intrauterine Devices in Clinical Practice. *Family Planning Perspectives.* 3:1, Jan. 1971.

CHAPTER 10

COUNSELING AND ABORTION

Cesar Villanueva, M.D.,
and Barbara Clancy, R.N., M.S.N.

Abortion is the removal or expulsion of a fetus from the uterus before it has reached the age of viability. In most situations, gestational age is the most important factor in determining fetal survival outside the uterus. Although there is some disagreement among perinatologists about when the period of viability starts, this logically should be at 28 weeks, because at present only 3.4 per cent of 20- to 27-week-old infants survive outside the uterine environment, and no infants less than 20 weeks old survive.[2] One can conclude from the most recent United States Supreme Court decisions on abortion that (1) a pregnant woman may secure an abortion during the first trimester essentially upon demand; (2) during the second trimester, the state may impose reasonable requirements and restrictions to protect the health and life of the pregnant woman; and (3) during the last trimester and particularly during the last 10 weeks of pregnancy, the state may also impose reasonable qualifications and conditions to safeguard the life of the fetus.[8]

STATISTICS

Since the landmark decision of the Supreme Court (Roe v. Wade) in 1973, there has been a large increase in the number of legal abortions in the United States (from approximately 6000 in 1966 to 500,000 or more in 1971).[14] The majority of these abortions are performed on young single white women with gestations of 12 weeks or less and who are pregnant for the first time. Uterine hemorrhage and infection appear to be the most frequent complications. Although the complication rate (9.6 per cent) of abortion seems to be high, this is probably not a true gauge, because a large number of trivial complaints were included in the rate reported. In 1971 the overall mortality rate of legal abortion in the United States was 8.2 per 100,000 abortions. This compares favorably with the British death rate from abortions in 1969 (one year after passage of a liberal abortion law) of 21 per 100,000 abortions. The latter figure is in turn smaller than the British maternal mortality rate of 24 per 100,000 pregnancies for the same year.[14]

Women considering therapeutic abortion are frequently confronted with a conflict between deeply ingrained values, primarily those of respect for life and the right of individual choice.[3] Those who argue that all abortions ought to be available on demand appear to be as unreasonable as those who believe all abortions are wrong. It is the view of the majority of Americans that while government and religious groups should not have the right to forbid abortions, the right of an individual to have an abortion should not be absolute.[7] Requiring that all abortions be performed on demand is untenable because it would infringe upon the rights of others. Physicians have the right to refuse to perform an abortion when it is contrary to their conscience or when, in their judgment, the abortion would be detrimental to the patient's health. Society has the right to regulate abortions because it has an interest in its own survival. It also needs to insure that abortions are performed safely and that women who are to have abortions receive adequate counseling about alternatives.[3] Women having abortions for a genetic indication exhibit a greater frequency of emotional side effects after the procedure than women having abortions for psychosocial reasons.[1] Emotional adjustment is easier when the pregnancy terminated was unwanted than when it was desired, but this does not eliminate the need for counseling before abortion.

When abortions are performed in large numbers, the procedure is a powerful agent in the regulation of birth rate and growth of population.[12] In fact, according to Maudlin, in modern times "probably no country has ever attained a low birth rate without widespread use of abortions, legal or illegal."[11] However, an increase in the gross pregnancy rate usually follows liberalization of abortion laws when the frequency of contraceptive use remains low or unchanged; increasing public awareness of and access to contraception are mandatory if abortion is to be merely an interim measure for fertility control.[6]

TEACHING AND COUNSELING THE PATIENT BEFORE ABORTION

The potential abortion patient needs to know that there are options other than abortion. These should be presented to her in the initial interview. If she has explored other possibilities and has given much thought to her decision, then the abortion should probably be performed. If there is doubt in her mind, or if she has consented to the procedure only because someone else wanted it done, then possibly the abortion should not be performed. In this situation, carrying the fetus to term and making plans for relinquishing the baby at birth may have a more satisfying long-term effect. Another question to ask the patient contemplating abortion is "Does the father of the baby know of your decision, and how does he feel about it?" If the relationship between the patient and the father is good and the patient wants the relationship to continue in this manner, the answer should be "Yes, he knows, and we came to the decision together." If informing the father about the pregnancy would be detrimental to the relationship, then it is the patient's option to withhold the knowledge. The patient should always make the final decision, and the health professional should support her in it.

Whatever the method of abortion, the procedure should be thoroughly explained with verbal and written illustrations. This should be done in such a way that the woman will not be frightened. She should understand the types of equipment that will be utilized during the procedure. She should be told of the risks involved, however minute these may be. There is always an element of risk in any surgical or medical procedure; therefore it is imperative that she and her family understand this and have signed appropriate legal papers.

The patient should understand what she will experience during the procedure. This should be explained prior to and again during the procedure, since anxiety decreases retention of information previously given. For example, several women have stated that they did not know that they would experience powerful uterine contractions during an abortion done by means of prostaglandin injection. They probably were told but just didn't hear.

Many women have no concept of the size or formation of the fetus at various stages of development. They need to know that the fetus is completely formed by 12 weeks and that maturation and growth occur after that time. This explanation should be given in a noncondemning manner that increases their understanding of what to expect during the labor and expulsion processes.

They should also know that they can receive pain medication after the cervix has begun to dilate. Some patients have the misconception that pain medication will completely stop uterine contractions. Generally, once contractions are of the intensity to cause cervical dilation, pain medication will not stop the process.

It is also very supporting to the patient contemplating an abortion to know that she may have someone, a significant person in her life, with her while she is having the abortion. Individuals can usually handle a stressful situation quite well if supported through the experience.

Teaching the patient what to expect after the abortion should be included in the pre-abortion counseling. Some patients may not be able to absorb extensive information; however, some exposure to expectations may enhance retention when the explanation is given again later.

METHODS OF ABORTION

EARLY FIRST TRIMESTER

The abortion method of choice depends upon the length of pregnancy, the size of the uterus, and, occasionally, the nature of previous pelvic surgery, if any.

Transcervical uterine aspiration after cervical dilation can be performed under paracervical nerve block anesthesia for the following women: (1) Those who are at six weeks' gestation or less; (2) those who are amenable to an operative procedure while awake; (3) those whose have not had a cesarean section or conization of the cervix. This procedure is safely done in a physician's office with the patient lying on an ordinary gynecologic examining table and an office nurse as an assistant.

The vaginal canal and cervix are visualized with a medium-sized Greaves speculum and cleansed with povidone-iodine (Betadine) soap. Approximately 5 ml. of 0.1 per cent lidocaine anesthetic is injected into each uterosacral ligament, through the vagina. After an interval of 2 to 5 minutes, a sterile uterine packing forceps is introduced into the cervical os and uterine lumen, and the jaws of the instrument are gently opened while in the uterine cavity. This will sufficiently dilate the cervix so that the forceps can be removed from the uterus and replaced with a sterile compliant plastic Karman cannula, 6 mm. in diameter. The proximal end of the Karman cannula is attached to transparent plastic tubing, which in turn is attached to two empty glass bottles connected in series and attached to a suction motor that is powered electrically. Products of conception are removed from the uterus with negative pressure of 50 to 60 cm. Hg. The Karman cannula is slowly rotated while gradually being withdrawn from the uterine cavity. With the suction motor turned off, the Karman cannula is reinserted into the uterine lumen through the cervical os. Uterine aspiration is repeated two or three times.

Gradual withdrawal of the suction cannula produces a sensation of rubbing against a coarse surface as the side fenestrations of the Karman cannula slide against myometrium (which would occur only after the uterine lumen had been emptied of placenta, embryo, and membranes). This sensation confirms complete evacuation of the fetus and placenta from the uterus. The operative instruments are removed, and the patient is asked to lie on her side with her knees bent and close to her chest. This maneuver reduces discomfort secondary to uterine contractions. No attempt is made to prevent the patient from having uterine contractions, because the phenomenon produces hemostasis after the abortion. Oxytocic drugs and intravenous isotonic fluids are not required for the procedure. The safety of early pregnancy termination by transcervical uterine aspiration using the Karman cannula is well documented.[10]

LATER FIRST TRIMESTER ABORTION

For those women who are more than six weeks but less than 13 weeks pregnant (or more than four weeks but less than 11 weeks after a missed period), the abortion procedure of choice also is cervical dilation and transcervical uterine aspiration, but the procedure is done in an operating room and usually under general anesthesia. The cervical os is gradually dilated (to 10 mm. in diameter if the pregnancy is of eight weeks' duration, and to 12 mm. in diameter if 10 to 12 weeks) with Pratt dilators. A transcervical plastic cannula 10 to 12 mm. in diameter is employed to empty the contents of the uterus. A small, sharp, spoon-shaped metal instrument (a curette) is then introduced into the cervical os, and the inner uterine walls are scraped. Again, a coarse rubbing sensation is produced when the curette is employed on an empty uterus. A sharp metal curette must be employed because large-diameter suction cannulae (which have outer diameters greater than 8 mm.) do not have side fenestrations. A coarse rubbing sensation is not produced when these large-diameter cannulae are slowly withdrawn from uteri that are empty of fetal and placental tissue. The patient is awakened from general anesthesia and is transferred to a recovery room, where her vital signs are monitored closely for any sign of bleeding. She is usually released from the hospital three hours after surgery if bleeding is minimal.

MID-TRIMESTER ABORTION

When the pregnancy is of more than 12 weeks' duration—or more than 10 weeks after a missed period—evacuation of the uterine contents by cervical dilation, transcervical aspiration of the uterine lumen, and uterine curettage is associated with severe blood loss and great risk of uterine injury (i.e., cervical laceration and perforation of the uterus). A surgical procedure similar to a cesarean section can be performed safely on these large fetuses. However, future pregnancies will frequently require delivery by repeat cesarean section in order to avoid dehiscence of the previous cesarean section scar in the uterus during labor. Dehiscence of the uterine scar and rupture of the uterus produce extrusion of the fetus and placenta into the peritoneal cavity, fetal death, and massive maternal internal hemorrhage, with possible maternal death.

Consequently, labor induced by injection of prostaglandin $F_{2\alpha}$ is the method of choice for these pregnancies. Injection of 40 mg. of prostaglandin $F_{2\alpha}$ and 40 gm. of urea into the amniotic sac of a woman who is more than 12 weeks pregnant or more than 10 weeks after a missed menstrual period usually produces powerful uterine contractions within 20 minutes, and rapid labor and delivery of the fetus and the placenta in about 12 hours. Prostaglandin $F_{2\alpha}$ is a potent stimulant of uterine musculature,[5] and hypertonic urea destroys both placenta and fetus by desiccation in addition to increasing intrauterine volume and augmenting the strength of labor.[15]

Since the onset of strong painful uterine contractions occurs rapidly, it is imperative that the patient and family understand what is happening and the expected effects of the drug. In a normal labor, the uterus contracts and relaxes; after prostaglandin injection the contractions are intense and very frequent, and the uterus does not relax fully. Diazepam (Valium) may be given to assist in calming the woman during early labor. When the woman is 2 cm. dilated, she may be given another more potent medication to decrease the pain and discomfort from the uterine contractions.

All methods of performing abortion may be psychologically traumatizing. This latter method, however, can also be physically traumatizing, because the woman cannot be anesthetized. Therefore, she should have a supporting, sustaining professional person, either a nurse or physician, with her as much as possible. In addition, a friend, husband, or any member of the family who is supportive should be encouraged to be with the woman experiencing an abortion.

These women undergoing mid-trimester abortion need to have hygiene and comfort measures and physical care similar to those afforded women experiencing a normal labor, including:

1. Monitoring of vital signs.
2. Measuring intake and output.
3. Encouraging voiding.
4. Providing cleansing and comforting measures.
5. Applying sacral pressure.
6. Administering oral hygiene.
7. Assisting with breathing and relaxing techniques.
8. Explaining progress to the patient and her family.
9. Giving medications as needed.
10. Watching for complications.
11. Including the family in plan of care.
12. Supporting the patient throughout the experience.[4]

It is most important that the woman not be left alone when the fetus is expelled. The cord is clamped and cut with sterile instruments so that the fetus can be covered and removed from the woman's presence as soon as possible. If the woman wishes to see the fetus, this is her right and she should be allowed to do so. This should be neither encouraged nor discouraged by any health professional; however, she should be supported throughout this experience.

TEACHING AND COUNSELING THE PATIENT AFTER ABORTION

Most patients express relief after the abortion. Some may cry; this should be encouraged if it occurs. Such statements as "go ahead and cry, it's okay, and you'll feel better" tell the patient you respect her as a person and you care about her. Not only verbal reassurance but also touch can be most therapeutic.

It is important to diminish the risk of Rh reactions. Therefore, all Rh-negative patients experiencing an abortion past six weeks' gestation should be protected with immune globulin. If the patient has been previously sensitized or if the mate or fetus is known to be Rh negative, the immunization need not be given.[13]

Every patient should be aware of signs of complications such as hemorrhage or infection. The bleeding is usually minimal after an abortion; however, a serous vaginal drainage will persist for two or three weeks. Once the red discharge has ceased, it should not reappear. If the bleeding continues and cramping persists, retained fragments of the placenta or uterine infection may be the cause. If this should occur, the physician should be contacted. In summary, the signs of complications are:

1. Persistent bleeding
2. Foul-odored discharge
3. Persistent uterine cramping
4. Elevated temperature
5. Pain, frequency, or burning on urination
6. Continued depressed state

If the patient is from out of town, she should be provided with medical and counseling resources within her locale. Family planning organizations as well as mental health agencies in any city can provide patients with information on available resources.

It is normal for the patient to experience the "blues" after an abortion. This is because of psychological reasons as well as the physiological effects of depletion of placental hormones. These feelings should be transient. If they last longer than three weeks or become intensified, the patient should seek counseling. If the couple has discussed the problems of the unwanted pregnancy and has agreed on the abortion as the solution, this experience usually does not produce sexual or marital problems, but if one of the persons involved opposed the abortion and consented because of coercion, marital and sexual problems may result. The patient should be encouraged to seek assistance through counseling if this should occur.

All patients should be seen two to four weeks after the abortion to ascertain whether healing is adequate. A thorough pelvic examination should be included. Normal activity can be resumed within a few days after the abortion if no complications arise.

Menstruation will usually resume in four weeks. The first menstrual period after the abortion may be heavier and last a day or two longer than usual. If bleeding persists, the physician should be contacted.

Sexual intercourse can be resumed as instructed by the physician, usually in two or three weeks. The patient should not use tampons, douche, or place anything in the vagina for two weeks, since it is possible to introduce infection.

Every woman should be given contraceptive advice following an abortion. It is important to ascertain what method of contraception had been used in the past and what is acceptable to her and her partner. To be effective, a contraceptive must meet the individual needs or it will not be used. It is imperative that the woman understand that she is very vulnerable to another pregnancy if unprotected intercourse occurs, even before her first menses after the abortion. Many women, especially teenagers, are under the false assumption that pregnancy cannot occur until after a menstrual period. This needs to be clarified so that the need for a repeat abortion can be reduced.

SUMMARY

As a means of population control, abortion is the last resort and should remain so. It is more problematic than contraception, yet for some is the only way out of a dilemma.

Whatever one's philosophy or values concerning abortion, consideration must be given for an individual's dignity, privacy, self-fulfillment, autonomy, and external freedom. This consideration should be given to both the physician and the person seeking an abortion.

The earlier in gestation the abortion is performed, the less the chance of physical and emotional sequelae. Information about facilities for abortion should be made readily available to the general public so that the decision and the initial contact with the physician can be in the first 12 weeks rather than in the second trimester of gestation.

More contraception information should be disseminated to all age groups capable of reproduction. Family living courses, including value clarification, foundations of satisfying relationships, and reproductive anatomy and physiology as well as contraception should be provided in junior high school curricula rather than senior high, which is too late for the majority.

It is hoped that new and improved means of contraception will be available in the near future. Until then, abortion will continue to be a means of solving the problems of an unwanted pregnancy.

REFERENCES

1. Blumberg, B. D., M. S. Golbus, and K. H. Hanson. The Psychological Sequelae of Abortion Performed for a Genetic Indication. *American Journal of Obstetrics and Gynecology,* 122:799–808, Aug. 1, 1975.

2. Brown, A. K. and J. G. Freehafer. Prenatal Risks—A Pediatrician's Point of View. In: *Risks in the Practice of Modern Obstetrics.* Aladjem, S. (ed.) St. Louis: C. V. Mosby Co., 1972, pp. 48–49.

3. Callahan, D. *Abortion: Law, Choice and Morality.* New York: Macmillan Co., 1970.

4. Clancy, B. The Nurse and The Abortion Patient. *Nursing Clinics of North America,* 8:469–478, Sept. 1973.

5. Corlett, R. C. and C. A. Ballard. The Induction of Midtrimester Abortion with Intra-amniotic Prostaglandin F-2-alpha. *American Journal of Obstetrics and Gynecology,* 118:353–357, Feb. 1, 1974.

6. David, H. P., and N. F. Russo. Abortion and Fertility Regulation in Socialist Countries of Central and Eastern Europe. In: *Abortion, Obtained and Denied.* Newman, S. H., et al. (eds.) Bridgeport, Conn.: Key Book Service, 1971, p. 90.

7. Gallup Poll. In: *Kansas City Star,* June 8, 1975.

8. Hirsh, H. L. Legal Guidelines for the Performance of Abortions. *American Journal of Obstetrics and Gynecology,* 122:679–682, July 15, 1975.

9. Hordern, A. *Legal Abortion: The English Experience.* Oxford: Pergamon Press, 1971, p. 190.

10. Liu, D. T. and I. Hudson. Karman Cannula and First Trimester Termination of Pregnancy. *American Journal of Obstetrics and Gynecology,* 118:906–909, April 1, 1974.

11. Maudlin, W. P., et al. A Report on Bucharest—The World Population Conference and the Population Tribune, August, 1974. *Studies in Family Planning,* 5:357, 1974.

12. Moore, E. C. Induced Abortion and Contraception: Sociological Aspects. In: *Abortion, Obtained and Denied.* Newman, S. H., et al. (eds.) Bridgeport, Conn.: Key Book Service, 1971, p. 144.

13. Queenan, J. Role of Rh (D) Immune Globulin in Induced Abortion. *Clinical Obstetrics and Gynecology,* 14:234–244, March, 1971.

14. Tietze, C. and S. Lewit. *Early Medical Complications of Legal Abortion: Highlights of the Joint Program for the Study of Abortion.* New York: The Population Council, 1972.

15. Walker, S. M., A. P. F. Flint, and A. C. Turnbull. Rate of Fall in Plasma Progesterone and Time to Abortion Following Intra-amniotic Injection of Prostaglandin F-2-alpha with or without Urea in the Second Trimester of Human Pregnancy. *British Journal of Obstetrics and Gynaecology,* 82:488–492, June, 1975.

SEXUALITY DURING PREGNANCY

Claudia Anderson, R.N., M.N.,
Barbara Clancy, R.N., M.S.N.,
and Barbara Quirk, R.N., M.N.

Sexual behavior has traditionally been an area that has not received high priority from either nurses or physicians in the routine health assessment. Unless trained in the area of human sexuality, health professionals tend to omit discussion of the topic or to provide only routine statements to patients. The addition of pregnancy provides a new dimension to the area of sexuality. Philosophies vary from advocating total abstinence with no alternative modes of sexual outlet to placing no restriction on sexual behavior during pregnancy. Few scientific guidelines have been determined along which to advise the pregnant couple.

CHANGES AFTER CONCEPTION

When conception occurs, the cyclic function of the ovaries is interrupted and is not re-established with regularity until after lactation is finished. Thus, the psychobiology of pregnancy can best be understood as an immense intensification of the luteal phase of the reproductive cycle. This accounts for the increase in hormonal and metabolic processes and their psychological manifestations, which are characterized by intensified receptive and retentive tendencies.

FIRST TRIMESTER

In the first trimester of pregnancy, the hormonal influences of pregnancy are felt in varying intensities of fatigue, sleepiness, nausea, and vertigo. Headaches appear to be prevalent around the fourth month of gestation. Certain tastes and smells may become repulsive because of increased sensitivity to these special senses. Some women may experience bleeding or "spotting" during the first trimester at or near the normal time for their period.

Sexual intercourse is not contraindicated in the first trimester unless there is a history of previous fetal wastage during this period. However, in a study by Quirk[17] it was found that there is usually decreased sexual desire in the first trimester resulting from the general malaise and nausea common in early pregnancy.

The vital energies of the mother are augmented by heightened hormonal and metabolic processes that maintain the normal growth of the fetus, and it is these interlocking physiological processes between mother and fetus that make the pregnant woman experience libidinous feelings. Because of the replenished libido reservoir of the mother, her primary narcissism becomes the source of her motherliness. However, differences among women may be noted according to how much the individual's libido increases her pleasure in childbearing, stimulates her hopeful fantasies, and diminishes her anxieties.

In many, there are realistic fears and insecurities motivated by out-of-wedlock conception, unwanted pregnancy, economic worries, or marital difficulties, and the frustrated pregnant woman may turn her anger toward rejection of the pregnancy as well as herself. In acute cases, anorexia and vomiting may cause severe metabolic disturbances if allowed to continue.

The integrative task of pregnancy and motherhood, both biologically and psychologically, is much greater than most women have been confronted with before, and in some cases the adaptive task appears greater with the first child, when the experience is completely new. Motherhood is usually made easier with the second and third child because of the physiological and emotional maturation achieved in the first pregnancy. However, there are cases in which women who are fatigued by the labors of motherhood and the burden of an additional child may experience depression and pathogenic regression during subsequent pregnancies.

Some women perceive pregnancy as a proof of femininity, of really being a woman, and of being able to conceive—corresponding to the male ego and pride in fathering a child, which establishes his masculinity. Therefore, it does not always follow that the wish to be pregnant is always the wish for a child. It is not infrequent that the wish for parenthood is to make up for a lack of a meaningful marital relationship.

Whatever the reason for the pregnancy, the development of the parenting response in the mother usually follows a pattern of primary attention to the physical changes during the first trimester, when the mother considers the embryo a part of her own body. In the second trimester, quickening brings with it feelings of ambivalence, in which the mother becomes aware of the separateness of the fetus and at the same time is usually delighted with the perceptions of fetal movement. From this point on, the most relevant person to the pregnant woman emotionally is now her mother, and she is flooded with memories of her relationship with her mother, even though outwardly she takes as her model her contemporaries. Strongly ambivalent feelings toward her mother may provide negative attitudes toward her own pregnancy.

By the third trimester the fetus is large and the movements often painful; the tenderness previously felt toward the fetus may turn to irritation or anger, and desire for delivery becomes strong. At the same time, there is a sad awareness that with delivery the child will never again be as close to the mother, and so delivery is thus anticipated with a mixture of positive and negative feelings. Fear of deformities or of harm to the baby or herself is also prevalent as delivery approaches. This completes the normal pattern for the development of parenting during pregnancy.

The familial support received by the pregnant woman, whether in terms of an affectionate partner (marital or otherwise), a secure marriage, or positive relationships with her children or parental family, provides her with the essentials for maintaining an emotional balance during this time. Husbands should be made aware of the personality changes that will occur as the pregnancy progresses to prevent a resulting disharmony in the family. The pregnant woman has increased needs for nurturance and becomes more preoccupied with herself, often creating resentment in her husband. These sometimes excessive needs for love and attention should be fully explained to both partners as a passing entity. Her mate should also be made aware that mood swings are not uncommon, and emotional lability, irritability, and sensitivity may occur with only slight provocation.

Changes in sexual desire and performance may result, and there are a variety of responses to and reasons for this. Some women use pregnancy as an excuse for curtailing sexual relations if they did not enjoy them prior to conception. On the other hand, many women find increased pleasure if they feel very much loved and nurtured by their partners, and may even experience orgasm for the first time. Some couples, through lack of knowledge, are afraid of sexual relations during pregnancy because of fears of harming either the mother or the fetus.

By many men, the pregnant woman's body is considered beautiful, but this opinion is not held by all. If the male in any way indicates repulsion at the sight of his partner's body, she will feel unattractive and will respond negatively both psychologically and sexually. Fears of sexual infidelity are sometimes the basis of a woman's continued interest in relations even if she has a decreased sexual appetite. Masters and Johnson found that pregnancy indeed appeared to be the point of time at which many men began extramarital activities if they were so inclined.[14] It is important, therefore, that both partners be aware of each others' needs for closeness and support as the developing crisis of pregnancy unfolds. For many, the act of intercourse is the culminating expression of the fulfillment of these needs.

MID TRIMESTER

The mid trimester of pregnancy is, for most, a quiescent period when the woman is feeling good physically and is more stable emotionally. Fewer serious complications are found from the twentieth to the thirtieth weeks of gestation. Masters and Johnson found that sexual appetites did increase in many women at this time, with noted elevation in eroticism and sexual performance owing to the increased vascularity of the pelvic organs.[14] However, it is not uncommon for uterine contractions to occur with orgasm, and a woman may feel some cramping and aching in the lower abdomen following sexual stimulation. According to Masters and Johnson, the only effect on the fetus at the time of orgasm is a slowing of the heart rate, which passes quickly.[14]

LAST TRIMESTER

In the last trimester, there has been a traditional proscription of sexual relations as early as six to eight weeks prior to the estimated date of delivery. It has been shown in studies by Pugh and Fernandez[16] and by Quirk,[17] however, that fears of infection, rupture of membranes, and premature delivery as a result of intercourse are unfounded, and today most physicians allow sexual relations to continue throughout the normal pregnancy. Because orgasm produces uterine contractions, some physicians may even encourage sexual stimulation in cases in which the mother is at term and the cervix is very ripe.

There are mechanical problems related to intercourse in the last trimester that can be overcome by changes in coital positions. Any position that is comfortable, does not apply pressure to the female abdomen, and does not allow excessively deep penetration is acceptable late in pregnancy. Entry from behind with both partners on their sides is usually comfortable and does not allow deep penetration (Fig. 11-1). The female atop the male in a sitting position allows her freedom from abdominal pressure, but penetration is deep in this position and it may be uncomfortable (Fig. 11-2). The female sitting with both knees drawn up and resting over the male who is on his side below her is also a possibility that does not allow very deep penetration (Fig. 11-3). In any position, however, the woman can place her hand on the shaft of the penis to control the depth of vaginal penetration. Couples should be encouraged to experiment with many positions until one is found that is satisfying to both partners.

With the availability of chemotherapy, vaginal infections do not present a contraindication to coitus even late in pregnancy if the membranes are intact. Once a woman is in labor or membranes have ruptured, intercourse or any tactile stimulation could cause infection in the woman and the fetus and is therefore contraindicated.

Figure 11–1. A position that does not allow deep penetration.

As a counselor, the health professional must explore with the couple what sexuality means to them, especially in relation to the pregnancy. Both may need to discuss the woman's changing body; pregnancy may be viewed as a very feminine period or a very awkward one.

Both partners may be afraid that intercourse will harm the baby and therefore either abstain from coitus and develop hostility, or continue to have intercourse and develop feelings of guilt. The health professional must utilize verbal and nonverbal cues in giving the couple scientifically based knowledge.

A grave error in practice is to give patients a routine statement such as "Abstinence must be observed for the last six weeks of gestation," without assisting the couple to explore alternatives. An even more serious error is to tell patients nothing about sex during pregnancy and to leave no room for discussion. Patients may continue to have sexual relations but may feel increasingly guilty for so doing. The role of the

Figure 11–2. A position that allows freedom from abdominal pressure, but deep penetration.

Figure 11–3. A position that does not allow deep penetration.

professional is to assist the couple in achieving a satisfactory sexual relationship without causing guilt or concern.

SEXUALITY IN LABOR AND DELIVERY AND THE POSTPARTAL PERIOD

Most women face delivery with ambivalent feelings of, "Yes, I want my baby born, but I also don't readily wish to give up a part of me."[11] It has taken several months for this symbiotic relationship to develop, and it is difficult for the woman to realize that soon this little being that relied on "me" solely for so long will be a physically independent being, capable of living outside "my" body.

Rubin has stated that it takes approximately three months into the pregnancy for a woman to accept the growth of a new being in her body.[18] Possibly, it takes longer than the average 12 to 16 hours of labor for a woman to physically and psychologically lose the fetus. Although pregnancy is a normal physiological process, the early adjustments are tremendous.

Some women may have difficulty disengaging from the past and orienting themselves to the future. Because of this, it is wise for health personnel to focus their care toward the laboring woman and mate more so than the fetus. This is not saying that the care of the fetus should be ignored, because this is also very important. All the physical and emotional care given to the laboring woman affects the fetus. However, the approach to the laboring woman and mate should be, "You are the important ones." Often we hear health personnel say, "Breathe more slowly, it will help your baby," or "We can't give you pain medication because it may harm your baby." Many women have expressed to the authors feelings of guilt because they were concerned about their own feelings more than the fetus. As health professionals, we should encourage feelings of narcissism and discourage feelings of guilt. The new mother must have feelings of self-love before she can find the strength to give love to this new infant.

The family-centered childbirth concept has become more popular throughout the country in the past few years. This is certainly a step in the right direction in enhancing spousal relationships and in assisting the new couple in incorporating this new being into the family circle.

Pregnancy, labor and delivery, the early postpartum period, and the first few weeks of home adjustment are crisis times in the lives of the persons involved. The health team should do everything possible to assist persons in meeting their goals and expectations. It has been shown that women have certain expectations of labor and delivery, and when these are congruent with outcomes, their adjustment to mothering and their mate's adjustment to fathering are enhanced. Conversely, when outcomes do not meet expectations—for example, when a woman desiring natural childbirth must have a cesarean section—this may well be a high-risk situation for poor parenting and poor sexual relationships within the family.[4]

Narcissism is a necessary trait not only for women in developing positive relationships with their infant and mate; it is also important that men "feel good about themselves" to enable them in turn to give to others. Often the men feel left out during pregnancy, and this can certainly be true during labor and delivery as well. Many hospitals do not allow fathers in the labor and delivery suite. This is changing slowly, however, and when consumers have more responsibility and authority for planning their own health care, we may see a rapid change in this policy. Childbirth education classes do encourage active participation of the fathers. Fathers can take an active part in helping the laboring woman with breathing and in monitoring progress. They need assistance and support from health personnel to feel like an active member of the team. It is a most insensitive professional who leaves the father "alone" with the laboring woman.

DELIVERY

The authors believe that if the father wishes to be in the delivery room and the laboring woman desires his presence, he should be allowed to participate in this experience. If he does not wish to observe the birth process, this should not be forced, because psychological damage may ensue.

Everyone experiencing the delivery process in a hospital must follow the delivery protocol, which involves the following concerns expressed by mothers: (1) being placed in an immodest position in the presence of strangers, with frequent intrusions made into one's body; (2) experiencing intense pressure and discomfort with the delivery of the infant's head and shoulders, and being caught between wanting complete relief from drugs and yet knowing that sedation must be limited to facilitate birth; (3) fearing the loss of control (bowel and bladder); (4) grunting and moaning to aid delivery; (5) feeling as if there is no escape because of being strapped down; and (6) experiencing build-up of anxiety about possibly sustaining serious injury or death.[7]

It goes without saying that a woman is exposed to unique and intense stresses during the delivery experience. Unless we as members of the health team can impress upon the couple the positive aspects of the experience, the unpleasant experiences may stay in the foreground. Positive aspects can be reinforced by showing the newborn to the parents and allowing them to "touch and see" as soon as it is physically safe for the infant. It is important to remember that the newborn has an immature temperature-regulating mechanism, and his body heat must be maintained with adequate covering. Another means of reinforcement is to congratulate the parents and impress upon them how well they worked together. Try to compliment them whenever appropriate. If the parents have chosen a name for the newborn, address the baby by name.

Many women have equated the delivery experience with similar sensations during orgasm.[15] The vasoconcentration and pressure, plus the exhilaration, exhaustion, and relief experienced certainly could be described as similar. Many women who are well prepared for labor and delivery have described the birth process as the ultimate expression of their feminine sexuality.

Immediately after delivery, when the woman's physiological state has stabilized, she and her mate need time to be alone. They need to reflect on what has happened and express feelings about their experience. Most parents who are well prepared and supported throughout the labor and delivery experience express their exhilaration by crying. The health professional should encourage them by stating that this is normal and should provide privacy.

If parents express a desire to see the infant in the recovery room, or if they wish to be alone, this should be respected.

POSTPARTAL PERIOD

Breast-Feeding. Breast-feeding can be a most rewarding experience if there is prior preparation for it, both physical and emotional. Physical preparation involves the mechanical toughening during the antepartal time as well as an understanding of the hygiene and care of the breasts. Emotional preparation involves understanding that successful breast-feeding will occur only if the mother really wants to breast feed. To comply with the wishes cf a mother or a mother-in-law or to go against the wishes of her mate may increase tension and interfere with success in breast-feeding. One woman expressed a repulsion for breast-feeding, but her family wanted her to do it. After she had expressed her feelings, the authors told her that she should bottle feed if repulsed by breast-feeding. She breathed a sigh of relief and said, "Oh, I wanted someone to tell me that."

Some men may have an adverse reaction to their mate's breast-feeding. On occasion they have expressed a possessiveness of the breasts and a feeling of jealousy when the newborn suckles. Through counseling, these feelings can often be expressed, examined, and possibly alleviated. If not, and if the couple's sexual relationship may be jeopardized, the value of breast-feeding should be examined.

Some women have expressed a feeling of attaining orgasm during breast-feeding. They may be due to the contractions of the uterus experienced during breast-feeding and the physical warmth and closeness of a human being suckling at the breast. In the authors' experience, many a man has expressed a feeling of exhilaration and loving similar to orgasm when watching his loved one nurse his child. Breast-feeding can be an experience that enhances a relationship if the persons involved are adequately prepared.

Postpartal Recuperation.   Adequate rest and proper healing are essential goals for postpartum recuperation. Explanations of proper hygiene measures and the physiological changes that are occurring are essential components of the teaching plan. Nursing care should be focused toward the new mother, and emphasis placed on her needs. It has been said that during the antepartum period the "mother-to-be" needs an "extra dose" of love so that she can then pass this love on to her newborn. Labor and delivery may cause additional physical and emotional trauma. If so, does it not seem feasible that the woman needs special attention and love after delivery so that she may again express love for her mate and the new member of the family? This may be a difficult concept for fathers to comprehend and should also be included in the teaching plan.

The "postpartum blues" have been described as a normal phenomenon of the early postpartal period. It is true that this is natural and normal; however, the emotional and physiological basis for such feelings needs to be explained to the couple during pregnancy and reinforced after delivery. This is the time when a woman needs to be fondled and caressed so that she knows she is loved and needed.

Women should be advised to practice "Kegel" exercises, or conscious abdominal and perineal tightening, after delivery. This will strengthen the muscles of the pelvis and perineum that have been stretched during pregnancy, labor, and delivery. One can teach this by having the woman sit on the stool with legs about 18 inches apart. She is then told to practice starting and stopping her urinary stream at least three or four times. This will give her a good idea of which muscles need strengthening and of the sensation of tightening. This exercise should be done several times a day in the early postpartum period, and a woman should be encouraged to do this several times a day for the rest of her life. The tightening and relaxing of the muscles will improve the healing process and possibly prevent the pelvic relaxation that may occur in the fourth or fifth decade of life. Many woman have stated that this exercise, if done during sexual intercourse, increases their pleasure and that of their mates.

Resumption of Sexual Intercourse.   Advice about the resumption of sexual intercourse is also a necessary aspect of the teaching plan. This expression of love is an important aspect of communication, yet many health professionals neglect to include it. If the topic of resumption of intercourse is omitted from the teaching, many persons feel they should not resume coitus until they are told to do so. If they do engage in intercourse, they may feel guilty. Often couples engage in coitus and the woman becomes pregnant before her follow-up examination at six weeks. The couple should understand how vulnerable to becoming pregnant a newly delivered woman is. It has been these authors' experience that many women have the false assumption that they cannot become pregnant until after they menstruate. An equally false assumption is that a woman can't become pregnant if she is breast-feeding. Correct information about the vulnerability to pregnancy and about available contraceptives should be given in the early postpartum period to all persons concerned about family planning.

Masters and Johnson found a greater orgasmic capacity in the postpartum period owing to increased pelvic vasoconstriction.[14] For many couples, parenthood may represent the ultimate test of masculinity and femininity, bringing a full acceptance of these roles. Often women who were timid regarding bodily functions are now "liberated" regarding what it's really like to be a "woman."[5]

It is important to realize that many physicians may advise abstinence from sexual intercourse from one month prior to delivery to four to six weeks post partum. These physicians fear stimulation which may cause early labor and endometrial infection post partum. There is a basis for the former concern: It is true that intercourse may cause uterine contractions sufficiently intense to be detrimental to an ill fetus.[8] As for postpartum infection, according to Krantz, the cervix is essentially closed 24 hours after delivery, and endometrial infection is unlikely.[12] If couples adhere to the usual advice regarding sexual abstinence, there will be approximately six weeks to two months during which they do not engage in sexual intercourse. This is difficult for many couples, since abstinence causes increased tension.

Many couples have stated that they did not wait the designated time to resume sexual intercourse. Those who began earlier were those who were experiencing sustained blues, depression, and anxiety during the postpartum period, as well as persons who had begun some means of contraception.[17]

The health professional should initiate the topic of resumption of intercourse. Some physicians are now advising couples to resume coitus when they feel comfortable. The episiotomy site will be completely healed by seven days post delivery, so infection of or injury to this area is not probable. The couple may be advised to use the side-lying position or the woman-on-top position for intercourse, which will keep pressure off the episiotomy site. Usually intercourse tends to soften the scar; therefore, discomfort will be decreased with time.[3] Although the cervix is essentially closed 24 hours after delivery, the couple should be advised of the possibility of infection, and proper hygiene of the genital area should be stressed. Adequate lubrication of the penis may also make the initial experience of post-delivery intercourse more comfortable.

Oral-genital contact may be a means of relieving tension, if this has been an acceptable means of expression for the couple in the past. Penile-breast stimulation may also be used if the couple prefers to wait the advised four to six weeks.

By talking with the couple about "sex" and "sexuality," the health professional is letting them know that this is an important aspect of their relationship. To say "we'll talk about contraception or the resumption of intercourse at your six-weeks checkup," is doing the couple a disservice. It may be advisable to show them illustrations of positions to make them feel comfortable with the topic. Generally, if the sexual relationship was satisfying prior to delivery, the couple will find ways to satisfy each other.

Adjustment to Parenthood. The arrival of a newborn is bound to cause some strain on the relationship between the couple. They may feel as if they may never be totally alone again. In one sense this may be true, because they now have the responsibility for another human being in addition to each other. The realization of this responsibility may cause some tension and a confusion of roles. Feelings and concerns should be expressed freely between the couple. They may experience some relief in knowing that most couples have such feelings. Several hospitals are including classes on adjustment to parenthood as an integral part of the childbirth classes. Parents have found this sharing of adjustment experiences most valuable.

The couple needs to have time alone whenever possible. As soon as the woman has regained her strength (usually two or three weeks), they should be away from the newborn for a few hours.

New parents are often tired in the early weeks after delivery. It is difficult to sleep a full eight hours at a time because of the newborn's adjustment to extrauterine life. Couples should be encouraged to "never be too tired" to express love and affection for each other.

The newborn should enhance family ties if one remembers that parenthood involves three roles to play: (1) first and foremost, an individual, involving personal feelings of worth and self-esteem; (2) a mate, which involves being the most intimate friend to another human being; and (3) a parent, the least important of the three roles. The role of parent is the only one we adopt with the explicit intention of eventually relinquishing it.[10]

SEXUALITY AND HIGH-RISK PREGNANCY

Few guidelines have been offered to the professional to assist couples with explorations of feelings of sexuality during problem pregnancy. Patients who have been classified as having a high-risk pregnancy need to have avenues of discussion open to them. The health professional is in a unique position to counsel the couple, since she often has more time to establish rapport with them than the doctor. The woman may hesitate to talk to a male health professional in relation to sexuality, whereas she would welcome discussions with a woman. The converse is also true. All regimens must be individualized and each circumstance must be considered when exploring methods of expressing sexuality. These patients often have feelings of guilt, frustration, and hostility that need to be expressed.

There are several high-risk circumstances in which vaginal or manual stimulation may be contraindicated during pregnancy. If this is the case, the health professional must explore with the couple alternatives to vaginal penetration. The next section discusses conditions in which traditional intercourse may be prohibited.

BLEEDING COMPLICATIONS

Old wives' tales have often prevented a couple from having sexual intercourse at the time menses would occur during the first trimester. This, as well as many other old wives' tales, has no scientific basis. When a spontaneous abortion does occur, the couple and the physician may try to search for a specific cause for it. Perhaps vigorous intercourse took place a short period before the woman began to bleed, and the intercourse was blamed for the abortion. In the case of a normal pregnancy in a woman with no history of habitual abortions, intercourse must not be blamed for the abortion. This must be thoroughly discussed with the couple to avert later guilt.

In cases of threatened abortion, abstinence should be observed for two weeks after the symptoms subside.[20] Intercourse may be resumed after quickening occurs.[2]

Coitus may be a secondary cause of abortion when an infection such as syphilis is transmitted.[19] If this happens, generally the fetus will die within the first trimester.

During the first trimester, cramps and aching may accompany orgasm. These may be considered harmless unless the woman has a history of premature labor or habitual abortions or is a threatened aborter for the present pregnancy. Manual stimulation causing orgasm is also contraindicated owing to the intense contractions produced in women at risk for pregnancy wastage.[14]

Bleeding in the second trimester is often attributed to an incompetent cervical os. If this problem is to arise, it will do so with or without intercourse. The process might be hastened, however, owing to the rhythmic contractions produced by orgasm and the intravaginal deposition of prostaglandin.[9] Patients who have this disorder need to be advised that premature labor will occur sooner or later even without orgasm. Patients with cerclages (suturing the cervix closed) should postpone intercourse for two weeks following insertion of the cerclage to promote a quiescent state of the uterus.

Whenever abruptio placentae or placenta previa is suspected, intravaginal penetration (manual as well as penile) should be prohibited. When placenta previa occurs, the trauma that may result from intercourse may cause profound bleeding and shock. Orgasm is contraindicated in abruptio placentae owing to the chance of initiating uterine contractions and causing more of the placenta to separate prematurely. The couple should be cautioned that any sexual activity that causes female orgasm is contraindicated.

When cervical erosions are present, bleeding following intercourse usually does not occur except when the erosions are infected.[2] Unlike placenta previa and abruptio placentae, cervical erosions are not a contraindication to coitus. Late in pregnancy (near term), spotting may follow either intercourse or vaginal examination. The historian must determine whether this is frank bleeding or spotting; the former would be a cause of grave concern, whereas the latter would be considered within normal limits.

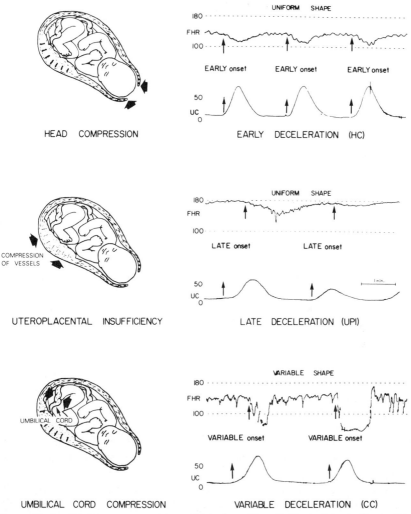

Figure 11–4.   Fetal heart rate patterns. (Data from Hon, E. H. *An Introduction to Fetal Heart Rate Monitoring.* Courtesy of Corometrics Medical Systems, Inc., Wallingford, CT)

UTEROPLACENTAL INSUFFICIENCY

When there is uteroplacental compromise, orgasm may be contraindicated in the female. Situations in which the placenta may not function optimally are conditions such as toxemia, diabetes, heart disease, and multiple gestation. Goodlin et al. monitored the fetal heart externally during orgasm in a woman at 39 weeks' gestation. This record showed evidence of variable and late decelerations in fetal heart rate (Fig. 11–4).[9] This woman and her fetus were healthy, and the female infant was born healthy. The fetal heart rate during orgasm dropped to 96 beats per minute. Patients who have a compromised placenta or a sick fetus may cause stress in the fetus during orgasm, which may not be reversible. Multiple late decelerations rapidly produce fetal acidosis and hypoxia, which can cause insult to an already injured fetus (see Fig. 11–4). It is imperative to make early accurate diagnoses of pregnancies at risk for placental insufficiency and of fetuses in jeopardy.

PREMATURE LABOR

Patients who have a history of premature labor or who have had episodes of premature labor during the current pregnancy should be cautioned against having orgasms, especially after the thirty-second week of gestation. This is especially true in patients with "ripe" cervices or with poor reproductive histories. Orgasm late in pregnancy may initiate painful uterine contractions, with or without the onset of labor. Orgasm may also cause an elevation of serum oxytocin levels. Intravaginal administration of prostaglandins may stimulate the onset of labor in the gravid female. Semen prostaglandins may likewise initiate labor following coitus.[8] The combination of elevated serum oxytocin levels, painful uterine contractions, and semen prostaglandin could set off true labor in patients. Size of the fetus, length of gestation, and condition of the cervix must be considered in counseling patients about sexual activity during pregnancy.

COUNSELING THE COUPLE

When advising the couple on sexual activities, several aspects must be considered. Automanipulation leading to orgasm produces stronger uterine contractions than does orgasm from coitus.[14] These contractions have been noted to have lasted 30 minutes post orgasm in the normal gravid, and they may be intense enough to initiate labor in a patient who has a history of premature labor. Owing to the role of intravaginal prostaglandin in inducing labor, manual manipulation may be preferable to the woman at risk. The woman's response to orgasm from manual stimulation as well as from coitus must be considered in advising the couple and in helping them identify alternative methods of sexual expression.

The woman who has uteroplacental insufficiency from any cause should be advised to avoid orgasm altogether, since this may produce late and variable decelerations in the fetal heart rate. This is easily compensated for in the healthy infant, but the sick infant may experience hypoxia.

If bleeding has taken place, coitus and automanipulation are contraindicated in the third trimester until delivery. In the first trimester, abstinence should be the rule until either abortion has occurred, there has been no bleeding for two weeks, or quickening is felt.

Cross-infection is likely in patients with venereal disease. When reinfection is possible, coitus and other forms of sexual behavior should be avoided until the infection has been completely eradicated.

Because of the possibility of infection, coitus should not take place when membranes are ruptured. Coitus has been blamed for rupture of membranes prior to the onset of labor. Although unlikely, if this occurs, it is a result of tension on membranes that would have ruptured spontaneously soon anyway.

OTHER MODES OF SEXUAL EXPRESSION

When the health professional advises abstinence, other modes of sexual behavior must be suggested. Whenever possible, counseling should involve both partners. During the third trimester, libido for both husband and wife may fall, and sexual activity may diminish voluntarily. Husbands who are concerned about their manhood or to whom the reasons for abstinence have not been explained may attempt to "prove" themselves away from home during this time. Often a simple anticipatory discussion will prevent this.

If indeed intercourse in the traditional sense is prohibited during pregnancy, other sexual outlets must be utilized. With creativity both people will find joy and satisfaction. The couple might be encouraged to make the most of the sensitivity of the breasts by utilizing the intermammary technique of intercourse. In this method, care must be taken not to compress the pregnant abdomen while penile thrusts are made between the breasts.

Another possibility would be to utilize the groin space between the upper thigh and the lower abdomen, creating a tube out of this space. This would not cause orgasm for the woman but would allow the man to release his sexual tensions.

Anal intercourse, if personally acceptable, is also an alternative to vaginal penetration. If this technique is to be employed, caution must be exercised not to contaminate either the vagina or the urethra. Hemorrhoids, common in pregnancy, might prohibit this practice.

Oral-genital stimulation may be utilized during pregnancy. According to a recent survey of women (*Redbook,* September, 1975), a large percentage engage in and enjoy oral sex. Many women indicated that this experience provided intense orgasm. If female orgasm is contraindicated, couples should be cautioned regarding the use of this method.[13] Also, couples must be warned not to inflate the vagina with air, since this has been known to cause fatal air emboli.[1, 6] The large dilated uterine vessels pick up the air, and embolism causes rapid death.

In patients who have high-risk pregnancies, an additional amount of sexual conflict may be present. The counselor must be aware of cues and work with the couple in an appropriate manner. If a crisis occurs with regard to the pregnancy, one must anticipate subsequent guilt and either assist the couple himself or make a referral to someone who can work with them. Patients who have a normal obstetrical history need no restrictions on their sexual activity during pregnancy. Patients who must alter their activities need a great deal of guidance and support from the health professionals. They may continue to have sexual relations and feel guilty because of this.

Touching and caressing techniques need to be developed to the utmost during pregnancy. A caring attitude is essential for the couple. The health professional should help the couple realize that alterations are only temporary, and that soon previously utilized techniques may be resumed.

SUMMARY

Sexual intercourse represents an integral part of life, and it should be dealt with in pregnancy in a realistic and understanding manner both by couples involved and by health team workers. These personnel should be concerned not only with the physiological aspects of the pregnancy and early postpartal period, but also with the emotional problems that may develop.

Sexual intercourse produces a feeling of closeness between couples in addition to satisfying a woman's need for nurturance during pregnancy and the early postpartal period. Many textbooks continue to advise sexual abstinence from four weeks prior to delivery to four to six weeks post partum. Many physicians are becoming more lenient regarding restrictions and are advising the continuance of coitus or genital play until membranes rupture, if there has been no problem with the pregnancy. Anything introduced into the vagina after membranes are ruptured could increase the possibility of intrauterine infection, threatening the welfare of the mother and baby.

By three weeks post partum, the vaginal discharge has probably ceased except for a slight brown effluent. Any tears that occurred in the vaginal wall or cervix have usually healed by this time. Physiologically, it is safe to resume intercourse at this time. Psychologically, couples must be assured that there is no physical danger and should be counseled regarding positions and techniques that minimize initial discomfort.

Health workers should counsel couples regarding sexual practice based on individual circumstances, needs, and desires. Sexual satisfaction should be geared toward strengthening the couple's relationship and enhancing the family unit.

REFERENCES

1. Aronson, Marvin E. Fatal Air Embolism Caused by Bizarre Sexual Behavior During Pregnancy. *Medical Aspects of Human Sexuality,* Dec. 1969, pp. 33–39.
2. Bourne, Gordon. *Pregnancy.* London: Cassell, 1972.
3. Clark, A. L. and R. W. Hall. Sex During and After Pregnancy. *American Journal of Nursing,* 74:1430–1431, Aug. 1974.
4. Coleman, A. D. Psychological State During First Pregnancy. *American Journal of Orthopsychiatry,* 39:788, 1969.
5. Falicor, C. J. Sexual Adjustment During Pregnancy and Post Partum. *American Journal of Obstetrics and Gynecology,* 99:991–1000, Dec. 1, 1973.
6. Fatteh, Abdullah, William Leach, and Charles Wilkinson. Fatal Air Embolism in Pregnancy Resulting from Orogenital Sex Play. *Forensic Science,* 2:247–250, May 1973.
7. Fisher, Seymour. *The Female Orgasm.* New York, Basic Books, 1973.
8. Goodlin, R. C., et al. Orgasm During Late Pregnancy, Possible Deleterious Effects. *Obstetrics and Gynecology,* 38:916–921, Dec. 1971.
9. Goodlin, Robert, William Schmidt, and Donald Creevy. Uterine Tension and Fetal Heart Rate During Maternal Orgasm. *Obstetrics and Gynecology,* 39:125–127, Jan. 1972.
10. Grams, Armin. 1970. (Editorial) Merrill-Palmer Quarterly, Detroit, April 1976, pp. 18–23.
11. Jessner, L., E. Weigert and J. L. Foy. The Development of Parental Attitudes During Pregnancy. In: *Parenthood: Its Psychology and Psychopathology.* Anthony, E. James and Therese Benedik (eds.) Boston: Little, Brown & Co. 1970.
12. Krantz, Kermit. Personal Communication.
13. Levin, R. J. and A. Levin. Sexual Pleasure: The Surprising Preferences of 100,000 Women. *Redbook,* Sept., 1975, pp. 51–58.
14. Masters, William H. and Virginia Johnson. *Human Sexual Response.* Boston: Little, Brown & Co., 1966.
15. Newton, Niles. Trebly Sensuous Woman. *Psychology Today,* July, 1971, pp. 68–71+.
16. Pugh, W. E. and Fernendez, F. L. Coitus in Late Pregnancy. *Obstetrics and Gynecology,* 2:636, Dec. 1953.
17. Quirk, Barbara L. *Coitus During Pregnancy.* Unpublished Master's Thesis, University of Kansas, 1972.
18. Rubin, R. Cognitive Style in Pregnancy. *American Journal of Nursing,* 70:502, March, 1970.
19. Slate, William. Coitus as a Cause of Abortion. *Medical Aspects of Human Sexuality,* January, 1970, pp. 25–32.
20. Taylor, E. Stewart. *Beck's Obstetrical Practice.* 9th ed. Baltimore: Williams & Wilkins, 1971.

12

DRIVES, DIFFERENCES, AND DEVIATIONS

Rosemary J. McKeighen, R.N., M.S.

DEVELOPMENT OF DIFFERENCES AND DRIVES

Sex differences begin to develop before birth. Each organism has tendencies to respond to external stimuli in certain ways. The framework of future behavior is thus set; whether it persists depends on whether it is reinforced, punished, or ignored.

The majority of sex abnormalities seen in young children show that the male child is at a significant disadvantage. Physiologically, males have a greater incidence of abnormalities of genetic and hormonal origin; behaviorally, emotional disturbance is reported with more frequency and at an earlier age for males. Psychiatric populations are still predominantly male. The most commonly reported deviancy for males is a tendency toward antisocial personality and behavior disorders. Depressive reaction is the most frequent manifestation in females.

Determinants of Sex Differentiation

A general assumption of geneticists is that differences between the sexes arose when one type of germ cell retained its power of locomotion and became a sperm, while the other type accumulated nutrients, grew larger, lost the power of locomotion, and became the ovum. It seems logical, then, that cursory sex differentiation is made from a biological frame of reference.

Physiologically, two discrete agents, genes and hormones, influence sex differentiation. Sex determination is genetically controlled, and sexual development is hormonally controlled. The basic difference between men and women genetically is that women have two X chromosomes and men have one X and one Y chromosome. Women have 23 pairs of homologous chromosomes; men have only 22. While the combined action of some genes in both X chromosomes is required to produce a fertile woman, the action of genes in only the lone Y chromosome produces a fertile man.

One of the functions of the Y chromosome is to ensure that fetal gonads develop into testes rather than ovaries. Even though the sex of the zygote is determined at conception, one cannot recognize the differences between male and female embryos until the seventh week of fetal life. The nucleus of normal female cells contains the sex chromatin (Barr body), while the cell nucleus of normal males is chromatin negative.

SEXUAL ANOMALIES

Developmental abnormalities of gonads caused by chromosomal aberrations result in sexual infantilism. Hypothalamic-pituitary deficiencies must be considered as causes of failure of sexual development when levels of pituitary gonadotropins are low and the gonads are responsive to exogenous gonadotropins. The gonadotropin deficiency may be temporary or permanent. Permanent deficiency may indicate eunuchoidism. If, however, the deficiencies are the result of malnutrition or chronic illness, the normal pattern of growth will evolve, but at a retarded rate.

Sexual infantilism becomes evident at the expected time of puberty. Reports of the sex drives of such children are misleading, since such a vast number of inhibitors can be operating. The sex drives seem to be related to various types of inhibitors, e.g., ambiguous external genitalia, mental retardation, coarctation of the aorta, physical appearance, or hypogonadism.

Conversely, initiation of puberty before the age of eight years in girls and ten years in boys is considered abnormal. It is difficult to determine whether or not the sexual precocity will lead to complete sexual maturity.

When the condition of ambiguous external genitalia is present, treatment with hormones is advantageous both medically and psychologically. Children with anomalous internal accessory organs rarely reach full function and maturity without medical intervention. However, sex-role rearing practices seem to be the crucial factor in full role enactment. Males, in particular, who are reared as males continue to relate to the masculine role even though they have a uterus.

THE ROLE OF HORMONES

In a multicellular organism, the cells are marshaled in tissues. In order for each tissue to perform its role, its cells must function cooperatively. The primary controllers are hormones.

A hormone is manufactured in a tissue or an organ, from which it is released into the bloodstream. It exerts specific regulatory effects on its target cells. Hormones need to be produced in only minuscule amounts, since they contribute nothing to the structure or energy supply of the organs they regulate. Hormones affect the activity of genes through their ability to alter the pattern of genetic activity in the cells responsive to them. The primordial male and female sex organs are identical when they first appear. For a male to develop, something must be added. Cells of a genetic male are dependent on the male hormone androgen, secreted by the Leydig cells, to differentiate the embryo sexually.

Androgen enhances the sex drive in both sexes. In contrast, estrogen is a functional castrating agent in the male. It may lower the intensity of the sex drive and lead to a decrease in sexual initiative and activity, thus serving as an erotic tranquilizer. Estrogen, for the female, appears to be more important to the cycle of nidation and gestation than to the sex drive and eroticism per se — with the exception that a vagina not receiving estrogen is unlubricated, so that intercourse is painful.

The Testicular Feminization Syndrome. The syndrome of androgen insensitivity or testicular feminization can also cause ambiguity in sex differentiation. A child born with this defect is a female externally, and the psychosexual characteristics are also feminine. Her gonads are two testes, always lacking spermatogenesis, either undescended or pushed down toward the labia. Her uterus is vestigial, making menstruation impossible. In some cases, the vagina is too short for comfortable intercourse and requires surgical intervention. Puberty is feminizing, since the cells of the body are unable to respond to the normal masculine output of androgen from the testes. They respond instead only to the amount of estrogen normally produced in a male. The nature of the resistance to androgen at the cellular level is unknown but is presumed to be enzymatic. This condition is hereditary, probably through sex-linked dominance.

DETERMINANTS OF GENDER ROLE

Gender imprinting begins at birth with sex assignment. The critical period is reached by 18 months, and by age 2½, a gender role identity is well established. Gender role incorporates all the behavior a person engages in to disclose himself or herself as being male or female. Sexuality is included but is not restricted to the sense of eroticism. It is judged in relation to the following areas: (1) general mannerisms, (2) conduct, (3) posture, (4) play preferences, (5) recreational interests, (6) impromptu conversational topics, (7) casual comments, (8) content of dreams, (9) daydreams, (10) fantasy, (11) projective tests, (12) erotic practice, and (13) reply to direct inquiry.

In regard to sex assignment, some believe that the sexual instinct is present at birth. In this formulation, sex drive then becomes a special example of haptic drive—that is, an urge to touch and be touched. Others believe the human species has erotically sensitive areas in the body, particularly the genital organs. In the course of growing up, a person's sexual organ sensations become associated with a gender role, and orientation as male and female becomes established through repeated encounters and transactions. This is referred to as *social* and *environmental determinism.*

It is much easier for a male child to be socially determined simply because of his anatomic structures. He soon learns that the penis is an important part of his role, and he is constantly reminded of his sexuality. These reminders form a psychological "groove," which enforces his maleness throughout his life. On the other hand, a female child's sexuality is hidden and protected. Instead of being immediately aware of her sexuality, she must learn about it. She has no constant reminders of her femaleness until puberty, when she is suddenly faced with it.

When sexuality is not imprinted at birth, the social hermaphroditic condition exists, causing sexuality to be determined through the various experiences of growing up. The most convincing evidence of the impact of social interaction upon gender identity differentiation is a series of conclusions drawn from studies of congenital hermaphrodites. The outcome of psychosexual differentiation is totally independent of genetic sex. A person can establish and be reared in a gender role consistent with assigned sex yet inconsistent with chromosomal sex. Seventy per cent of persons with gonadal sex discrepancies take on a gender role that is concordant with their socialization practices. Only the remaining 30 per cent act according to their genetic sex.

Gender identity differentiation is also independent of hormonal sex. The ovaries of the hyperadrenocortic female pseudohermaphrodites are inert. Even though their adrenals produce an excess of both estrogens and androgens, androgenic activity dominates and the body is excessively virilized. However, the majority establish a female gender role. The testes of male pseudohermaphrodites produce estrogens which feminize the body. Yet as many as 80 per cent of these individuals establish male gender roles despite the embarrassment caused by hormonal contradictions.

SOCIALIZATION AND SEX DIFFERENCES

An important component of this formulation is how physiological differences can affect the socialization process. Clinical observations of children reveal that males and females exhibit differing sleep-wakefulness patterns. At three weeks and at three months, males sleep less and cry more—thereby experiencing a more stimulating interaction with their mothers. In a sex-linked interaction, mothers' contact increased with their irritable daughters but decreased with their irritable sons.

Mothers touched and talked to their six-month-old daughters more than to their six-month-old sons. When re-evaluated at 13 months, the same daughters touched and talked to their mothers more than the same sons did.

When age is held constant, some modal differences between the sexes are identified. Boys have higher activity levels, are more prone to act out aggression, are physically impulsive, are genitally sexual earlier, and appear to have less well developed cognitive and perceptual skills. The opposite is true for girls. They are behaviorally more passive, display less overt aggression, are more sensitive to pain, have greater verbal, perceptual and cognitive skill, and realize their genital sexuality later.

SEX-RELATED DIFFERENCES IN ADULTS

Outgrowths of these differences are recognizable even in adults. While men are readily aroused to a casual or promiscuous liaison, women are more dependent upon long-term romantic attachments. Men and women also respond differently to visual images representative of sexual desire. The male views pinups as a substitute object of sexual desire. The female projects herself into the image and becomes the seducer. Normal men do not identify with pictures of males in this manner. It is true that the male homosexual responds to photographs of other males, but only as sexual objects, not as extensions of self. Dream content that triggers erotic arousal also elaborates these sexual differences. Dreams of sexual organs are found twice as frequently and in much younger age groups in males than in females.

Another source of difference is perceptual distractability. The male demonstrates his distractability by moving from one love object to another over a period of time. Conversely, the female is typically steadfastly anchored to a single romantic object or concept. However, in the act of copulation, it is the male who demonstrates such an absolute singleness of purpose, in that he is likely to be unable to complete the act successfully if distracted.

A hormone-controlled difference that has sexual significance is related to the sense of smell. Smell acuity, governed by estrogen levels, is greater in women than in men. There is a rare clinical syndrome (Kallman's syndrome) seen in males, consisting of hypogonadism and sterility, in which congenital absence of the sense of smell is a pathognomonic sign.

An odor may serve as a pheromone, or long-distance excitor, for mammals. Many marriage and sexual counselors endorse this belief by recommending aphrodisiacs and emollients as a requisite for sexual practice in order to enhance compatibility and enjoyment. Some interpret oral-genital sex as fulfilling an erotic pleasure need dictated by the sense of smell, rather than as one that emerges from boredom with a ritualistic sexual pattern.

DEVELOPMENTAL ASPECTS OF SEX DIFFERENCES

Some persons suggest that the less organized physiological functions of the male make him less able to initially respond favorably to his mother. The fact that the effect of one person's behavior shapes the response of another causes a circular and perpetuating process. The response of the mother is shaped by the child in earliest infancy, and the child likewise responds to the behavior of the mother. These behavior differences are common in the sexes when they are older; in the first year, they may be related to the quality of the relationship between the mother and child at birth. That these characteristic behaviors are responded to differently by mothers, fathers, and siblings adds further confusion to role development and expectation for the child.

Studies of varied societies by anthropologists reveal that, regardless of culture, in a disproportionate number of instances, boys tend to be somewhat more aggressive than girls. While levels of aggression vary from culture to culture, in only a few societies studied are girls more aggressive than boys. Also, in most societies boys are not specifically trained to show more aggression than girls. Most anthropologists agree that in all cultures, the tendency toward aggression can be modified by experiences of children within the culture. Evidence is emerging to substantiate the theory that activities associated with aggression are generally assigned to men because of the male's somewhat greater constitutional readiness to be aggressive. This worldwide difference in task assignment may be another sign of the human tendency to adapt to the world by matching the facts of biology with the requirements for survival.

In most societies, impulsive, aggressive children are forced to restrain these tendencies. Girls' more mature skills enable them to respond to stimuli, especially from other people, more swiftly and accurately than boys. Girls are better at analyzing and anticipating environmental demands. Thus, the characteristic behavior of girls is less likely to disturb parents than boys' characteristic behavior.

These differences in response tendencies, along with another factor, specify group differences between boys and girls. Any behavior, either feminine or tomboyish, is sanctioned for girls, while for boys, neither "sissy" nor "bad boy" behavior is acceptable. Beginning at age 2½, boys experience greater prohibitions than girls on behavior. Dependent behavior, normal for all young children, is permitted for girls but discouraged in boys.

Girls today are not encouraged to give up old techniques of relating to adults and using others to define identity, to manipulate their physical world, and to supply their emotional needs. Girls' self-esteem remains dependent upon acceptance and love from others; therefore they continue to react to others rather than evolving their own responses. The boy's impulsiveness and sexuality are sources of enormous pleasure that is independent of anyone else's response. These pleasures are central to the early core self. Negative sanctions from powerful adults threaten not only the obvious pleasure, but also self-integrity. Thus, boys are pressured by their own impulses and society's demands to give up their dependence on the response of others for feelings of self-esteem. Forcing the male to continually reaffirm himself leads him to develop a sense of self and a criterion of worth, both of which are relatively independent of others' responses. He turns to achievements in the external world to value himself in the form of tangibles.

In the world of the growing child, both male and female systems of behavior are models with positive or negative values. The child's psychosexual identity is not written at birth in either the genetic code, the hormonal system, or the nervous system. The child becomes conditioned through his rearing to adhere to the positive model that, in the normal course of events, is congruous with his anatomic structure.

Today, this simple stereotype is becoming less valid for the middle-class man and woman. Men are rejecting tangible success as the sole source of esteem. Women are becoming freer to participate in the professional world. For both sexes, both old and new norms exist and a clearly defined role is not visible. As a result, it becomes difficult to achieve a feminine or masculine identity. Thus, the search for this identity must be simplified by the socialization process. Children must be directed toward their role model in order for them to comfortably assume their sexual identity.

SEXUAL DEVIATION PATTERNS

Throughout the socialization process of man, physical expression has been an important area of study and comment for artists, philosophers, academicians, and clinicians. Sexual expression has always held a prominent place in man's value system and has played a prominent role in understanding his behavior.

Until now, knowledge about sexuality has been shared in a limited and covert manner; recently, however, society has sanctioned an open exchange of this knowledge. In fact, the exchange has become so open that the American social system has begun to evaluate its own sexual behavior. The result is society's identifying certain sexual behaviors as problems resulting in the inhibition of ultimate self-fulfillment. Practitioners are charged with evaluating these behaviors, designing interventions, providing prescriptions, and applying treatments that will modify this human condition by changing these behaviors.

The sexual behaviors that have been selected to be presented and discussed in this chapter are contained within Cohen's interpretation of deviance as "behavior which violates institutional expectations—that is, expectations which are shared and recognized as legitimate within a social system."[1]

Within this context, it is important to realize that the point of reference determining deviance is the discriminating factor. Deviance is not something inherent to the behavior. Instead, reference to a socially defined scale of evaluation, as well as shared expectations about what behavior is suitable and conforms to the social norms, decides which behavior is to be called deviant. Sherif emphasizes this point by stating that "an item of behavior, taken in and by itself, cannot be labeled either conformity or deviation. There is no such thing as conforming or deviating behavior in the abstract."[3] It is possible then that the same behavior may or may not be judged as deviant, depending upon its relation to the social norms that exist at the time and place of its occurrence. Take, for example, extramarital intercourse. In contemporary American society, it digresses from social norms regulating sexual behavior; this is not true among the Eskimos, however, where wife sharing is an integral part of hospitality.

As important as the fact that deviance is not a property of the behavior per se is the realization that the term "deviant" is used to describe the behavior, and not the person manifesting the behavior. Many times the classificatory leap is made from the labeling of certain actions that depart from social norms to the labeling of the person as deviant. This is a common occurrence when theories and concepts of psychopathology are used to interpret behavior. Such reasoning operates on the assumption that the personality disturbance provides the sole explanation for a person's failing to conform to normative expectations. This position states not that personality, in general, is separate from deviant behavior, but that all behavior, deviant or not, can be construed as being the outcome of the simultaneous operation of both personality and sociocultural determinants.

Viewing the family milieu as a microcosm of the larger society, Jessor et al.[2] believe that the socialization system develops from exposure to three parental structural categories: reward, belief, and control. The child's socialization system becomes an integration of his perception of these interrelated sources of parental pressure. He then incorporates these into a behavioral system of his own, which he uses to justify his future behavior. Jessor et al. further hypothesize that "the more fully the variables in the three structures characterize a given family situation, the more likely it will be that the child will develop personality attributes conducive to deviance and will actually engage in deviant behavior."[2]

Because sexuality is closely associated with integration of the personality, it is not surprising that disturbances in the relationships between men and women may be exposed in sexual inadequacies. Sexual difficulties are a mode of expression that often provides clues to the basic impediments people have to their growth as individuals.

This background information on the definition and sources of deviance helps one to understand the study of deviance. The next step is the recognition, modification, or eradication of a few specific deviant behaviors. Later chapters will deal with some behavior patterns more commonly identified as "deviant," e.g., homosexuality (see Chapters 15 and 16). The remainder of this chapter will cover two types of prevalent sexual problems not usually labeled as "deviant" but rather as dysfunctions—namely, psychosomatic infertility in the female and impotence in the male.

PSYCHOSOMATIC INFERTILITY IN THE FEMALE

When appraising a response to sexual intercourse, one must realize that the response of the female—that of climax of coitus—will not be the same as the orgasm of the male. They are not analogous and should be evaluated independently. Their differences lie in the fact that the genital tracts of men and women differ anatomically in both structure and sensory cell distribution. Sensory cell distribution similar to that of the glans penis can be found only in the clitoris, lower vaginal muscles, and parts of the labia minora, and since the vagina is homologous with the penile shaft, the response to sexual stimulation could not be comparable with that of the phallus. The unrealistic expectation on the part of women that they can attain a rapid and climactic orgasm similar to that of men is common. Women must be given appropriate stimulation to achieve a slower but more enduring gratification.

Education to clarify this difference through demonstration of physical sexual routines may or may not remedy this situation, depending on the complexity of the problem. The critical role of psychological aspects in this situation causes the complexity. Even after biological and physical discrepancies are remedied, the psychological status of the participants continues to be the greatest influence on achieving satisfaction, particularly on the part of the woman. Unfulfilled expectations of their sexual response arouse in some women feelings of shameful inadequacy and, in others, rage at their partner. For a woman to have satisfactory sexual adjustment and fulfillment, she must perceive her partner as desirable, become sexually aroused, and be free of guilt and anxiety.

Etiology. Women manifest guilt and anxiety in many ways within the sexual realm, the most common being psychosomatic infertility. Frigidity arises from attitudes that the woman has adopted as operants for her behavior within a relationship. Such causes may include a belief that the love relationship is not reciprocal, conscious resentment of her partner for any reason, doubts of her physical attractiveness or sexual technique, or simple envy or hostility. Frigidity also is often related to fear of venereal disease, pregnancy, or injury during intercourse.

Muscular activity of the vagina under these conditions may rapidly expel the spermatic fluid and result in the inability to conceive. Suppression of ovulation due to persisting anxieties and subtle avoidance of coitus have the same effect. The woman may also develop and report physical conditions such as spasms of the uterine tubes, rapid expulsion of spermatic fluid, failure to ovulate, and vaginismus. Gynecologists report that more than 5 per cent of all infertile women have a body chemistry that produces antibodies that destroy the husband's sperm. They classify these women as being allergic to their husbands' sperm. They also report an equal number of women who unconsciously recognize and are sensitive to the chemical changes occurring at ovulation and engage in the unconscious avoidance of any sexual contact during this time. These women have great difficulty being artificially inseminated and complain of vaginismus.

History.   Family histories of such women reveal a paternal pattern of belittling her as a young girl, at the same time making it clear that father expected her to care for him in his senior years. Frequent warning against sexual activity and overt jealousy of boyfriends were also common. Deep-seated attachment to father arouses guilt reactions during sexual activity. During therapy, these women reveal unresolved incestuous desires for their fathers and admit to having discomforting feelings when they see father display any physical contact with a young woman, however platonic — i.e., putting his arm around a young female relative.

In a review of the socialization process and personality conditioning of other frigid women, one discovery was that maternal dependence, founded on hostility for the mother, was, and continued to be, great. The threat of motherhood is overwhelming for this type of woman, but she has difficulty admitting that she really does not desire to have a baby but would prefer to compete with her husband. These women generally exhibit an overcompensation in such areas as active physical expression and academic pursuit, and they often suffer from spasms of the uterine tubes.

Anger toward overprotective parents, accompanied by childhood fantasies of running away or dreams of parental death, can cause failure to ovulate. Frequently these women report their initial identification and socialization patterns to be masculine. They were given men's first names, grew up as father's "little boy," indulged predominantly in masculine play, and recall having had difficulty in engaging in primary sexual expressions (e.g., kissing boys) because daddy disapproved. As adults, they retain the masculine behavioral patterns and remain overly dependent on parents — father may telephone daily. Intense feelings of shame or guilt about sexual relations permeate their attitude and inhibit their function. They hold the belief that being an adequate woman is synonymous with producing a child, and they are fearful that they will lose their husbands if they do not do so. It is obvious that the wish to be pregnant is not always the wish for a child.

Another form of troublesome behavior within the sexual sphere is the one-child infertility pattern that many American families portray. Psychodynamically, this infertility pattern establishes for the wife a child-mother relationship between the woman and her own mother that was nonexistent. The completeness of this dyad (mother-child relationship) does not permit the intrusion of a third person such as the husband or another child. The sexual deviancy of this woman is an outgrowth of her basic conflicts over dependency and hostility. As a child, she believed that her existence was the cause of her mother's unhappiness and experienced guilt whenever she felt hostility toward her parents, to the extent that she believed her mother would die if her anger was expressed. To protect herself from such an unacceptable childhood situation, this woman either developed an extremely dependent identification with the hostile mother or overidentified with the father. Either stance results in a woman's developing insecure and immature attitudes regarding her femininity, development of tomboyish attitudes, and sexual maladjustment.

When husband and wife are sexually compatible and have common social interests, they establish a natural condition that operates against a mother-child monopoly. Time and energy are required for maintaining the husband-wife dyad, thereby diminishing the potential for development of the exclusive parent-child relationship. Many pediatricians attest to the frequency with which the problem of maternal overprotection reveals the mother as being an aggressive woman experiencing sexual maladjustment. Psychiatrists describe these mothers as frigid women who seek refuge from a loveless marriage by vicariously finding love in an ecstatic attachment to their children. This interpretation suggests that a consequence of frigidity could be pervasive devotion or hatred.

IMPOTENCE

At the present time, there is no meaningful evidence to substantiate the possibility that emotional factors in the male may produce biophysiological changes resulting in reduced sperm count or defective sperm. A reduced emission is reported at the time of collection and examination of the ejaculate, which is generally ascribed to the male's anxiety when his performance ability is being questioned. However, there is sufficient evidence to support the belief that emotional factors are responsible for certain types of impotence.

Impotence can be measured in two dimensions: physical ability to attain an erection, and interest in coitus. The varying degrees of impotence may extend from (1) complete failure to obtain an erection with no interest in coitus; (2) a partial or inadequate erection with limited interest; (3) periodic failure of erection coupled with limited interest; (4) ability to establish erection, but lack of sexual gratification with ejaculation in coitus; to (5) premature ejaculation. Most clinicians categorize the disabilities within three broad categories: erectile impotence, ejaculatory impotence, and phobic coitus avoidance, or premature ejaculation.

Etiology. For successful completion of the sex act, the male requires a sex drive, a partner he deems desirable, and a situation devoid of distraction and anxiety. These prerequisites allow for erection, penile insertion, and the necessary muscular activity to provide penile friction and stimulation and to build to eventual ejaculation, which is accompanied by a distinctive pleasurable feeling and climactic orgasm. Impotence, then, may occur whenever there is discrepancy that causes a disruption in any of these areas—i.e., no desire, lack of attraction to the partner, or a distracting or threatening environment.

The anxiety of the male can stem from internal or external stimuli. Internal stimulus anxiety is derived from the pressure of performance he places upon himself to consummate the act. The external source of anxiety can be anything in his environment that can evoke a negative connotation for him—for example, ridicule, unsafe situations, satisfying his partner's expectations, or time or space limitations. When disease, trauma, and organ disease are ruled out, clinicians almost always view impotency to be the product of a psychological conflict in the male under 55, and in 90 per cent of all cases.

Guilt, anxiety, and shame may also lead to impotency if the male fears disapproval by parents or society, has unconscious wishes to damage the partner, or considers exposure of his body or his sexual performance as subject to ridicule. There is agreement, though, that the most common psychogenic causes are unconscious and conflicting loves, due to either persisting infantile attachments to the mother figure, latent homosexual attachment, or an extramarital love attachment.

During psychotherapy, these men reveal a masochistic attachment to the mother figure and derive pleasure from being refused consummation of the act. Because the man interprets this as revenge against women, who are considered to be the symbolic representation of the mother, he seeks this refusal of pleasure. The anxiety that prevents his proficiency is due to the underlying hostility he feels toward women—a hostility that stems from childhood experiences in which the female was perceived as critical, punitive, and capable of damaging the male genitals.

Psychoanalytically, there seem to be two major attitudes toward the sexual partner that underlie the impotence. The first is the guilt felt in response to the partner's modest apprehensions during early sexual activity. This may cause resentment in the man because he is confronted with a living reproach for his more aggressive sexual wish; a result may be the fantasy equation: wife equals frustrating mother. The second is the emergence of a split in the husband's objectives. He gains the need to deny the sexuality of the woman. He quickly desexualizes, idealizes, and fuses her with the maternal image in its possessive, restrictive aspect. Her sexual demands arouse anxiety and disgust. His feelings may entail components of adolescent revolt against maternal authority, an identification with the weak father, or both. These feelings conflict with the demands made upon his freedom, which he interprets as wounds to his male status and his role needs. Both of these may be inflated by the male into enormous sacrifices, such as giving up all male "fun things." Because he feels caged and fears being totally devoured, he retaliates with impotency.

Psychiatrists have demonstrated the existence of a strong association between the symptom of retarded ejaculation and mild paranoid tendencies. Frequently, males whose highly competitive and ambitious drives were inhibited during childhood by excessive parental intimidation perceive all future competition in terms of murderous violence. Sex relations, then, are seen as a symbolic extension of a competitive struggle with men. Successful completion means not only validating the masculine role, but simultaneously destroying the competitiveness by sustaining an erection but inhibiting orgasm. In this way, the male can ward off the fantasy of retaliation while maintaining his illusion of hypermasculinity.

The sex-related fears that men in therapy repeatedly identify as unconscious motivators are those concerned with contracting a venereal disease or dying during coital activity. Many times the problem of impotency is associated with a depressive reaction in which the man complains of frequent backaches. In these instances, when he recalls the initial situation in which the trauma and failure occurred, symptoms disappear and activity is restored. These situations are usually associated with the attitudes of the partner toward sexuality, frequency of the sexual act, and disgust for precoital stimulation practices. Fantasies during sexual activity and traumatic environmental distractors can also bring on impotence. Both men reporting an acute onset of symptoms and younger males suffering from transitory or secondary impotence are easily treated with supportive therapy. Such therapy consists of re-education and training of sexual function using conditioning techniques.

Conclusions

Usually, when communication between the partners becomes strained, sexual activity ceases or becomes markedly diminished. There are many reasons for this. Sexual intercourse is the most intimate of all social relationships, and disharmonious emotions are very likely to interfere despite the control either partner exerts. These reservations, along with the unconscious conflicts, set the stage for either impotency in the man or frigidity in the woman.

Communication and honesty are all-important in a sexual relationship between two people. This honesty can occur only when each individual is accepted by the other as what he is, and nothing more or less. The study of what our society refers to as "deviant" behavior becomes valuable as a tool in working toward this open communication. With study and correction, these deviances can be accepted for what they are, enabling each individual involved to understand the problem. In this way, each person will be able to feel confidence and security in his own sexuality.

REFERENCES

1. Cohen, A. K. The Study of Social Disorganization and Deviant Behavior. In: *Sociology Today: Problems and Prospects.* Merton, R. K., L. Broom, and L. S. Cottrell, Jr. (eds.). New York: Basic Books, Inc., 1959, p. 462.
2. Jessor, R., T. D. Graves, R. C. Hanson, and S. L. Jessor. *Society, Personality and Deviant Behavior.* New York: Holt, Rinehart & Winston, Inc., 1968.
3. Sherif, M. Conformity-Deviation, Norms, and Group Relations. In: *Conformity and Deviation.* Berg, I. A. and B. M. Bass (eds.) New York: Harper & Row, 1961, p. 159.

13

INFERTILITY

Paul Hensleigh, M.D.

The basic premise of fertility is that conception will occur as a normal consequence of coitus if the ovary has produced an egg, a viable sperm has reached the egg at the optimal time for penetration, and the tubes provide an unobstructed pathway for sperm and egg migration. In order for these dramatic though silent and unobtrusive events to occur, we now understand that they must be preceded by complex messages between the hypothalamus and pituitary gland in the brain. The final messages from the pituitary gland are carried by hormones called *gonadotropins,* which stimulate the ovary of the woman and the testis of the man to produce the single egg and sperm required. Gonadotropins also stimulate production of the potent hormones needed by each partner to insure the optimal nourishment of the tiny ova and sperm cells as they migrate over vast distances from the gonads to their appointed meeting in the uterine tubes and, ultimately, to the uterus.

As the complexity of the reproductive process becomes increasingly apparent, it becomes less surprising that pregnancy does not result inevitably after properly timed coitus, even in couples who are "normal" by all the tests available. Information obtained from the Growth of American Families Studies[5] indicates that pregnancy will not occur in more than half of couples with previous known fertility until after the third menstrual cycle of unprotected intercourse. It is on the basis of such probability statistics that extensive infertility evaluation is delayed by most physicians presented with a young couple with no apparent abnormalities who have attempted for only a few months to achieve pregnancy. Similarly, patients in whom a significant problem has been identified and treated should be allowed several months' exposure before one can assume that yet another infertility factor is present. A more realistic premise for infertility might be that if pregnancy has not occurred after a year of properly timed coitus in an apparently normal couple, there may be an identifiable problem that can be recognized and corrected, thereby significantly improving the chances for successful pregnancy.

Rapport between health professional and patient(s) is a vital ingredient for successful management of infertile couples. The frustration of prolonged evaluation and treatment, the seemingly fruitless investment of significant effort and money (which is often not covered by medical insurance), and the inevitable feelings of guilt and inadequacy (which may not be limited to patients) must be dealt with in an open and honest manner. The health professional is often, and appropriately, relied on by the couple for encouragement in the face of seeming failure. At the same time, however, he must guard against unrealistic optimism. For some couples, all efforts will be futile, and the health professional should not be reticent to admit to failure or advise referral to another specialist with expertise or special interest in a highly unusual aspect of reproductive failure.

INITIAL INTERVIEW

It is essential that both husband and wife be included from the beginning of an infertility evaluation. Some health professionals prefer interviewing each separately, especially in obtaining a sexual history. Whether it is a gynecologist, a urologist, a nurse, or a family physician who is first consulted, the couple should be oriented toward viewing the failure of conception as a mutual problem rather than as an inadequacy of one partner or the other. The overall probability for the primary factor responsible for infertility being in the female is about 60 per cent; therefore, about 40 per cent of identifiable fertility problems occur in the male.

Obtaining an accurate sexual history is most essential, for this alone may lead to the factor responsible for the failure to conceive. Individual libido and orgasmic capacity with the partner are significant elements in the history, not because they play a physiological role in fertilization (which they don't), but because they reveal to the health professional the significant ways in which this couple view themselves, each other, and the prospects of an addition to their family unit.

Subtleties of coital technique can play a significant role in failure of couples to conceive. It is important to establish that: (1) ejaculation occurs regularly with intercourse; (2) the wife does not assume a position during or immediately following coitus that contributes to the loss of sperm from the cervix; (3) excessive douching or douching immediately after intercourse is not employed; and (4) lubricants, which could interfere with sperm migration, are not used.

Some couples focus inordinately on the timing of intercourse in relationship to ovulation. The use of basal body temperature records to document ovulation contributes to a preoccupation with planning the optimal moment for intercourse. Other couples seek assistance for infertility of several years' duration, when, in fact, the husband has been assigned to a foreign country for work or military service for most of the time interval. Intercourse frequency of three times weekly provides adequate exposure, since the ova are viable at least 48 hours, and viable sperm may be stored in cervical mucus and released into the female genital tract for three days or more. The anxiety and stress generated by unnecessary attention to the moment of ovulation may, in fact, result in blockage of ovulation by interference with the intricate and critical coordinating functions of the brain. Resolution of anxiety related to the infertile condition is the most common explanation for the unexpected incidence of conception associated with the first visit to the infertility specialist or the adoption of a child. Thus, patients should be counseled that the optimal frequency of intercourse (for conception) is about every other day, and that they should adjust their desires accordingly during the second and third weeks after the menses begins. Precise identification of the optimal fertile moment is counterproductive and should be discouraged.

Specific questions regarding the wife's gynecologic history may reveal the cause of infertility. The woman should be questioned in detail about *any* previous pregnancies, including those by a previous marriage, those ending in spontaneous miscarriage, or those terminated by therapeutic abortion. Infertile patients with previous pregnancies are said to have "secondary" infertility as opposed to those who have never conceived, who are defined as having "primary" infertility. Statement of the implications regarding possible causes of these two types may facilitate arrival at the correct diagnosis. The menstrual history, including date or age of menarche (first menses), interval of menses (number of days from the beginning of one menses until the beginning of the next), and average duration of each menses may help in recognition of patients who have menses without having regular ovulation or normal hormonal production — termed "anovulatory" cycles. Special note should be made of any hormonal medication used in the past (including oral contraceptives) and the effects of these hormones on the menses during and after their usage. Cyclic symptoms that are suggestive of ovulatory cycles (as opposed to anovulatory cycles) include: (1) predictable regularity of 26- to 34-day interval; (2) pain in the lower abdomen at midcycle (Mittelschmerz); and (3) characteristic mood changes and vascular changes sometimes associated with headaches and fluid retention that occur preceding menses (collectively called "molimina").

The history of lactation during the time of infertility, either due to breast-feeding or unrelated to previous pregnancy (called galactorrhea), is not compatible with normal ovulation and indicates a likely starting point for subsequent diagnostic studies.

Previous medical (or surgical) illnesses of either the husband or wife should be documented. Special attention should be given to thyroid disorders, venereal diseases, adulthood mumps, surgical procedures done in the pelvis or external genital area, and *any* medications routinely used by the patient. Occupational exposure of the husband to high environmental temperature may also be a significant determinant of marginal sperm production.

Throughout the interview with the couple, while one is collecting the significant background information needed for a rational approach to the infertility, one should recognize the attitudes of the couple toward their inability to conceive. After dispelling the common guilt feelings, one should provide a realistic orientation for the couple, emphasizing the probability for success, the scope of evaluation planned initially, the time frame for re-evaluation, the overall cost, and the number of office visits or duration of hospitalization that they should anticipate. If the workup or therapy extends beyond 3 or 4 months, the couple should again be seen together for an interview to review the findings and to make decisions about the extent of further workup or treatment desired.

PHYSICAL EXAMINATION

In the general physical examination, particular attention should be directed toward the body habitus of both the husband and wife, particularly the fat and hair distribution. These observations may be the first indication of a hypogonadotropic condition, i.e., inadequate sex hormone production, in either partner. In the female, distribution of hair in the pubic area (escutcheon) extending toward the umbilicus may be a critical point in separating patients who are androgenized and probably anovulatory from those with familial or "constitutional" hirsutism.

Enlargements or nodules in the thyroid gland should be evaluated in either sex, for this may be associated with either increased or decreased thyroid function. Deviations from normal thyroid function may also contribute to failure to ovulate or, in the male, to a decrease in sperm production.

The genital examination in the male should be directed toward identification of cryptorchidism, inguinal hernia, atrophy of the gonads, and the presence of varicocele (dilated veins along the spermatic cord). The most significant aspect of the male examination is the sperm analysis, which will be considered as a part of the workup.

The examination of the female pelvis is essential and usually conclusive in identification of congenital abnormalities, uterine or ovarian tumors, acute infection (usually nonvenereal) of the cervix, or chronic pelvic inflammatory disease (PID), often the result of remote gonorrhea. Endometriosis, which is commonly associated with infertility, may not present with striking findings on physical examination. Only the more advanced cases are associated with enlargements of the ovaries or masses in other regions of the pelvis. A pelvic examination should not be completed without obtaining a Pap smear as a screen for cervical cancer, and if there is clinical evidence of estrogen deficiency, a smear from the vaginal wall may help to document possible lack of hormone stimulation.

In addition to the interview and physical examination, at the time of the first visit, it is common practice to obtain a battery of laboratory screening tests that relate to the general health of the couple. Urinalysis, blood counts, a blood test for syphilis, a test for thyroid function, and blood type analysis are usually done on both husband and wife. In addition, a rubella screen for the wife may be indicative of the need for immunization prior to conception, particularly if she is commonly exposed to many children in her daily work. Nothing could be more frustrating than for the happy occasion of a conception to be followed by unprotected exposure to rubella in the early weeks of gestation.

Male Workup

SPERM ANALYSIS

The essence of the male examination and workup is the sperm analysis. The specimen should be examined in the first few minutes following ejaculation, and this should in turn be preceded by at least two days of abstinence. Most urologists request that the specimen be obtained in their office by masturbation — only a few of them have the finesse to carry out this procedure without causing considerable embarrassment to the patient. One of the characteristics of semen that may occasionally contribute to infertility is failure of liquefaction. This phenomenon, which normally occurs during the first half-hour following ejaculation, consists of a transformation from a semisolid gelatinous state to a liquid state. Obviously, this information will not be recorded accurately if the specimen is obtained elsewhere and then transported to the urologist's office or the lab.

A normal volume of semen for a single ejaculation is about 2.5 to 5.0 ml. Volumes smaller or much larger than this are frequently associated with other abnormalities such as lower counts, abnormal sperm forms, or decreased motility. Normal numbers of sperm range from 60 to 150 million per milliliter of specimen. Counts in the 40 million per milliliter range are sometimes associated with subnormal fertility, and men with counts less than 20 million per milliliter are only occasionally fertile. Associated with low counts or extreme volume variations, or both, one often observes less than the expected fraction (80+ per cent) of active vs. inactive sperm and less than the expected 80 per cent with normal shape or morphology. Thus, when an abnormal specimen is examined, one commonly observes not an isolated deviation such as low count alone, but rather a composite in which none of the characteristics is optimal.

Men with very low sperm counts (oligospermia) or no sperm (aspermia) should be evaluated with other tests to identify possible causes. X-ray examination of the skull around the pituitary gland will sometimes identify tumors, which could interfere with production of gonadotropins. Gonadotropin assays can also be performed on a blood sample. A pituitary tumor can be identified by the destruction of nearby bone and would be associated with low levels of blood gonadotropins, resulting in failure of spermatogenesis.

HORMONE PRODUCTION

Testicular hormone production is sometimes decreased when the semen analysis is abnormal; this can be evaluated by measurement of serum testosterone. Other endocrine disorders that can affect the sperm count include thyroid and adrenal disorders. Each of these can be diagnosed by measurement of their hormone products in the blood or urine. Men with no sperm may have chromosome studies done to identify intersex problems and should have a testicular biopsy to rule out neoplasms of the testes.

Female Workup

EVALUATION OF CERVIX

Role of Cervical Mucus. The production of mucus by the endocervical glands is primarily in response to the estrogen produced by the ovaries. The character of cervical mucus is dependent on the amount of estrogen stimulation. The ovaries produce increasing amounts of estrogen just prior to ovulation, and this causes the endocervical glands to produce an increased amount of mucus with physical properties favoring sperm transport. Current studies of cervical mucus suggest that under normal conditions, this material acts not only as an optimal medium for transfer of sperm to the upper female genital organs, but also serves as a reservoir for storage of sperm, which are subsequently released into the uterus and tubes during the following hours and days. In addition, there is evidence that the physical properties of normal mucus favor transfer of normally shaped, active sperm and blockage of abnormally shaped, inactive sperm. Thus, normal cervical mucus functions not simply to transfer sperm, but also to store and provide an extended supply of sperm, which are transferred after selection for normal shape and motility.

The optimal time to examine cervical mucus is near the time of ovulation — at other times the mucus will be scanty, thick, and not conducive to sperm transport. The finding of such abnormal mucus could mean that the examination was done at the wrong time in the cycle, that the patient is anovulatory, or that there is inadequate estrogen stimulation, even in the presence of ovulation.

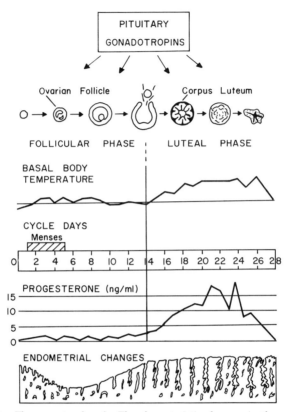

Figure 13–1. The menstrual cycle. The characteristic changes in the ovary, basal temperature, serum progesterone, and the endometrium that lines the uterine cavity are shown.

At this point, mention should be made of the terms used to identify parts of the menstrual cycle. In Figure 13–1, the cycle is illustrated in two parts: the follicular and the luteal phases. These terms refer to the development of the ovarian *follicle*, which will produce the ova to be released with ovulation, and the development of *corpus luteum* from the ruptured follicle. The particular cycle shown is 28 days long, i.e., there are 28 days from the beginning of one cycle until the beginning of the next. The first day of menses is called "cycle day 1," and ovulation, which separates the two phases, occurs on day 14. In patients with longer cycles, ovulation occurs later, so that the luteal phase is consistently 14 days long, whereas the follicular phase may vary in length. Thus, if a patient has 31-day cycles, the maximal development of cervical mucus will occur on day 17.

For some patients with more irregular cycles, the time of ovulation can only be estimated retrospectively when the next menses begins. Therefore, if the cervical mucus is examined on day 14 and found to be scanty, thick, and tenacious, the patient should be re-examined at two-to three-day intervals thereafter, and the onset of the next menses should be used to count back 14 days to the time when ovulation should have taken place.

The most common technique for examination of cervical mucus is to ask the couple to abstain for two days just before ovulation, then to have intercourse at a predetermined interval (usually between two and eight hours before the examination). The mucus is obtained by placing a speculum into the vagina without lubrication and aspirating the mucus either from a small plastic tube placed into the cervical canal or with a special aspirating instrument designed for this purpose. Care must be taken not to traumatize the tissues because hemorrhage interferes with the examination. The mucus is then expelled onto a glass slide; the amount obtained is noted; and a cover slip is then touched against the mucus and lifted away to determine the elasticity of the mucus. This quality is called the Spinbarkeit, and the length the mucus can stretch before breaking should be 8 to 10 cm.

The cover slip is then applied over half the mucus on the slide, and the remainder is left uncovered. The covered portion is examined under high power on the microscope; the number of sperm present, whether or not there is motile action of the tails, and whether or not this activity moves them about in the mucus are noted. Normal specimens will have 20 motile sperm moving about in each high-power microscopic field, and very few inactive sperm will be present. These males essentially never have deficiencies on semen analysis, and on this basis alone may have an evaluation delayed.

In a study of the mucus examinations of 200 infertile patients, Jette and Glass[1] found that if there were 20 or more sperm present per high-power field, the eventual pregnancy rate for the couple would be 72 per cent. In contrast, when no sperm were found in cervical mucus, the expected pregnancy percentage was only 33. Motility of sperm in mucus was a less reliable test, with an anticipated pregnancy rate of 53 per cent with 100 per cent motility, and 36 per cent with no motility. In all cases with more than 20 sperm per high-power field, the men had sperm counts greater than 20 million.

The presence of an excessive number of white cells in the specimen may indicate infection (cervicitis), which can be an infertility factor. Excessive amount of red cells should be noted, since they will interfere with sperm motility and the physical properties of the mucus. After the area under the cover slip has been examined for all these findings (the uncovered area having had an opportunity to dry), the last quality to be noted is the so-called *ferning* of the mucus as it dries (Fig. 13–2). In the absence of estrogen stimulation and the changes in salt balance associated with estrogen effects, ferning will not take place.

To summarize the findings on a normal cervical examination, there should be an abundant amount of glassy clear mucus that contains more than 20 fully mobile sperm per high-power field, stretchability to 10 cm.,

Figure 13–2.   Ferning of cervical mucus, magnified 100 times. Lack of ferning at mid-cycle indicates poor estrogen stimulation.

and a good ferning pattern upon drying. Failure of appearance of these findings could be due to localized infection within the cervix, failure of ovulation, or improper scheduling of the test within a normal ovulatory cycle.

THE UTERUS

Anatomical Problems. Most of the common anatomical variations do not contribute to infertility, though they may lead to spontaneous abortion. Included in this category would be congenital duplication of the uterus, uterine fibroid tumors, and incompetence of the uterine cervix. Cervical stenosis or sclerosis of the endometrium (Asherman's syndrome) may be the cause of infertility but usually presents as a problem of amenorrhea. Hysterosalpingography is an x-ray technique whereby contrast medium is injected through the cervix and is subsequently viewed as it passes upward to outline the cavity of the uterus and the uterine tubes. Each of the significant variations in uterine and cervical anatomic structure give characteristic findings with this x-ray technique.

Other diagnostic aids include direct visualization of the uterine cavity with a device called the "hysteroscope," and visualization of the outer surface of the uterus with a laparoscope. Hysteroscopic examination is a relatively new technique in this country and is not widely accepted or available as a tool for infertility evaluation. It is possible that hysteroscopy may be developed into a satisfactory outpatient procedure that will give more precise information than that obtained from radiologic techniques. Within the last 10 years, the laparoscope has become popular in this country for diagnostic evaluation of the pelvic organs of patients with infertility problems as well as those who are thought to have a disease process in the pelvis. This instrument allows direct visual examination of the uterus, tubes, and ovaries after its insertion through a small incision near the umbilicus. Although the procedure is commonly done under general anesthesia, it is usually considered a semioutpatient operation and seldom requires hospitalization overnight.

EVALUATION OF TUBAL PATENCY

In normal reproduction, the uterine (fallopian) tubes have the function of transporting the sperm to the ovum in order that fertilization may occur in the distal portion of the tube (the ampulla). Subsequently, the fertilized ovum is transported to the uterine cavity, where implantation occurs about a week following ovulation. The uterine tubes are not viewed as simple conduits through which these tiny cells migrate; there is now much evidence that they function as a source of energy for motion and nourishment of the gametes and the developing zygote during the critical first week after fertilization. Thus, while tests of the uterine tubes are performed and decisions about the prognosis are based on the tests, it should be remembered that the tests indicate only that a passageway or potential passageway exists. No information can be obtained from the usual tubal tests that relates to the more intricate and very critical role of the tube as the only support system for maintenance of the fertilized ovum prior to implantation.

Rubin's Test. The simplest tubal test to perform is Rubin's test for tubal patency, which is performed in the office by passing carbon dioxide gas through the cervix. This can usually be done without much discomfort or risk, although it is important to use a special device designed for this test in order to limit the gas pressure to about 150 mm. Hg and to limit the volume of gas instilled to no more than 250 to 300 ml. Often the test can be done satisfactorily with much less gas and lower pressures than these limits indicate. The carbon dioxide is instilled through the cervix by means of a cannula with an acorn tip that fits tightly against the external cervix to prevent external escape of gas. The physician places a stethoscope bell over the suprapubic area to listen for escape of gas as he watches the pressure and volume indicators. Inserting only one earpiece allows the physician to listen for external gas escape with one ear while listening for tubal gas escape with the other. In order to avoid interference with an early conception, studies of the tubes should not be done following midcycle in patients not using some form of contraception. Following completion of this study, the patient is asked to sit upright — free gas will rise to the subdiaphragmatic area and often give referred pain to the right shoulder, a positive sign of tubal patency.

Hysterosalpingography.   The second type of tubal investigation is hysterosalpingography — an x-ray procedure previously mentioned in the uterine workup. By injecting contrast medium through the cervix and into the uterus and tubes, one can obtain x-rays that show not only whether each tube is open but also the distance from the uterine cavity (the cornua) to the location of tubal obstruction. This procedure is more costly, more time-consuming, and somewhat more risky for the patient than Rubin's test, but it has the advantage of localizing an obstruction to one tube (or both) and outlining the area of obstruction.

Laparoscopy.   The most discriminating tubal test is that done at the time of diagnostic laparoscopy. With the tubal fibria under direct vision, the instillation of a dye solution such as indigo carmine through the cervix allows the physician to determine if there is free passage through the two uterine tubes. If there is not, then attention can be directed toward identification of any obstructive lesions that might be treated. Unless one specifically suspects a lesion in the uterine cavity or is trying to determine the extent of tubal patency from the cornua outward, it has become common practice to omit x-rays of the uterus and tubes, relying instead upon Rubin's as a screening test and following this with the laparoscopy evaluation, which is also a part of the evaluation of other pelvic organs.

EVALUATION OF OVARIAN ACTIVITY

The two functions of the ovary that are critical to reproduction are the cyclic release of ova and the cyclic production of hormones. In most cases, these two functions are intimately coupled, so that documentation of normal hormone production is also taken as evidence of ovulation. Specifically, the tests used to document ovulation are all based on the measurement of progesterone, metabolic products of progesterone, or the physiological effects of progesterone stimulus.

Basal Body Temperature.   The basal body temperature record is the classic method for documenting ovulation. The patient is instructed to take her temperature (preferably rectal) each morning before arising and to record this graphically for several cycles. One of the physiological effects of progesterone is elevation of the basal temperature, probably owing to its effect on the thermoregulatory center of the brain. Therefore, if the patient is ovulating she would be expected to form a corpus luteum (and have a luteal phase), which produces progesterone and causes the temperature to increase slightly during the two weeks preceding the onset of menses. The problems associated with this method include its inaccuracy, the inconvenience to the patient, the tendency to record fictitious data, and the uncontrollable focusing of the patient's attention on identifying the exact time of ovulation. For the latter reason alone, one may prefer to discourage patients from recording basal body temperatures and to rely, instead, on more objective tests of ovarian function.

Endometrial Biopsy. The most widespread objective test for documentation of ovulation and progesterone production is endometrial biopsy. Based on the anticipated changes in the endometrial tissue throughout the menstrual cycle (which have been outlined in detail by Rock, Hertig, and Noyes[3]), a single properly timed biopsy can be used to determine not only if ovulation has occurred but also if there has been normal progesterone secretion. Although sometimes associated with moderate patient discomfort, the biopsy is an office procedure that can be done any time between the sixteenth and twenty-fifth days of a typical 28-day cycle. After this, there is some risk of interrupting an unexpected conception, and therefore the biopsy should not be done more than about ten days following the expected time of ovulation if the possibility of conception exists.[2] An alternative, which is preferred if one is trying to document adequacy of progesterone production, is to perform the biopsy within a few hours of the onset of the next menstrual period. If more than 24 hours have passed, the results are almost universally ambiguous.

Although the endometrial biopsy has become a standard of reference for documentation of ovulation and progesterone production, there are some drawbacks to the method, not the least of which is patient discomfort. Frequently, documentation is necessary in more than one cycle, and the expense is generally approximately $75, which includes the physician's fee for performing the procedure and the laboratory costs for preparing and analyzing the tissue. Because of these factors, there has been interest recently in direct measurements of progesterone in the blood as an index of ovarian function.

Radioimmunoassay. Until recently, the laboratory techniques for progesterone measurement were not sensitive enough to measure the very minute quantities that circulate in the blood. Therefore, the laboratory determination of progesterone production required collection of urine for 24 hours to submit to the laboratory for determining

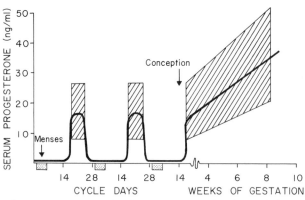

Figure 13–3. Serum progesterone levels in two normal cycles and during first eight weeks of gestation.

the amount of pregnanediol, which is the major metabolic excretion product of progesterone. Patients who excrete more than 2 mg. per 24 hours of pregnanediol almost certainly ovulate. Because of the inconvenience and the time needed for collection of urine and performance of a rather laborious assay technique, this method has not been widely used.

Newer methods of radioimmunoassay for steroids in blood have emerged in recent years, and a number of physicians have reported successful application of radioimmunoassay for progesterone measurement to determine not only whether the patient has ovulated, but also that her ovaries (specifically the corpus luteum) have produced enough progesterone to sustain a pregnancy. Deficient production of progesterone may result in miscarriage in the first few weeks of gestation. Figure 13–3 shows the normal level of serum progesterone in three cycles; in the third cycle, conception took place. The normal range, as shown by the shaded areas, is large. However, most investigators consider luteal phase levels of less than 2 mg. per milliliter to be indicative of failure to ovulate. Luteal peak levels consistently between 2 and 10 mg. per milliliter are considered subnormal, and these patients may be infertile or may experience recurrent early miscarriages.

Although serum progesterone assays have not yet been widely used by practicing physicians, the convenience, low cost, patient comfort, and probable accuracy of the method suggest that it may become a cornerstone in the armamentarium of the infertility expert. The samples can be sent by mail to a laboratory some distance away, for an immediate answer is seldom necessary in caring for the patient.

EVALUATION OF PERITONEAL FACTOR

Inflammatory processes in the pelvis may give rise to adhesions that interfere with conception and can be associated with infertility even when no large masses or extensive adhesions are present. Common underlying conditions that may contribute to inflammation of the peritoneal surfaces include ruptured appendix, salpingitis due to gonorrhea, abdominal surgical procedures of any kind, endometriosis, and perforation of the uterus at the time of D. & C. (dilatation and curettage) or IUD insertion. Most of these conditions should become apparent in taking a medical history, but some (endometriosis) may not present with typical histories.

Endoscopic procedures such as laparoscopy or colposcopy are necessary to make an accurate diagnosis. These two procedures provide a means of visualizing the abdominal surfaces of the organs, and they differ only in the site of insertion of the endoscope — the laparoscope being inserted through an incision near the umbilicus, and the colposcope through an incision at the apex of the vagina. For either of these devices, there are attachments for performing minor operative procedures such as lysis of adhesions or fulguration of endometriosis implants. Care must be taken to avoid injury to the tubes and the vascular supply to the tubes and ovaries. Endoscopic examination for diagnosis of peritoneal factors is recommended for any infertile patient who has a negative history and physical examination and no explanation of infertility after the other factors discussed previously have been studied. In some reported series, more than half these patients have had correctable problems discovered on endoscopic examinations.[4]

GENERAL APPROACH TO INFERTILITY

The evaluation of infertile couples is generally done through a step-by-step progression, beginning with a complete health history and a careful physical examination. These are followed by fundamental laboratory studies, which in conjunction with the history and physical examination may alert the health professional to potential problems. Simultaneous studies should be undertaken on both husband and wife to confirm normal spermatogenesis and ovulation. Examination of the cervical mucus within a few hours following intercourse (Sims-Hunter test) may be acceptable as a substitute for semen analysis, for if more than 20 active sperm are seen in each high-power microscopic field, the probability of an abnormal semen analysis is practically zero.

After completing studies of sperm and ovum production and Rubin's test for tubal patency, the physician may have identified some possible explanations for the infertility. The initial findings should then be discussed with the couple, and any more extensive evaluations that seem appropriate should be described in terms of risks versus probability of gains. This is also an appropriate time to suggest exploratory laparoscopy as a final diagnostic procedure for those patients in whom no problems have been identified.

MALE INFERTILITY

In males with very low sperm counts (< 5 million per milliliter), the concern should be ruling out the possibility of gonadal or pituitary tumor rather than fertility. For men with moderate to severely depressed counts (5 to 30 million), only limited therapy is available. If a varicocele is present, there may be significant improvement following surgical correction. Of those without varicocele but with low counts, a few have improved after empirical treatment with ascorbic acid, testosterone, or clomiphene citrate therapy. To date, no test has been discovered that will predict whether any one of these will be of value in a particular patient. For patients whose semen fails to liquefy, some urologists have advocated amylase vaginal suppositories following intercourse or amylase treatment of the semen followed by artificial insemination; neither method is documented as efficacious. A few men with low counts, especially those with high volumes (8 to 10 ml. or more), have been found to have higher sperm concentration in the first part of the ejaculate. Some success has been achieved with collection of this first fraction and subsequent artificial insemination.

Frequently, when the only identifiable problem is a low sperm count that does not respond to any of the empirical drug regimens, the only alternative left to consider is adoption or artificial insemination with donor semen. The latter is chosen by some couples but is usually available only in the larger medical centers, where the anonymity of donors and recipients can be maintained. Legally, the status of conceptions following artificial insemination varies from state to state, some even requiring the husband to adopt the child. Technically, this procedure is usually done at the anticipated time of ovulation by placing a small cervical cap around the cervix with a vaginal speculum, as in a routine office vaginal examination. The semen is then placed in the cap with a syringe. The following day, the cap is easily removed by the patient, using gentle traction. Overall success rate with artificial insemination is about 50 per cent, assuming that the patient continues therapy for six to eight months.

FEMALE INFERTILITY

For female fertility problems, the therapy may be as simple as topical vaginal cream for infection of the external cervical os, or as complex as the most intricate plastic surgery on the uterine tubes. Diagnostic studies should be pursued until the most appropriate therapy becomes apparent. For patients who have failure of ovulation in the absence of anatomical disorders of the tubes or uterus, studies should be done to eliminate the possibility of thyroid or adrenal disease, which could block ovulation. If these factors are not present, the treatment of choice is clomiphene citrate. This is a relatively inexpensive drug, taken by mouth, with limited side effects, which will induce ovulation in most women who do not have complete pituitary or ovarian failure. Clomiphene acts by stimulating the pituitary to release gonadotropins, which then stimulate the ovary to produce an ovum and make cyclic hormones. Serious common side effects include the possibility of hyperstimulation of the ovary, which can enlarge, burst, and bleed. Twinning is also more common after clomiphene therapy—about 1 in 15 incidence rather than the usual 1 in 80. However, triplets are rare, and multiple births other than twinning have not been associated with clomiphene therapy.

In patients who fail to respond to clomiphene, or in those with consistently low levels of serum gonadotropin, the only remaining effective treatment may be gonadotropin replacement. In contrast to clomiphene therapy, gonadotropin replacement is expensive; side effects such as hyperstimulation are more common; and multiple conceptions are often reported. It is generally believed that the multiple ovulation problem can be controlled with meticulous monitoring of therapy with daily blood measurements of estradiol, but obviously this goal is not always attained. Patients beginning therapy should be advised that the cost may be between $1000 and $2000, and that the overall success rate is no better than 50 per cent.

ADOPTION

Finally, as the workup and therapy of an infertile couple continues, the possibility of adoption should be considered. If any interest is shown, they should be encouraged to begin working with a social agency in the area. This is appropriate not only for those who have failed to respond to therapy after a problem has been identified, but also for those in whom no problem can be identified, for this is the group in which ultimate conception rates are very low.

SUMMARY

Couples who experience either primary or secondary infertility may have problems with the concept of their masculinity and femininity and with marital relations. They may need assistance from health professionals to talk about these feelings if they do exist. The infertility tests for both the male and female are expensive and time-consuming and may interfere with the spontaneity of sexual intercourse. Counseling the couple regarding these aspects may be necessary so that their marital and sexual relationship will not be jeopardized during infertility therapy.

REFERENCES

1. Jette, N. T. and R. H. Glass. Prognostic Value of the Postcoital Test. *Fertility and Sterility,* 23:29–32, Jan. 1972.
2. Karow, W. G., W. C. Gentry, R. F. Skeels, and S. A. Payne. Endometrial Biopsy in the Luteal Phase of the Cycle of Conception. *Fertility and Sterility,* 22:482–495, Aug. 1971.
3. Noyes, R. W., A. T. Hertig, and J. Rock. Dating the Endometrial Biopsy. *Fertility and Sterility,* 1:3–25, Jan. 1950.
4. Spangler, D. B., G. S. Jones, and H. W. Jones, Jr. Infertility Due to Endometriosis. *American Journal of Obstetrics and Gynecology,* 109:850–857, March 15, 1971.
5. Welpton, P. K., A. A. Campbell, and J. E. Patterson. *Fertility and Family Planning in the United States.* Princeton: Princeton University Press, 1966.

PROBLEMS IN ADOLESCENT SEXUALITY

Robert Crist, M.D.,
and Gale Hickenlooper, B.S.N.

Teenagers have become a major force in American society. The American population increased 13 per cent, from 179 million to 203 million, between 1960 and 1970, but the number of Americans aged 15 to 19 jumped by 46 per cent, from 13 million to 19 million, or 9.4 per cent of the total population. This teen society has continued to expand as the children who were born during the baby boom of the late 1950's enter their teen years. The 1975 percentage increased to an estimated 10.3 per cent. This boom in number of teenaged Americans has coincided with significant changes in sexual attitudes and behavior, women's roles, and the family structure and with the erosion of faith in established social values. The adolescent, who is rapidly changing through physical maturation, quickly grasps new ideas and concepts and consequently has become a banner bearer in the increasing rejection of established mores. For today's youth, sexual activity is being approached more and more as a casual encounter rather than a deeply moving emotional experience; it has become an experience in light-hearted play, although unquestionably female sexual expression is still primarily and profoundly related to being in love and "going steady." The resulting teen subculture, pressured into a group by a rejecting "establishment," has found identity in their rebellion.

HISTORICAL PERSPECTIVE

American adolescents are oriented toward an ideal of premarital chastity, but at the same time they are systematically bombarded with sexual stimuli. Hence, there is a conflict between the ideal and the reality, and the adolescent must choose between observing standards and feeling frustrated and cheated, or violating them and feeling guilty and risking social disapproval.[13] The myth of Victorian and Puritan virginity before marriage is widely accepted. Church records indicate that 200 years ago, in Groton, Massachusetts, one in every three brides confessed fornication to a minister.[1a] Similar evidence exists for the Victorian era of the late nineteenth century. Prostitution was widespread at that time, and though there was likely a higher precentage of virgin brides than today, many females were experienced sexually. Kinsie estimated that about one in every four females born before 1900 in his sample was not a virgin at the time of marriage.[21] This conflict and its resolution can clearly be seen to have existed throughout the 200-year history of the United States.

FROM THE PARENTS' VIEWPOINT

Most of us tend to generalize about others from our own point of view. Our own sexual experiences are applied to the sexual experiences of others. Most of us in the professional "adult" world grew up with relatively firm ideas of what constitutes appropriate sexual conduct between males and females. Awareness of contemporary sexual behavior and its perspective within the teen culture can place the health professional and parent in an uncomfortable role. In order to avoid this unfamiliar and uncomfortable situation, it is traditional for parents to restrain teenagers' curiosity about sexuality by not mentioning it, or by being very serious, distant, and negative about the subject. Parents unfamiliar and uncomfortable with their own sexuality are poor tutors for the new initiate into the "rites of sexuality." Parents may feel jealous, may fear growing older, or may see a discussion of sexuality as a symbolic violation of incest taboos. Parents, therefore, appear especially conservative to their children and often are unable to communicate openly about love, sex, contraception, and abortion, except in a negative way.[7]

Family conflicts are not unique to any one family or child, but occur in all families to varying degrees. The social changes that occur over a 20- to 30-year span mean that adolescent behavior that was appropriate for parents may not be appropriate for their children. Another societal source of adolescent-adult value discrepancy derives from cultural discontinuities, which involve almost complete reversals of expected behaviors as the individual progresses from childhood through adolescence and into adulthood.

The differences in sexual permissiveness between generations may, however, relate more closely to marital and parental status than to age alone. Reiss found greater differences between 50-year-old men who were single and 50-year-old males who were married and had a teenage daughter than between single teens and single 50-year-olds.[17] Thus, the assumption of responsibility for someone else's sexual permissiveness through marriage and parenthood is associated with conservative views. Parents want to see their children move into an adult world of maturity, independence, and responsibility, but are at the same time reluctant to give up their status as parent.

TEENAGERS AND PREGNANCY

The teenage girl today remains for the most part uneducated by enlightened adults. She is told by cultural forces to be sexy, responsive, emancipated, and uninhibited. "It is every woman's right to enjoy an orgasm," she is told by the journalistic media, but she is totally unaware of what a heterosexual orgasm is. She turns to an understanding but unknowledgeable peer group for guidance.

Her failure to find information, guidance, and reassurance from the nurturing family comes at a time when she feels a surge of sexual development and self-awareness. The result is the familiar adolescent rebellion. Teenagers face a value-behavior discrepancy, and it is not surprising that teen peer values are irrational about sex and contraception. They begin to act out their frustrations. Adolescent girls provide the lure of physical availability without overt sexual initiative. They desire, but dare not act. Intercourse, which is something that happens *to* them, is not their responsibility.

Romantic love is a theme that pervades literature, movies, television, and advertising. While many of these media imply sexual activity, rarely do they include "how to" or "do it yourself" references. The teenage male, in an air of bravado, acts as if he understands this new-found sexuality, but in truth is a bumbler in the act of sexual intercourse. This lack of knowledge frequently results in pregnancy.

In the past ten years, the birth rate has fallen in the United States. In only one age group, those 18 years old and under, has there been an increasing birth rate.[2] The fertility rate is falling less among teenagers than among older women, and the percentage of births to teenagers is rising.[12] The National Center for Health Statistics reported a 10 per cent increase in illegitimacy in 1973. The increase in the teenage birth rate is indicative of the amount of sexual activity. A survey of Michigan teenagers indicated that in 1970, 27.8 per cent of the males and 16.1 per cent of the females aged 15 to 19 had experienced premarital coitus. In 1973, these figures increased to 33.4 per cent of males and 22.7 per cent of females, with the greatest increase in the 14- to 16-year-old age group.[19]

The culturally propelled increase in teenage intercourse is not associated with the knowledge, maturity, or responsibility of planning. Our pleasure-seeking, self-gratifying society pushes the teens toward their peers for all positive reinforcement. The suburban pressure of early social maturity may be a conscious or an unconscious message from parents to become sexually active. Pregnancy is a ready exit of escape from an undesirable family situation.

Perhaps not all teenage pregnancies are unplanned. In some cultures, having a baby has become a peer group status symbol. The teenage girl may want to get pregnant to validate her femininity by proving that she *can* get pregnant, just as boys validate their masculinity as culture defines it, by doing dangerous things.

The classic cultural concept of attainment of adulthood for girls has been defined as motherhood. Motherhood had for centuries been the only culturally acceptable occupation open to women. It should not be surprising that motherhood represents the ultimate in the teenage declaration of independence and brings with it the rights of adult decision making. Pregnancy carries an unequaled impact for attention-getting for the troubled teen. To have a perfect baby as portrayed by Madison Avenue is to produce the ideal love object.

PROBLEMS IN TEENAGE PREGNANCY

Whether incurred by intent or by accident, pregnancy brings the new teen mother many problems. Her partner is rarely prepared to support a family or to emotionally accept the responsibility of parenthood. Her parents, rejecting her because of anticipated peer pressures, are unable to relate to her problems. She therefore lacks the two primary supports of older pregnant women: a husband and an extended family. There are very few sources of social support for the unwed schoolgirl; she is ostracized and rejected.[7]

During 1972, there were 200,000 unwanted births to teenagers and 400,000 abortions.[17] Of the female teenagers experiencing coitus, three in 10 will become pregnant. What, then, are the problems of teenage birth and pregnancy?

Adolescent pregnancy causes a syndrome of failure.[20]
1. Failure to fulfill the functions of adolescence.
    a. separation from parents.
    b. determination of a sexual role.
    c. development of a value system.
    d. choice of vocation.
2. Failure to remain in school.
3. Failure to limit family size.
4. Failure to establish stable families.
5. Failure to be self-supporting.
6. Failure to have healthy families.

The adolescent frequently fulfills these functions by challenging existing parental values and authority figures. The search for a value system requires experimentation. When taken to the extreme, male adolescent rebellion results in shoplifting, vandalism, and running away from home. Delinquency for the female is often sexual, and pregnancy is an ultimate form. Pregnancy may be the final attempt by a young girl to make her parents and the community aware of her social or emotional problems. Petty crime can be easily covered up by an influential parent, but a baby cannot. Birth of a child forces separation from rejecting parents, a clear declaration of sexual role, acceptance of a poorly defined and distorted value system, and child care as a vocation. This "adult" role is premature and self-limiting.

The adolescent trapped in this untested lifestyle becomes frustrated, retreats to childlike ways, and continues to fail. When the tasks of a phase of development are not completed or are completed unsatisfactorily, there is a withdrawal back to the last successfully completed developmental level.[6]

TEENAGERS AS PARENTS

Adolescents who continue their pregnancy face two overwhelming problems statistically: (1) repeat pregnancy — 27.9 per cent had repeat pregnancy and delivery;[5] 60 per cent aged 12 to 16 years had repeat pregnancies before they reached the national age of primiparity;[11] and (2) school drop out — 43.4 per cent withdrew from school within two years of the postpartum visit.[5] These problems, which result in the syndrome of failure, are not unique to any social, racial, or ethnic group.

The teenage parent fails to fulfill the developmental tasks of adolescence and is trapped in an unwanted lifestyle. The risks to the children of adolescents are profound. Because many adolescents deny their pregnancy initially, they often do not receive prenatal care until the second or third trimester of pregnancy and may arrive in the delivery room having never been seen prenatally. This lack of prenatal care and the generally poor teenage diet result in a high incidence of delivery of premature and low birth weight infants.

When the adolescent assumes the responsibility for the care of her infant, she has unrealistic expectations of its behavior, and she usually lacks knowledge of normal childhood growth and development. Adolescents have a low tolerance for frustration, and they are impulsive and easily frustrated. They may interpret many normal infant behaviors as being malicious and intentionally directed toward them. Discipline of their children tends to be irrational, inappropriate, and unnecessarily harsh, to the point of even being physically abusive.[18]

Children born to mothers less than 18 years of age are more likely to be characterized as "outgoing," dependent, and distractable. They display infantile behavior problems and acting-out difficulties. These children are more likely to be underweight, to be shorter, and to have lower reading performance and I.Q. levels than children born to mothers older than 18. These mothers are less likely to remain with their children, less likely to be attentive to them, and less likely to give their offspring guidance.[14]

How common is this problem? In 1970, living births to mothers aged 15 to 19 years accounted for 17 per cent of all live births in the United States.[22] Statistics for the same period of time disclose that 24 per cent of abortions performed in Population Council Joint Program for Study of Abortion (JPSA) institutions were on patients younger than the age of 20.

ROLE OF CONTRACEPTION

Twenty-five years ago, dating was chaperoned and controlled by the familial unit. Today, the extended family unit is no longer prevalent, and dating has become a matter of casual pairing within the framework of teen hangouts. The father of one generation ago who insisted on meeting his daughter's date before she could go out in the evening has been supplanted by the daughter who announces her departure for the local drive-in restaurant. With this liberalization and release from structural control, there has not been a concomitant increase in knowledge of sexual conduct and contraception.

The history of mechanical contraception in human sexuality goes back approximately 100 years. The 1876 Philadelphia centennial was made famous by the offering for sale of the first vulcanized rubber condom. In 1880, the vulcanized diaphragm was introduced as a contraceptive, and for nearly 80 years these two methods were the best available means of preventing pregnancy. Even today, they are used by the majority of people. A connection between the introduction of highly efficient modern contraceptive methods (the condom, the diaphragm, the pill, and the IUD) and an increase in freedom of sexual relationships cannot be established. It should be clear that prior to introduction of these methods, most people copulated outside of marriage without benefit of effective contraceptive techniques. This fact is no less true today than 200 years ago.

Social patterns determine sexual behavior and, in turn, influence contraceptive use. Boy/girl relationships, attitudes of parents, patterns of sexual activity, levels of awareness, the girl's readiness to disclose her sexual activity to others, and her perceptions of the risks and benefits of contraception all affect the use of contraceptive methods.[13]

STAGES IN CONTRACEPTION

Unmarried young women go through three stages in finding a means of avoiding pregnancy:[13]

1. Natural Stage, in which they do nothing to avoid pregnancy;
2. Peer Stage, in which they get information from peers and experiment with various methods;
3. Expert Stage, in which they consult an expert to seek an effective method.

Natural Stage. For the young initiate, the frequency of sexual activity and the unpredictability of coitus in time, place, and partner falsely appear to make contraceptive planning unnecessary. The casual social atmosphere and less structured dating arrangement have placed today's teen couple in a totally unpredictable sexual environment.

The spontaneity of social activity, emotional caring, and physical involvement has placed a high priority on the naturalness of sexual activity. The prior planning necessary to institute oral contraceptives or the immediate precoital introduction of mechanical devices such as condoms, foam, and diaphragms distracts greatly from this desired spontaneity and naturalness. Further, the infrequency of coitus makes long-term planning such as insertion of an IUD or long-term use of oral contraceptives seem inappropriate. The longer the period of time since first coitus, the more likely it is that a birth control method will be used. The opposite psychology also exists. The young adolescent who has been engaging in heterosexual activity for some time without getting pregnant may adopt the attitude, "I haven't gotten pregnant yet, so why worry about birth control?"

These attitudes are well illustrated by statistics gathered from a sexually active group of 15 to 19 year olds. In this group, 53 per cent had failed to use any kind of contraceptive the last time they had intercourse; only 20 per cent of the sexually experienced 15 to 19 year olds reported that they always use some form of contraception. Sixty per cent failed to use contraceptives, citing some of the following reasons:[10]

1. "I am too young to be able to get pregnant."
2. "I have sex too infrequently."
3. "I only have intercourse at the 'wrong' time of the month."
4. "I feel I shouldn't have intercourse at all, so I won't plan ahead for it."
5. "Deep down, I might want to get pregnant."
6. "I'd be afraid I'd get hassled if I went to get birth control."[7]

Three of four teenagers who became pregnant did not intend for it to happen at the time it occurred, but only 13.1 per cent of those who did not intend the pregnancy were using any form of contraception. The methods that were being used were frequently the most ineffective—douche and withdrawal.[22]

The greatest deterrent to the use of contraception by teenagers is the infrequency of their sexual activity. During a sexual encounter and for a short time afterward, there is a heightened awareness of the need for contraception, but this awareness fades during the period of time between sexual encounters.[13]

Peer Prescription Stage. During the peer prescription stage, the teenage girl becomes aware of her sexual activity. She learns to define herself as sexually active, capable of reproduction, and in need of contraception. She also becomes willing to divulge her sexual activity to peers in order to gain information. A number of factors can either increase or decrease the adolescent's level of awareness of sexual activity. A teenage girl under the influence of drugs or alcohol may not even know she is having sexual intercourse, let alone be aware of the risk of pregnancy and the need for contraception. She may "drift" into a sexual relationship and feel that intercourse is an accident or a fluke. An increase in awareness may occur quickly after a "scare" from a late menstrual period, a friend becoming pregnant, or becoming pregnant herself.

The most commonly used methods of contraception during the peer prescription stage are rhythm, withdrawal, foam, douche, and condoms. These methods are seldom used consistently, and there is a great deal of switching from one method to another. They are also the methods most readily available to the adolescent. They do not require a prescription or a visit to a physician or clinic. By using any contraceptive technique on a fairly regular basis, the adolescent demonstrates that she has become aware of both her need to prevent pregnancy and her reproductive capability. She is anticipating coital activity, and her advance preparation for it obligates her to accept responsibility for the act. She is ready to move to the expert stage and seek professional advice and a more effective method of contraception. There are problems involved in entering this stage, however.

Expert Stage. There is a conflict between the need for and the ability to get contraceptives and professional information. The dominant view of society continues to be that coitus is an adult marital function, and, therefore, unless you are adult and married, there is no need for contraception. Many teenagers hesitate to approach a physician for contraceptive advice because they fear rejection or are afraid the physician will tell their parents. The names themselves of many clinics where contraceptives are available imply marital status for use—"Family Planning Clinic," "Planned Parenthood."

Many teenagers believe they must have parental consent in order to be examined and given contraceptives. There are many states in which "touching" a minor without parental consent may constitute assault or battery, or both. However, no prosecution has been instituted for such a case.[15]

The teenage girl may not realize that a pelvic examination is necessary before contraceptives can be dispensed. Her first experience with a pelvic examination may be so frightening and embarrassing that she may not return to a clinic or physician but instead will revert to the peer prescription stage. Health professionals must ensure that the first pelvic examination is a positive experience so that the patient may continue to receive professional help. She may also regress because of side effects of the chosen method or because she may not see a continued need for an effective method.

The introduction and widespread availability of contraceptives such as the pill and the IUD have been blamed for a number of social problems, such as the increase in the incidence of adolescent sexual activity and the recent surge in reported cases of venereal disease. The availability of the pill and the IUD to teenagers cannot account for their increased sexual activity or the increase in the birth rate among teenagers, since statistics have shown that only the most "expert" teenage girls are using these methods, and that their sexual activity was established before these methods were sought. Very few teenagers appear to be taking advantage of the availability of contraceptives. Just as sexual activity cannot be blamed on contraceptives, neither can the surge in venereal disease be blamed entirely on "the pill."

VENEREAL DISEASE

Three changes have been used to explain the trends in incidence of venereal diseases: (1) changes in the use of antibiotics by physicians and the antibiotic susceptibility of pathogens; (2) changes in social controls and governmental regulations; and (3) changes in sexual behavior patterns among the American people. While all these changes can explain the trends in venereal disease to some extent, none of them in itself offers conclusive reasons for the increase in venereal disease.

Incidence

The Center for Disease Control statistics on trends in reportable cases of venereal disease are listed in Table 14–1. The incidence of both syphilis and gonorrhea doubled between 1941 and 1948, and then declined until 1957. The incidence of gonorrhea has been increasing by 12 per cent per annum since 1957. That of syphilis increased from 1957 to 1965, but between 1967 and 1969, a decreasing number of cases were reported.

TABLE 14–1.   Venereal Disease Incidence

| YEAR | NUMBER OF CASES | |
	Syphilis	Gonorrhea
1941	68,231	193,468
1948	106,539	363,014
1957	6,251	261,476
1973	25,000	809,681

The first theory regarding these trends concerns the use of antibiotics by physicians. During the late 1940's and early 1950's, there was widespread use of penicillin—the miracle drug—to treat any and every disease. Therefore, it is possible that many cases of gonorrhea and syphilis were treated without ever being diagnosed. The marked increase in venereal disease during the late 1950's and early 1960's, according to this theory, is attributable to the fact that physicians recognized the limitations and hazards of widespread antibiotic use and cut back on their prescriptions. Concurrently, the pathogens causing venereal disease became more resistant to antibiotic therapy.[4]

In the second theory, Anderson[1] hypothesizes that "the amount of disease in a social system is inversely related to the social restraints placed upon the people." During wartime and other emergency situations, the government is able to control interpersonal relationships somewhat, while in peacetime, civil liberties take command. In peacetime, government measures to control and prevent venereal disease are less likely to be effective.

The third theory explores the relationship between the sexual behavior patterns of the hosts and that of the victims. It takes into account the common use of the pill and the IUD as contraceptives, the existence of an increasingly permissive society, and the increase in promiscuity. The introduction of the pill resulted in a decrease in the use of condoms and, because of the emotional security it induced, led to promiscuous behavior, thus increasing the incidence of venereal disease.[4]

The actual causes and increasing incidence of venereal disease probably incorporate or lie somewhere between these three categories. Our society has experienced a marked increase in the degree of social permissiveness, associated with an open expression of sexuality. Our advertising and communication media have equated sexual adjustment with health and happiness and have implied an association between sexuality and many popular consumer products. The expansion of human rights and equality and the liberation of both racial and sexual minorities have led to a marked decrease in the double standard. Women today at all ages are claiming their right to freedom and sexual gratification.

Social trends during the Vietnam War did not conform with earlier experiences of this country or the predicted patterns of societal behavior presented by Anderson.[1] In 1967, in the midst of the Vietnam War, the government lost social control, and Anderson's predicted pattern of behavior was no longer applicable. Society began to question the integrity of government, and the adolescent segment of our society led a rebellion against the established values. Social and sexual permissiveness, instead of decreasing during the time of war, increased markedly. Promiscuity increased to an all-time high. Kaats and Davis reported that 41 per cent of co-eds at the University of Colorado had engaged in premarital coitus, as contrasted with approximately 22 per cent one year earlier.[9] By fall of the same year, this number had increased to 44 per cent. It is pertinent to the overall argument that the incidence of premarital coitus in college men remained essentially the same for 11 years.

The association between promiscuity and VD (presented in theory number two) is clearly refuted by California state statistics for the summer of 1971. Patients at a VD clinic were questioned regarding the number of sexual partners they had had in the 30-day period prior to their clinic visit. The average number of sexual partners named by all patients who were examined was 1.45, with 66.4 per cent of the patients indicating only one sexual partner in the period of time preceding their clinic visit.[4] These statistics do not support the concept of indiscriminate promiscuity involving brief and random sexual relationships. The assumption that there is a direct relationship between the number of different sexual partners encountered per unit of time and an increased risk of acquiring any sexually transmitted diseases requires considerable support. This postulate should not be accepted a priori and, based upon only limited statistics, cannot be accepted a posteriori.

There is an association between the introduction of oral contraceptives and IUD's and an increase in venereal disease, but likewise there is lack of significant statistical support. In 1968, statistics show that only 7 per cent of college couples engaging in premarital intercourse relied upon oral contraceptives.[4] As discussed previously, this relatively infrequent use of oral contraceptives and IUD's also applies to the younger adolescent group. Further statistics derived from the Sacramento, California, study showed that women who relied on condoms to prevent unwanted pregnancy did not seem to be at lower risk for venereal disease than women using other methods of contraception. Among women visiting the clinic, those who used oral contraceptives and were infected with gonorrhea were not statistically different from the women using oral contraceptives who were not infected.[4] The significant association is not between the method of contraception used and the incidence of venereal disease; rather, the individual's risk of infection depends upon the sexual behavior patterns of the individual and the sexual partners. No predictive correlation can be made between the use of condoms and the prevention of gonorrhea. Likewise, no statistical association can be proved between use of the pill and an increase in gonorrhea.

ABORTION

Sexual behavior has long been recognized as a major concern of adolescents and, more particularly, of others in charge of adolescents. A statement is never more germane than one regarding the adolescent and abortion. Since the 1973 Supreme Court decision Roe v. Wade, which legalized abortion, white teenage middle-class American girls have been the largest recipients of abortion services. Throughout this two-year span of time, abortion has represented more of a way out of an embarrassing social predicament for parents than a means for the rebellious adolescent to escape a self-created predicament. Abortion has rescued parents from the consequences of a mistake made by their errant teenage daughter but is not, as idealized in the minds of many social planners, a means to assist the pregnant teenager to escape unplanned motherhood.

This situation has been clearly demonstrated in the approach of most clinics to the use of operative permits. The adolescent female enters with her mother and must have her mother's signed consent to legally qualify for an operative termination of an unwanted pregnancy. The lowering of the age of legal majority from 21 to 18 has changed this situation only slightly, since the vast number of physicians and institutions providing pregnancy termination services require parental consent until age 21.

Statistical surveys published on attitudes regarding abortion clearly equate general attitudes about abortion with the religious background and degree of religious feeling of the individual.[16] This association is not maintained, however, when one examines statistics regarding adolescents seeking abortion services. In a review of 2000 abortions done at the University of Kansas, the distribution of expressed religious preference of patients seeking abortion corresponded within one percentile to the stated religious preference of the general population of the metropolitan area provided by the greater Kansas City Ministerial Alliance.[3] While general public acceptance and attitudes regarding abortion may determine its future, for the pregnant adolescent and her family there are only two types of reasons for terminating a pregnancy: hard and soft. Hard reasons include: The life of the mother is endangered; the baby will be born deformed or retarded; or rape has occurred. The soft reasons often heard are: "We can't afford a pregnancy now;" "we don't want to be hassled now;" "this pregnancy was unplanned;" or "I have a bad feeling about this pregnancy."[8] Legal abortion in the United States is still new. The public's attitude toward abortion depends to a great extent on who is trapped in an unwanted pregnancy. A person's attitudes might well change drastically if she or her child were involved in this situation. The effects of the syndrome of failure experienced by the teenager who becomes pregnant, carries to term, and delivers might theoretically be averted. In practicality, however, this adolescent must return to the same environment that pushed her toward the rebellious act that ended in pregnancy.

CONCLUSIONS

It is evident that the facts and situations just described constitute a direct blow to the establishment, to parents, and to our social system.

Nevertheless, we feel that adolescents are making commitments and decisions earlier, and are more capable of making them, than was the case with previous generations. They have heard the cry for human rights and the rights of minorities, have accepted the open expression of sexuality, and have practiced and lived these concepts to a far greater extent than other sections of American society.

Counseling and education are the two ingredients necessary for the successful maturation and adjustment of the American adolescent today. However, we wish to urge that counseling and education be directed equally to the adult segment of our society. Adults have prepared the script for a liberal life style, have been elected to public office on the strength of espoused views of human equality, have prepared advertisements and sold time on television bombarding us with the equation of sexuality with happiness. Yet they have failed to provide the information and education necessary to meet the resulting feelings and actions.

REFERENCES

1. Anderson, O. W. Syphilis and Society—Problems of Control in the United States, 1912–1964. Chicago: Center for Health Administration Studies, Health Information Foundation, Research Series 22, 1965.
1a. Calhoun, A. W. *A Social History of the American Family.* Vol. 1. New York: Barnes and Noble, 1945.
2. Cook, Cynthia W. Contraceptive Usage Among Teenagers. *Journal of the American Medical Women's Association,* 28:639–642, 1973.
3. Crist, Robert D. (Kansas University Medical Center). Unpublished data.
4. Darrow, William W. Changes in Sexual Behavior and Venereal Disease. *Clinical Obstetrics and Gynecology,* 18:255–267, March 1975.
5. Dempsey, John J. Recidivism and Post Delivery School Withdrawal: Implications of a Follow-up Study for Planning Preventive Services. *Journal of School Health,* 42:291–297, May 1972.
6. Erikson, E. H. *Childhood and Society.* 2nd edition. New York: W. W. Norton and Company, 1963.
7. Gabrielson, I., S. Goldsmith, L. Potts, V. Mathews, and M. Gabrielson. Adolescent Attitudes Toward Abortion: Effects on Contraceptive Practice. *American Journal of Public Health,* 61:730–738, April 1971.
8. Jones, Elise F. and Charles F. Westoff. Changes in Attitudes Toward Abortion: With Emphasis Upon the National Fertility Study Data. In: *The Abortion Experience: Psychological and Medical Impact.* Osofsky, Howard J. and Joy D. Osofsky (eds.). New York: Harper & Row, Publishers, Inc., 1973.
9. Kaats, G. R. and K. E. Davis. The Dynamics of Sexual Behavior of College Students. *Journal of Marriage and Family,* 32:390, 1970.
10. Kantner, John F. and Melvin Zelnik. Contraception and Pregnancy: Experience of Young Unmarried Women in the United States. *Family Planning Perspectives,* 5:21–41, Winter 1973.
11. Keeve, J. Philip, Edward R. Schlesinger, Byron W. Wright, and Ruthann Adams. Fertility Experience of Juvenile Girls: A Community-wide Ten-year Study. *American Journal of Public Health,* 59:2185–2198, Dec. 1969.
12. Klein, Luella. Early Teenage Pregnancy, Contraception, and Repeat Pregnancy. *American Journal of Obstetrics and Gynecology,* 120:249–255, Sept. 15, 1974.
13. Lindeman, C. *Birth Control and the Unmarried Young Woman.* New York: Springer Publishing Company, 1974.
14. Oppell, Kathy C. and Anita B. Royston. Teen-Age Births: Some Social, Psychological, and Physical Sequelae. *American Journal of Public Health,* 61:751–756, April 1971.

15. Pilpel, Harriet F. and Nancy F. Wechsler. Birth Control, Teenagers and the Law. *Family Planning Perspectives,* 1:29–36, Spring 1969.
16. Popoff, David. What are Your Feelings About Death and Dying. *Nursing '75,* Sept. 1975, pp. 55–62.
17. Reiss, Ira. Heterosexual Relationships of Patients: Premarital, Marital, and Extramarital. In: *Human Sexuality: A Health Practitioner's Text.* Green, Richard (ed.). Baltimore: The Williams & Wilkins Company, 1975.
18. Schwartz, Betty A. Rock and 'Bye' Baby. *Journal of Obstetrics, Gynecologic and Neonatal Nursing,* 4:27–30, Sept./Oct. 1975.
19. Stewart, Cyrus S., and Arthur M. Vener. More Teenagers Sexually Active, in Michigan Study. *Family Planning Perspectives,* 7:54, March/April 1975.
20. Waters, James L. Pregnancy in Young Adolescents: A Syndrome of Failure. *Southern Medical Journal,* 62:655–658, June 1969.
21. Winick, C. and P. M. Kinsie. *The Lively Commerce.* Chicago: Quadrangle Books, 1971.
22. Zelnik, Melvin and John F. Kantner. The Resolution of Teenage First Pregnancies. *Family Planning Perspectives,* 6:74–80, Spring 1974.

CHAPTER
15

SEXUAL DEVIANCY

Richard O. Sword, D.D.S., M.D.

DEVIANCY VS. NORMALITY

In discussing deviancy, sexual or otherwise, one must first define deviance and normality. When an activity is extremely different from the normal, there is a tendency to define it negatively or as a deviation. The man who can achieve an orgasm only by hiding in the bushes and watching a couple having intercourse would be termed a deviant. Yet what about the man who becomes aroused in a topless bar or while watching an X-rated movie? Indeed, it is these nuances between what is obviously abnormal and what is obviously normal that cause the difficulty and confusion. Even authorities in the field of sexuality disagree about the behavior they observe, describe, and classify.

The word normal can be used in several ways:

1. *Statistically* — how most people behave
2. *Socially* — what is acceptable
3. *Medically* — what is healthy

Therefore, whatever parameters are used to define normality and deviancy must be flexible enough to meet the needs of the patient, as well as the needs of the various cultures and subcultures. In some medical and legal settings, certain terminology has moralistic and judgmental overtones that are inappropriate in professional interactions. For example, a distinction must be made between what is deviant and what is pathological. Statistically, a genius is deviant, yet so is an idiot. Socially, both might be termed normal if their behavior adhered to group norms. Medically, however, the former is normal and the latter is pathological.

An additional aspect of deviancy concerns the synonymous use of the words "perversion" and "pervert." Such usage, still prevalent even in some medical and legal settings, has a definite moralistic and judgmental overtone that is inappropriate in a scientific discourse.

Finally, a distinction must be made about whether a sexual act is central or peripheral to a person's sexuality and also whether the act is a free choice or the result of restriction or other extenuating circumstances. To illustrate the former, oral-genital contact or mutual masturbation might be the only way an orgasm can be achieved, or it might be part of foreplay or simply an occasional change of pace. As an example of the latter, homosexuality is common in a prison population, where heterosexual contact is denied; yet most prisoners return to a heterosexual orientation when released. Similarly, an incidental homosexual experience while intoxicated does not mean a person is homosexually oriented.

What, then, is sexual normality? Since a person's sexuality is part of his totality, it affects his self-concept. It concerns his individual and group sexual identity—being male among men or being female among women—and his behavior, which must be learned by identifying with the group. Thus, the self is experienced as being masculine or feminine—manly or womanly—which is a psychological quality distinctly different from the physical quality of being male or female. This total sense of self, then, is the first aspect of sexual normality; that is, there must be a harmony between being male and masculine or female and feminine.

The second aspect is how a person relates to others. In an ideal relationship, a sense of basic self-esteem exists coupled with a desire to be close to the partner, who engenders thoughts and feelings of respect, concern, and admiration. This necessitates the capacity to love. It involves total intimacy, not just physical intimacy, because the partners have no need to be defensive or to feel vulnerable. It is complete openness. In such a relationship, psychological and physical sexual urges with orgasmic capability are directed toward the loved one in a wide variety of sexual activities undertaken for the purpose of reproduction, tension reduction, communication, or recreation.

Such is sexual normality. This concept does not include the desire to procreate as an essential ingredient; it may or may not be present.

THE ORIGINS OF DEVIANCY

Explanations of sexual deviancy, like many other explanations of human behavior, center on the "heredity versus environment" controversy. While there is some evidence that seems to support a genetic theory of deviancy (such as Kallman's twin studies), most authorities attribute greater significance to developmental environmental influences—what happened during the "growing up" years.

For the purpose of this chapter, Freud's psychoanalytic theories, which combine biogenetic and psychoanalytic hypotheses, are used to provide the framework for understanding and treating sexual deviancy. Central to this theoretical framework is the assumption that something went wrong during the developmental years of the deviant. His experiences with people, and the influences he was subjected to, were of such a nature that he became extremely uncomfortable when he attempted to continue to develop normally. Therefore, he did one of three things: (1) He retreated to an earlier and more comfortable way of handling things (regression); (2) he simply stopped (fixation) and didn't develop further, thereby avoiding further discomfort; or (3) he continued to develop but in a distorted way that was less uncomfortable.

Thus, in adulthood, the behavior of the sexual deviant represents a compromise—a conditioned way of releasing sexual energy while avoiding the extreme discomfort that would accompany a normal heterosexual experience. The deviant is not attracted to his abnormal sexuality; rather, he is retreating from the anxiety that accompanies normal sexuality.

PSYCHOANALYTIC THEORY OF DEVELOPMENT

Early in life, especially the first five or six years, sexual feelings are different than at the time of puberty. They tend to be more generalized and diffuse. They can be stimulated by many different experiences and are not yet localized in the genital organs. Freud termed them "polymorphous perverse" sensations. However, these feelings are primarily experienced in certain target organs—one at a time, in sequence—during the early years. Hence, the concepts of developmental stoppage (being "stuck" or fixated) and retreating from a developmental position already achieved (regression) are of prime importance in understanding deviancy, and they tend to be more difficult to grasp than the concept of distortion—developing in an abnormal way. In any instance, if the individual gets stuck, retreats, or gets sidetracked in the early stages of growth and development, then he will seek sexual pleasure in a way that would be normal at some point in time for the growing child but is regarded as deviant behavior for an adult.

What also must be understood is that many types of sexual behavior—such as masturbation, oral-genital contact, anal sex, biting, or viewing—are not necessarily considered deviant unless they become the preferred or only way to achieve an orgasm. They simply represent residual derivatives of early sexual experiences.

Freud postulated that during a sequence of stages of development, different organs of the body become exquisitely sensitive and are the primary organs through which sexual pleasure is obtained. They are, in chronological order:

1. The mouth
2. The anus
3. The urethra
4. The entire genital organ

Children obtain sexual pleasure from the mouth first by sucking and then by biting. They obtain pleasure from the anus by first extruding and then retaining feces. Pleasure is then obtained from the emission of urine through the urethra. Finally, sexual satisfaction is obtained by a progressive localization to and eventual orgasm in the primary sex organs. As the developing child passes through these stages, his experiences with those around him, especially the parents, markedly influence his rate of progress or potential blockage at any one stage.

ORAL STAGE

Getting "stuck" or fixated at the first stage is called *sexual oralism* — the obtaining of sexual pleasure exclusively through the use of the mouth. Examples are fellatio, in which the male sexual organs are sucked, or cunnilingus, in which the female sexual organs are sucked. Sexual oralism can occur in either a heterosexual or homosexual relationship.

ANAL STAGE

In the second stage of development, the anal stage, the child plays with his feces and experiences pleasure by holding in or releasing a bowel movement. This normal physiological substance is a part of the body in the toddler's eyes, and he can sometimes be heard saying "bye bye" as he flushes the stool. This is a necessary and normal stage of development. In the case of adults fixated at this stage, sexual analism is the obtaining of sexual pleasure exclusively through the use of the anus (legally known as sodomy) and, again, can occur in either heterosexual or homosexual relationships. Some authors relate this deviancy to the pleasurable experiences during the anal stage of early development (fixation), while others insist it is related to a fear-induced flight (regression) from the first experiences with heterosexual genital urges.

URETHRAL STAGE

The third stage of development is the urethral stage, when sexual pleasure seems to be linked to the emission of urine. Of all four stages, this one is the most poorly understood and most vaguely described. Some deny that it exists and cite as evidence that no known deviancy has ever been exclusively linked to it. Others argue for its fleeting presence, citing as evidence some of the various urinary acts associated with sexual behavior — such as partners urinating on each other in the shower.

GENITAL STAGE

The fourth stage of development, the genital stage, encompasses the Oedipal situation, also known as the Oedipal complex or Electra complex, which is a love affair with the parent of the opposite sex. As the entire genital organ becomes the center of sexuality, the child develops exceedingly intense sexual feelings—physical urges—for the parent of the opposite sex. At the same time, the parent of the same sex is perceived as a rival, and becomes the recipient of the child's murderous feelings. Hence, the child finds himself in an overwhelming situation, feeling guilty for the feelings and fearing reprisal (retaliatory punishment from the parent of the same sex).

Castration Anxiety.   The situation is not the same for the boy as for the girl; this may be the reason sexual deviancy is more common among males. The boy experiences his mother as a sexual object (or love object)—someone outside himself that his sexual feelings, now centered in the genitals, are directed toward. He also experiences feelings of both hate and fear toward his father—hate because the all-powerful father is a rival, and fear that the father will punish the boy for his incestuous desire for the mother.

What kind of punishment does the boy fear? Castration, of course! Aren't there people around without a penis—namely, girls and women? Well, they must have had a penis that was taken away as a form of punishment, in the same way that toys and other things are taken away as a form of punishment. Such is the small boy's thinking. The accompanying fearful feelings, which are extremely intense, are called *castration anxiety.*

The boy is in a jam and he's got to get out of it. He is so uncomfortable (castration anxiety) that he must do something—and he does. He decides, "If I can't have Mom as a sexual object, then I'll give her up; but when I grow up I'll have someone just like her. And the best way to make sure I do is to be like Dad." Hence, the boys resolves the Oedipal conflict by identifying with his father—being like him in dress, behavior, mannerism, and so forth. This identification process is easier for the boy if the father has remained close, involved, warm, and especially understanding.

Penis Envy.   The genital stage and accompanying Oedipal conflict is not quite the same for the girl. Like the boy, she is psychologically more strongly bound to the mother. Instead of extending her feelings toward the mother to now include sexual strivings, as the boy does, however, she must make a shift to the father. The basis of this shift is her discovery that she doesn't have a penis—and neither does her mother. She experiences males as being equipped differently and begins to envy them (called "penis envy," another type of castration anxiety). Consequently, she begins to feel a sense of loss and injury and to resent the mother intensely for bringing her into the world less well equipped than males. In an attempt to make up for her "inadequacy," the girl turns to her father in the hope that he will give her a penis, or a baby in place of the "missing" penis. The subsequent diminution of the girl's sexual love for her father finally occurs both because of his failure to satisfy her needs and because she fears the mother's disapproval. She returns to identifying with the mother, whose warmth and understanding facilitate the process.

The most significant difference beween the male and the female is that with the boy, the discomfort of castration anxiety rapidly leads to a resolution of the Oedipal conflict, while with the girl, it is the discomfort of castration anxiety (penis envy) that evokes the Oedipal conflict. In both instances, it is by the process of identification with the parent of the same sex that the Oedipal conflict is resolved. The conflict is less intense for the girl and the process, therefore, takes longer.

MASTURBATION AND AGGRESSION—TWO ISSUES IN NEED OF CLARIFICATION

MASTURBATION

Masturbation is considered a normal preliminary experience to sexual encounters with another person. Perhaps no single act has been more publicly condemned while being privately practiced; nearly all men and three fourths of women masturbate. Yet some persons still believe that this behavior will turn one's brain to jelly and cause idiocy.

Central to masturbation, and later to object-related sexual behavior, is the ability to achieve an orgasm. Perhaps the most significant information of recent origin with regard to orgastic behavior of both men and women has been described by Masters and Johnson. It is their concept that in a well-functioning sexual relationship, each partner is doing something *with* the other and is responsible for his or her own sexual responsiveness. In light of this concept, masturbatory behavior early in life can be seen as the training period for future object-related sexuality.

The growing child first directs his psychological energies inward during the pre-Oedipal phase of development. He initially loves himself, a necessary learning experience preliminary to loving another person. Likewise, he first experiences an orgasm as a result of self-stimulation, another learning experience in responding to another person in a maximal manner. It is only when one knows himself quite well sexually that one can give the most effective cues and directions to a sexual partner.

AGGRESSION

The expression of aggressive energy is usually normal, not deviant. The couples who fight the most efficiently also get along the best sexually. In his book *The Intimate Enemy,* Dr. George R. Bach states that "couples who can't display their hostilities are not polite but phony"; they also make lousy bed partners.

Hence, a detailed study of how the individual (or couple) handles aggressive feelings is an essential ingredient of sexual counseling. There are differences between constructive and destructive uses of anger. When a person can express how he or she feels to the partner, then the air is cleared. The psychological tensions that can be barriers to a maximal orgasmic response are thus removed.

Dr. Bach's approach to sexual counseling includes the use of fight clinics—teaching couples how to fight more effectively in order to achieve greater sexual intimacy—and it works. How, then, does one fight effectively? The many specific techniques can be learned in *The Intimate Enemy* and *Creative Aggression,* by the same author. However, a basic principle that is useful in sexual counseling is that in a fair fight, each person tells how he or she feels; neither "puts down" the other. When a person speaks from the viewpoint of how he or she feels, rather than attacking, there is less tendency for the partner to become defensive and counterattack. Each is an expert in his own feelings and should limit remarks to that area.

HOMOSEXUALITY

Homosexuality is the most discussed and possibly the most widespread of all variations of human sexual behavior. The word homosexual is used both as a noun (calling a person "a homosexual") and as an adjective (as in a homosexual story). It is also used indiscriminately to describe sexual behavior with both sexes, which more properly should be called bisexuality. The term "lesbianism," denoting female homosexuality, has become obsolete. Slang words such as "fairy," "pansy," "queen," and "queer" are so predominant that it is difficult to use them in ordinary language without bringing male homosexuality to mind. Among homosexuals the term "gay" is most often used, both as a noun and as an adjective. Homosexuals sometimes refer to heterosexuals as "straight."

Homosexuality has been defined as sexual behavior between members of the same sex. Although this definition sounds clear, one might ask, "What exactly does sexual behavior include?" When two women greet each other with a kiss on the cheek as they meet in a restaurant, is this homosexual behavior? When the singing of a male quartet at a party, now liberally laced with alcohol, goes up a few decibels and the arms go around each other, is this homosexual behavior? Most would agree that neither of the aforementioned examples is "sexual" unless erotic interest and excitation occur. But even this is difficult to establish because sometimes it happens outside conscious awareness. What does seem to be agreed upon is that people who exclusively or preferentially engage in "same-sex" erotic activity are "homosexuals."

A condition upon which there is little agreement is that of "bisexuality." Some maintain that everyone is bisexual—at least in a latent sense. Others define the bisexual as a person who repeatedly engages in homosexual activities and at the same time also engages in heterosexual activity, no matter which predominates. This readiness to switch differentiates those who engage in even quite sporadic or infrequent homosexual encounters from those who are exclusively heterosexually oriented.

Although homosexuality occurs in both sexes, male homosexuality has been given more attention. Its incidence and prevalence, especially in the United States where it is still illegal, are virtually unknown. According to most estimates, approximately 5 per cent of white adult males remain exclusively homosexual after adolescence. There is thought to be a higher percentage among members of artistic professions, but it may simply be that they are freer to declare themselves.

There are as many differences among male homosexuals as there are among male heterosexuals. Only a small percentage—those who emphasize feminine characteristics—are visually identifiable. Those who are exclusively homosexual tend to live in large urban centers where they have built up their own social system and where they can more readily blend into a large group. Although some pair up for long periods of time, most lead a relatively lonely life, ironically epitomized by the term "gay life," constantly pursuing new partners with whom they maintain tenuous and usually temporary relationships

A less prominent group of homosexuals live in a heterosexual world, often are married and have children, and conform to heterosexual cultural norms. Their homosexual activities occur in secrecy; they are known as "closet queens" and live in constant fear of being discovered.

Another group of homosexuals reflect intact ego functioning and conduct themselves effectively and constructively in society. It is probably this group that has been affected most by the recent decision of the American Psychiatric Association to remove the diagnosis of "homosexuality" from their *Diagnostic and Statistical Manual—II*, removing the connotation of pathological disorders from the term.

Homosexual behavioral practices include all types of kissing, mutual masturbation, and use of the mouth and anus as sexual orifices. There is no reliable correlation between appearance, social behavior, and preferred sexual practices. A large penis is highly valued. Only a small minority of homosexuals consciously seek out partners with feminine characteristics. Many male homosexuals are capable of establishing deep friendships with females, provided they are assured that nothing is expected of them sexually.

Most believe that homosexuality results from unfavorable psychological experiences during childhood years. Statistical evidence indicates that the typical mother of a male homosexual was close, overintimate, possessive, and dominating. She babied her son and may have been inappropriately intimate, sometimes exposing her nudity. The typical father was usually detached and unaffectionate and sometimes hostile. He spent very little time with his son, whom he minimized and humiliated. Thus, a detached, hostile father and a close-binding, seductive mother (who may have dominated and minimized her husband) are believed the most likely to produce a homosexually oriented son.

In this proposed family situation, as the son encounters the Oedipal conflict his sexual attraction to the mother is enhanced and the feelings of rivalry toward and the fear of reprisal from the father remain unmodified because of the distance and hostility of this parent. The child finds himself in an intensely anxious situation and has to continue to deny a heterosexual involvement in order to continue developing. Heterosexual involvement is subsequently avoided for life because of the fear of attack from a male competitor.

Psychoanalytic theory thus emphasizes castration anxiety as the main cause of homosexuality, that is, a fear of castration as a reprisal for the incestuous strivings. The female genitalia may be perceived as a castrating instrument. At the same time, identification with the mother following the Oedipal disappointment takes the form of a wish to obtain sexual gratification in the same way as the mother, and leads to the choice of a male partner.

Female homosexuality is less prevalent than male — about one-third as common. Ellis[4] gave the following explanation of the lesser incidence of female homosexuality:

1. Adolescent male sexual demands are more intense, requiring more of an outlet, while female demands are less so and can be more easily suppressed.

2. In our society females who are highly sexed and desire frequent outlets can more easily find them with males than can highly sexed males find fulfillment with females.

3. Females who for neurotic reasons suppress their heterosexual drives often develop frigidity and become sexless while males turn to homosexuality.

Relationships between female homosexuals tend to be longer-lasting and more stable than those between males, although in many cases the partners are somewhat ambivalent toward each other. Usually a heterosexual masquerade is acted out, with the male ("butch") and female ("femme") roles adhered to or interchanged. Sometimes a symbolic mother-daughter relationship develops.

Female homosexuals are particularly obsessed with maternal characteristics, best symbolized by the breasts. Their sexual practices vary a great deal but may include hugging and kissing, manual and oral stimulation of the breasts and genitalia, and simulated intercourse with or without an artificial penis.

The prevailing explanation of this condition is similar to that of male homosexuality, although there is somewhat greater agreement that the condition is completely acquired with no genetic factors Here, too, it is the encountering of pathological qualities in the parents early in life that leads the female to this orientation. In order to attain heterosexuality, the female must renounce the mother (first-loved) and be able to be attracted to the father. Those who cannot make this renunciation become "fixated" and develop a homosexual orientation. In addition, the girl develops a castration anxiety with the discovery that she lacks a penis and may then become preoccupied with her clitoris (protuberance), thereby denying her vagina (receptacle). To resolve the conflict she must identify with the passive receptivity of the vagina at the expense of the primacy of the clitoris or she cannot enter into a heterosexual relationship. Finally, if the attachment to the father is too intense in the Oedipal complex, she must retreat from her feared incestuous impulses and turn instead to a woman as a love object.

The typical mother of the female homosexual is ambivalent and often hostile and competitive. Rather than enhancing her daughter's femininity she attempts to minimize it, perhaps even denying the wearing of girlish clothes as well as being fault-finding and rejecting. She interferes with the closeness of a father-daughter relationship and even with heterosexual peer relationships. The typical father is usually submissive to the mother as well as distant and unprotecting of the daughter.

The fears under which the homosexual lives can hardly be overemphasized; the realities of persecution and the fear of discovery, with resulting shame and possibly loss of employment, realistically contribute to paranoid thinking.

The matter of treatment is controversial, some contending that homosexuality is not a disease and does not in itself require treatment. For those who desire to become heterosexual, authorities differ on the aims of therapy and the degree of effectiveness, but all seem somewhat more optimistic than Freud, who considered homosexuality untreatable. Therapeutic aims include getting at the root of the problem while assuring the homosexual that the pleasures of his present life will not be removed but rather added to by a new adjustment toward heterosexuality. Discomfort with a homosexual orientation, with a sincere desire to change, is the most favorable prognostic indicator. Other helpful factors are respect for one's father, beginning treatment early in adult life, a history of having attempted heterosexual intercourse, and heterosexual dreams.

If the homosexual is satisfied with his or her orientation, therapy may be directed toward achievement of self-acceptance and maintenance of self-confidence in a world in which the emphasis on heterosexuality is so pervasive.

Prevention, by early psychotherapy of both the child and the parents, would be a better approach, if it were possible to recognize children at risk. Within the context of the family situations described earlier, children who tend to isolate themselves from their peer group, shun typical play activities of their sex, and consciously avoid members of the opposite sex during adolescence should perhaps be evaluated, with cautious awareness of individual variation in rate of development.

FETISHISM

In fetishism, the sexual energy is attached to an object that symbolizes the heterosexual partner—primarily a female, since most fetishism occurs in males. A common fetish is a female shoe, which must be looked at or touched in order to produce orgasm—sometimes without the use of masturbatory activity.

Some authorities call a fetishist someone who substitutes a part of the body (foot or lock of hair) for the total human being, while others designate this individual as a Partialist. Some connect fetishism with sadomasochistic behavior because of the aggressive quality of some of the objects used to achieve sexual excitement (whip or tight corsets).

In fetishism, a person can be sexually aroused only by certain objects or specific conditions which are often unrelated to coitus. The most commonly erotically endowed objects are a woman's shoe, stocking, glove, handkerchief, corset, undergarment, or hair. Some fetishists feel that it is necessary to commit burglary—steal the necessary object—which has legal significance. Many go to great lengths to make a collection of different types of the specific fetish. Another variation of fetishism concerns the use of specific practices during intercourse, such as insisting that a prostitute smoke a cigar or wear leather boots.

Historically, the fetishist has a strong attachment to his mother and was introduced to the sight of either his mother's or his sister's genitalia at a very early age—causing severe castration anxiety, according to Freud. The fetish (substituted object) is symbolic of the penis, and fetishism is a defense against castration anxiety. Fetishism is demonstrated almost exclusively by males as a result of the overwhelming castration fear originating from this early childhood experience. The absence of a penis in females is a reminder that this could happen to him, and he therefore refuses to accept the fact that women have different genitalia from men. He withdraws from the living object to replace it with the fetish, which stands for a female penis. This substitution is the only way he can keep his castration anxiety under control. The patient thus experiences both sexual excitement and castration fear simultaneously. While the chosen fetish is erotically endowed and necessary for the achievement of orgasm, at the same time it symbolically denies the absence of a penis in the female.

Successful treatment depends on the strength of the patient's desire for change. Psychoanalysis, which is most effective only with great tact, is necessary to uncover and work through unconscious repressions and early fixations.

SADOMASOCHISM

Sadism and masochism are two sides of the same coin. Sadism involves obtaining sexual gratification from acts of cruelty — inflicting pain upon another person — and is of major significance because of its social effects. Masochism involves obtaining sexual gratification by being hurt, humiliated, dominated, or degraded — experiencing pain inflicted on the self. It must be emphasized that in both conditions, the infliction of pain is necessary for sexual gratification.

These conditions result from a lack of refinement of the aggressive instincts experienced by the young child. Contrary to popular belief, the very young child is not sweet and innocent. He is a ruthless savage who has death wishes for those around him. In sadism and masochism, the aggression lacks social refinement and remains unchanged. Sadomasochism is particularly associated with the oral and anal stages of development.

In addition, psychoanalysis defines this type of deviation as a means of avoiding castration anxiety. The sadist avoids the fear of castration by doing to others that which he is afraid will be done to him. The masochist, on the other hand, responds more to the guilt feelings derived from his incestuous desires and must be punished by suffering in order to achieve orgasm. Freud emphasized that sadism and masochism are related in that when the outwardly directed sadistic impulses become unacceptable, they are turned around and directed against the self instead, causing masochism.

Freud considered this condition extremely important, emphasizing that there is an intimate connection between aggression and the sexual instinct. Anthropological studies of some societies emphasize violence, such as biting, scratching, and spitting, during the sexual act.

Like many conditions, milder forms fall within the realm of normality. Some assertiveness or aggressiveness (sadism) is not only entwined in sexuality but is essential to it. With two totally passive partners, the act would never be accomplished. In the same manner, passivity or receptiveness can be seen to be a milder form of masochism and is complementary to the aforementioned assertiveness in normal sexual intercourse. Some authorities link sadism to the male and masochism to the female, stating that a certain amount of sadistic behavior tends to be characteristic normal male sex behavior, just as a certain amount of masochism seems to be characteristic of the normal female.

There is a certain compulsive quality to sadistic behavior, though it tends to be periodic rather than continual. The classic example is the sadistic husband obtaining pleasure from beating his masochistic wife, who patiently endures it, subconsciously enjoying her misery. The most serious of all are acts of cruelty associated with sexual pleasure, such as lust murders, which are often committed by very mild men.

With the masochist, fantasies of being punished as a means of alleviating guilt feelings and castration anxiety are common—being whipped, driven, bound, or tortured. There is no consistent sex-linked relationship in sadomasochism. Neither is found in just one of the sexes. Sadomasochistic relationships likewise occur among homosexuals.

The prognosis of this condition is fairly favorable when treatment is sought by the patient. In general, masochism is of less social significance than sadism, since others are not affected.

TRANSVESTISM AND SEX-ROLE INVERSION

These two conditions are different, although they bear a superficial resemblance to each other. Transvestism refers only to the desire to wear the clothing of the other sex, while sex-role inversion involves a total identification with, preference for, and adoption of the entire role of the other sex (of which dress is only one aspect).

TRANSVESTISM

Transvestism literally means to dress opposite, or "cross-dress." Its occurrence has been known since the beginning of recorded history and may be considered universal. In many cultures the transvestite is accepted into the world of the opposite sex; some of these instances may actually represent a sex-role inversion rather than simple transvestism.

One criterion is a strong desire to look like the opposite sex. American women who wear slacks and Scotchmen who wear kilts are not transvestites because there is no emotional accompaniment to wearing the particular apparel. The incidence of transvestism is 1 to 3 per cent of the general population—difficult to determine accurately, because the majority of transvestites do not come to the attention of health professionals or are not arrested for their behavior, which occurs only in private. However, some males do wear feminine items of clothing under their outer masculine clothes. The condition is more common among males than females, estimates ranging as high as 50 to 1. This may be because in our culture females are given more freedom in cross-dressing. In fact, the incidence of female transvestism is so limited that little is actually known about the condition.

The typical male transvestite has a rather elaborate and complete wardrobe of feminine apparel. The intensity of desire to wear this clothing is different in each individual. If he is married, the wife often knows about the condition and helps him choose his wardrobe. Characteristically, the transvestite feels more relaxed and natural when cross-dressing, but the frequency of occurrence of this need varies greatly. The actual visual experience of seeing one's self in the mirror and the tactile experience of feeling the clothing are fundamental factors. Many transvestites complain about the drabness of the clothing of their own sex, compared with cross-dressing.

Etiology. Transvestism is regarded as an acquired behavioral pattern directly traceable to conditioning during early childhood. In the earliest years of life the child was exposed to wearing and fondling clothes of the opposite sex, leading to the imprinting process. The boy's hair was kept long. He was given extra attention and praise for wearing feminine clothing. This feminization conditioning process was carried on by the mother even before the boy could verbalize his feelings and preferences.

One explanation for the greater incidence of transvestism among males is the more frequent occurrence of boys dressed as girls, rather than the reverse, in the first two or three years of life. In such situations the typical father is either absent (little or no contact with the son) or negative and hostile, rejecting the son. The father may also be dominated by the mother. Presumably a reverse pattern would be found in the childhood of female transvestites — an extremely rare phenomenon.

Psychoanalytically, the boy deals with his castration anxiety by convincing himself that his "phallic-type" mother has a penis, and thereby he identifies with her. The centering of attention on the mother's clothes rather than her body is a means of avoiding the anatomical difference between males and females, thereby denying the threat of castration. "Being like mother" primarily refers to wearing clothes similar to those she wears.

Some writers consider transvestism a form of homosexuality in spite of clinical studies that indicate that the majority of male transvestites are either predominantly or exclusively heterosexual throughout their lives. Others link transvestism with fetishism in spite of clinical evidence that indicates that the majority of transvestites desire the opposite sex's clothes in their own right rather than for purposes of masturbation. Only a minority of homosexuals are transvestites; only a minority of transvestites are homosexual. Likewise, most transvestites are not fetishists, and most fetishists are not transvestites.

Exhibitionism is also confused with transvestism, but there is a difference. The transvestite does not gain gratification from exposing his genitals. Rather, he obtains satisfaction from having other people look at him while cross-dressed, as well as from looking in the mirror.

Treatment. Transvestism is highly resistant to treatment, probably because it becomes fixated in early childhood. Most transvestites do not want to be cured. Prevention is the only answer—making sure that the infant child is exposed to and wears clothing that is appropriate to his or her sex, and creating a close affectionate relationship with both parents. In particular, mothers should be educated about the hazards of cross-dressing their children.

SEX-ROLE INVERSION

Sex-role inversion is a much more pervasive condition, in which a person of one sex thinks, feels, and acts like the other sex by identifying with, preferring, and adopting this role. Inversion, then, involves a disharmony between physical and psychological characteristics. Inverts, predominantly male, often state, "I'm really a female in a male body—nature made a mistake." The identity with the other sex is so compelling that many male inverts go so far as to imitate menstruation by scratching their thighs to produce bleeding. They may also pretend they go through pregnancy and childbirth.

Differential Diagnosis. The diagnostic criteria are psychological (having to do with masculinity and femininity) rather than physical (having to do with being male or female). Motives, feelings, manner of walking, bodily movements, and general demeanor are all acquired behavioral traits through which masculinity or femininity can be expressed. Thus, the diagnostic criteria differentiate sex-role inversion from hermaphroditism.

Inversion is often confused with transvestism and homosexuality. While inversion includes transvestism (since cross-dressing is part of the total sex role), the reverse is not true. Inversion is not found in all instances of tranvestism. Likewise, that type of male homosexuality that is passive and feminine is often seen in the male invert who experiences himself as a female and seeks sexual gratification from the "other" sex, namely, males. The same would be true about the relationship between female inversion and the active and masculine type of female homosexual.

Another term with a more specific meaning is transsexualism, a condition referring to the invert who has undergone surgical transformation to the opposite sex. The most well-known transsexuals are

Christine Jorgensen and Jan Morris. The male to female transformation includes hormonal (estrogenic) inhibiting of testicular functioning, surgical removal of the testes, amputation of the penis, electrolytic removal of facial hair, and transformation of the scrotum into an artificial vagina; often, breast augmentation is included.

Etiology.   While some authorities hold to a genetic explanation for inversion, the most reasonable is still psychosocial. Inversion is probably established very early in life by a continuing identification with the parent of the opposite sex. The child forms a close attachment to the parent of the opposite sex and gets little or no satisfaction from the parent of the same sex. The mother reinforces the development of femininity while discouraging masculinity in the boy. A conditioning process surrounds him with femininity in dress, mannerisms, and attitudes. He is encouraged to play with girls, learn their ways, and renounce his masculinity. As adolescence and then adulthood are approached, there is no attempt to conceal the compelling drive toward becoming a woman. Characteristically, a male invert has no desire to marry a woman and father children, while a male transvestite often does.

Treatment.   With regard to treatment, there is not one historically documented case of inversion being cured. Prevention is the only hope and centers on educating the parents to love the child as a male if he is a boy and as a female if she is a girl.

EXHIBITIONISM AND VOYEURISM

EXHIBITIONISM

Exhibitionism is the impulsive and compulsive exposure of the genitalia as a means of achieving sexual gratification. The act of exhibition does not usually end in orgastic gratification; this is accomplished later by masturbation. The compulsive quality of this act is important, since self-control is obviously lacking. The subject is spellbound, in a high state of anxiety, and unable to control his impulses to exhibit his genitalia. The compulsion refers not only to the act itself but also to the time and place of performance. Many exhibitionists return time and time again to the scene of their "crime."

The male exhibitionist frequently suffers from potency disturbances and may have little interest in a normal sexual relationship. He performs his act only in the presence of strangers, and if he has a family, they are often unaware of his abnormality. The act has an aggressive aspect in the sense that women are shown the penis against their will, as are children. Some reaction on the part of the onlooker must occur, such as shock, horror, or excitement. Some authors state that male exhibitionism occurs in timid men who are dominated by an assertive wife after being raised by an assertive mother. It is the obsessive-compulsive qualities of exhibitionism and voyeurism that can make these practices "normal" if controlled and practiced in privacy and in culturally approved settings.

This condition differs from the normal exhibitionism of childhood growth and development, which is practiced by mutual consent and closely tied up with a voyeuristic element. The adult exhibitionist's susceptibility to visual sexual stimulation is usually weak; he is typically not stimulated by the sight of the female breast or genitalia.

Exposure of and a desire to look at the genitals are normal in young children; these activities often occur in conjunction with various games. In pure form exhibitionism is rarely found among women in Western culture. One explanation is that females are granted some social permission to display their legs and upper parts of their torso in normal wearing apparel. When female exhibitionism does occur, it consists of the desire to show the nipples.

Etiology. Psychoanalytic theory states that exhibitionism serves as a reassurance against castration anxiety in three ways. (1) By exhibiting his penis the male exhibitionist says to his audience, "Reassure me that I have a penis by reacting to the sight of it." (2) By evoking a fearful reaction from others (especially children), the exhibitionist is saying, "Reassure me that you are afraid of my penis and therefore fear me and won't castrate me." (3) Finally, to the female observer, the exhibitionist is saying, "I wish you could show me what I show you in order to reassure me that you have a penis also and therefore have not been castrated." All these feelings are aimed at relieving the anxiety of castration. The compulsive quality of returning to the scene of the crime is a manifest symptom of his deep sense of guilt and need to be punished.

In exhibitionism the mother is dominant and aggressive, and she resents her feminine role. She tries to live her life through her children, especially the sons. The father is often weak and ineffective, having little influence in shaping the son's emotional development. Thus, the incestuous wishes stimulated by the unusual intensity of the mother's affection, and the associated castration fear, must be defended against by the compulsive exhibiting of the genital organs.

Exhibitionism also contains an aggressive element indicative of a maladjustment to early authority figures who stimulated the rebellious aspects of the behavior. Exhibitionists are repetitious transgressors of moral and social taboos. Consequently, they keep reinforcing a strong sense of guilt and need for punishment by repeatedly returning to the scene of their "crime" until they succeed in getting caught.

Treatment. With regard to prognosis, the exhibitionist rarely seeks therapeutic help, and prognosis is generally unfavorable. Psychoanalysis has been effective at times, especially for young individuals.

VOYEURISM

Voyeurism means the achieving of sexual gratification by watching nude women or a man and woman engaging in sexual intercourse. This condition involves women as well as men, though only about one third as many are affected. Certain voyeuristic activities are socially acceptable, such as strip-tease shows and pornographic pictures and films.

Sexual curiosity and excitement as a result of seeing the love object is part of normal sexual development. Although in early childhood this curiosity focuses on the parents, the adult voyeur is given to spying on strangers. The voyeur is fixated on this expression of his early sexual curiosity or has regressed from the aroused castration anxiety of the Oedipal complex. Social derivatives such as gossiping occur in both sexes. Voyeurs are infantile or adolescent personalities who are nuisances but not dangerous.

In voyeurism, practices range all the way from "peeping," which is carried out without the cooperation of the person or people being observed, to spectatorship at elaborate performances, for example, in houses of prostitution. Underlying voyeurism are the same infantile fixations or regressions relating to primal scenes as in exhibitionism. Hence, this condition can be interpreted as an attempt at attaining reassurance against castration anxiety, but because such reassurance cannot be obtained, the voyeuristic tendencies usually become insatiable and repetitious. Also, the original aggressive impulse is transformed into a milder one — to, "Look, I didn't do it, I only watched it being done."

According to Freud, visual impressions remain the most frequent pathway along which sexual excitement is aroused. Natural selection counts on this accessibility when it encourages the development of beauty in the sexual object. The progressive concealment of the body deemed necessary by civilization keeps sexual curiosity awake.

Etiology. Psychoanalysts believe that the reversion to some primal theme, such as a wish to deny the lack of a penis in women (that is, mother) or the wish to observe parental intercourse, lies behind this behavior. However, there may be more to it in that there seems to be considerable identification with the object observed, and sexual excitement often occurs. Like the exhibitionist, the voyeur seldom comes in for treatment on his own. However, his fear of being discovered or punished by the law can become a focal point for initiating treatment using a psychoanalytic approach.

PEDOPHILIA EROTICA (Infanto-Sexuality)

The pedophile requires the cooperation of a child or a sexually immature partner of the same or opposite sex in order to achieve sexual gratification. While it is known that homosexual pedophilia was common in ancient Greece, precise current statistics are difficult to obtain. Police records about complaints of child molesting provide some clues, but other factors must be considered. The adolescent "victim" may have deliberately concealed his or her age or may have behaved in a seductive manner. Also, children lend themselves to fondling and lap-sitting, which may be accompanied by friction with adult genitalia and consequent arousal.

The pedophile avoids coitus with an adult love object (male or female) because of the overwhelming castration anxiety. Instead, he is attracted to children, who do not elicit the same anxiety because they are weak and approachable. The selection of an immature object is the result of an unresolved Oedipal complex and the accompanying castration fear and sense of inadequacy in adult relationships with either sex. In addition, the pedophile is in love with himself as he was as a child and treats his immature love object in the same way he would have liked his mother to have treated him as a child. He functions on an immature psychosexual level because of his fearfulness and doubt concerning himself. He expects rejection and failure in adult heterosexual advances (and homosexual as well), and his sexual expression is therefore released toward children.

Clinically, most male pedophiles are psychologically weak and either partially or totally impotent. Their sexual activities consist of masturbation and exhibitionistic behavior. Occasionally, a child may suffer a major physical injury because of an attempt at intercourse. However, most activities are confined to fondling, exhibitionism, and masturbation.

A pedophile may be homosexual, heterosexual, or bisexual in his choice of objects, and theoretically, his activity can take almost any of the forms characteristic of heterosexual or homosexual activity with an adult partner. In evaluating a pedophile, one must keep in mind that the behavior of the child may have been seductive and played a major role which, because of the acting out of the Oedipal strivings, is indicative of a more serious disorder than the pedophile's response to the child's actions. Prognosis is poor, and the condition must be differentiated from a primary disorder such as an organic brain syndrome.

INCEST

Incest refers to coitus between members of the same family: father-daughter, brother-sister, mother-son. Some anthropologists have extended this definition to apply to a genital union between members of the same tribe or clan as well. Incest can be considered a form of intrafamilial pedophilia. It can be homosexual as well as heterosexual.

Freud described the incest taboo as "one of the most powerful prohibitions of mankind." The taboo serves at least two useful purposes. First, it tends to cut down on competition within the family unit and on jealousy that might interfere with the functioning of this most important social group. Second, it insures that mating will take place outside the family and thus widen the circle of people who will cooperatively band together in the face of danger.

Many authors have stated that in all cultures, sexual liaisons between parents and their offspring are forbidden. Thus, the taboo crosses cultural lines. The only known exception occurred among certain Egyptian dynasties: it was permissible for the Pharaoh, and only the Pharaoh, to impregnate his daughter or granddaughter in order to assure his lineage.

Incest prohibitions are not inborn or instinctually determined. Rather, the barrier is a cultural demand made by society and, therefore, learned. Clinically, the acting out of the Oedipal complex by actually breaking the incest barrier is a regressive phenomenon implying a serious defect in personality development. It is sometimes seen in schizophrenia, in which the desire for incestuous intercourse is expressed openly.

Attempts at sibling incest as part of exploratory sex play have frequently been reported in pre-adolescent development. Mother-son incest is far less common than father-daughter. The prognosis for treatment is poor, since this behavior represents a serious lack of impulse control, and in most instances a more basic and pervasive underlying pathology is present. Separating the child from the parents is usually necessary.

BESTIALITY (Zoophilia; Sodomy)

Bestiality means achieving sexual gratification by some type of activity with a living animal, though it is not necessarily limited to intercourse. During various periods of history, this practice occurred openly. Kinsey's sampling indicated that among those living on farms, there was a significant incidence of bestiality. One third of the males who lived on farms admitted to some form of sexual activity, often intercourse, to the point of orgasm with an animal.

This condition can take any one of three possible forms: (1) sexual arousal by observing sexual activities of animals (voyeurism); (2) animal objects — especially fur — acquiring a special sexual significance (fetishism); (3) actual intercourse or other sexual activity with an animal.

In adulthood, this condition represents reaction against castration fear. Animals don't talk; with them, a person is safe not only from rejection but also from retaliation. One of the most widespread activities concerns permitting a domestic pet, especially a dog, to masturbate by rubbing against the human. Also, fellatio and cunnilingus are not infrequent techniques of bestiality; dogs, cats, and even calves have been trained to lick human genitalia. While observation of the sexual activities of animals is a frequent occurrence in young children, there are also instances of adults of either sex deriving gratification from such observations — such as watching horses being bred. Of diagnostic importance is the significant incidence of this condition among schizophrenics and those with a schizoid personality — people who have a great anxiety in human relationships. Prognostically, farm boys are apt to overcome bestiality spontaneously when they are no longer isolated socially and are able to establish sexual relationships with girls. Treatment includes looking for a possible underlying schizophrenic process, toward which therapy should then be primarily directed.

SUMMARY

Sexual deviants, mostly males, never successfully attained adequate development. They lead miserable lives and usually are not physically harmful, though they can be psychologically disruptive, especially to growing children. The health professional's role consists of (1) diagnosis; (2) counseling patients regarding the need for help; (3) evaluating effect on the family and counseling appropriately; (4) making referrals to the appropriate health professional; and (5) continuing follow-up. In any consideration of sexual deviancy, it must be kept in mind that if one is going to understand the deviant pattern, then the reasons for the retreat, blockage, or distortion are far more important than the specifics of the deviancy. One should always be reassured that help can be obtained.

REFERENCES

1. Arieti, S., et al. (eds.). *American Handbook of Psychiatry*. 2nd ed. New York: Basic Books, 1974, Vol. I, pp. 589–607.
2. Bach, G. R., and H. Goldberg. *Creative Aggression*. New York: Doubleday & Co., 1974.
3. Bach, G. R., and P. Wyden. *The Intimate Enemy*. New York: William Morrow & Co., 1969.
4. Ellis, A., and A. Abarbanel (eds.). *The Encyclopedia of Sexual Behavior*. New York: Jason Aronson, 1973.
5. Freedman, A. M., and H. I. Kaplan. *Comprehensive Textbook of Psychiatry*. 2nd ed. Baltimore: Williams & Wilkins, 1975, pp. 258–264, 959–988.
6. Kolb, L. C.: *Modern Clinical Psychiatry*. 9th ed. Philadelphia: W. B. Saunders Co., 1977, pp. 619–627.
7. Masters, W. H., and V. E. Johnson. *The Pleasure Bond*. Boston: Little, Brown & Co., 1975.
8. Redlich, F. C., and D. X. Freedman. *The Theory and Practice of Psychiatry*. New York: Basic Books, 1966, pp. 384–392.

16

HOMOSEXUALITY: ESPECIALLY IN ADOLESCENCE

Lorraine Wolf, R.N., M.A.

The subject of human sexual partner choice has been of interest to mankind since the beginning of recorded time. With the evolution of the family and social "legislation" for survival, homosexual and heterosexual choices were prescribed in terms of the defined mores of each community.

HISTORICAL PERSPECTIVES

Rules and regulations abound in all cultures regarding the social role and sexual practice ascribed to the male and female of that society. Anthropologists have observed and recorded the extant sex and role assignation of both literate and preliterate people. On the basis of her comparison among peoples, Margaret Mead postulated that the characteristics labeled "female" or "male" were indeed not innate, but socially learned responses.[15] Anthropologists Ford and Beach noted that 64 per cent of the preliterate societies (with available information on sexual activities) consider some form of homosexuality as normal.[6] Of the remaining societies, some accepted premarital heterosexual activities, but not homosexual relationships; some had rigid rules and regulations governing heterosexual premarital relationships but were unconcerned about homosexual activities. In a few societies, there was a class of men who were intermediate between men and women and were identified variously as shaman, alyhar, or heduches.[17]

At the apex of the Greek civilization, as well as during its decline, homosexuality was accepted and expected between males. Plato, in *Symposium*, wrote:

> and if there were only some way of contriving that a state or
> army should be made up of lovers and their loves, they would be

the very best governors of their own city, abstaining from all dishonors, and emulating one another in honor, and when fighting at each other's side, although a mere handful, they would overcome the world. For what lover would not choose rather to be seen by all mankind than by his beloved, either when abandoning his post or throwing away his arms? He would be ready to die a thousand deaths rather than endure this. Or who would desert his beloved or fail him in the hour of danger? The veriest coward would become an inspired hero, equal to the bravest, at such a time; Love would inspire him.[16]

In this tradition, the Theban and Spartan armies made sacrifices to Eros before battle. These armies were made up of pairs of lovers who fought and died together as an example of excellence and manliness, according to their cultural mores. West stated that a study of the sexual habits of Greece and Rome serves to confirm what has already been deduced from anthropological studies, namely, that homosexual instincts soon make themselves apparent whenever they are given free rein.[17]

It is evident from recorded history that both homosexuality and heterosexuality have flourished with or without social sanction.

Western Perspective

The history of Western civilization from the advent of the Christian era shows the development of a severely repressive attitude that has labeled homosexuality as a repugnant, immoral, and abnormal choice of sexual expression. Homosexuality has been described as a "dislocation in heterosexual organization of biologically normal children . . . as a consequence of pathological relationships between parent and child."[3] Around this attitude have evolved rationalizations to support this thesis. Some of the more common arguments are

1. There is a direct cause-and-effect relationship between disturbed parent-child relationships and homosexuality.
2. People who persist in immoral life styles are neurotic and have a developmental fixation.
3. Homosexual practice is biologically unnatural.
4. Homosexuals are a menace to society and a moral threat to the community, especially the young.

From reading and hearing these arguments, it is not difficult to understand how the oppressive laws (including loss of civil rights) and social taboos came to be that surround the choice of or preference for a sexual and love partner of the same sex.

CHANGING PERSPECTIVES

The rationalizations reported in the previous section are now countered by eminent psychiatrists, theologians, and anthropologists. Briefly, they postulate:

1. All homosexuals do not have impaired family constellations, and "to call homosexuality the result of disturbed sexual development says nothing more than that you disapprove of the outcome of that development."

2. If all people who persist in unusual life styles are to be labeled as having a psychiatric disorder, the following conduct will have to be included: celibacy, revolutionary behavior, and religious zeal.

3. Biological evidence is to the contrary in the remainder of the animal kingdom.

4. A conservative estimate of the existence of one hundred million people with an identified homosexual orientation indicates that they cannot all be disturbed or peculiar.

It is only during the last decade, however, that individual sexual expression has publicly been considered the prerogative and sole right of the two consenting adults, quite outside the boundaries of theology, psychiatry, or jurisprudence. Contributing factors to this point of view are seen by this author as:

1. The choice to marry or remain single.

2. The choice to have children, to determine when to have children, or not to have children (all choices made from either a single or married position).

3. The redefining of marriage (since the liberation of women) from a "subject-ruler" or "object-owner" relationship to a "partner-peer" relationship.

4. The development of alternative life styles, i.e., communal living or mutual commitment to one another without marriage.

5. The development of gay liberation movements demanding "choice in social contacts as well as equal rights and fair treatment under law . . ."[9]

The result of these social changes and the more vociferous demands for control of one's own sexual destiny has been a polarization of individual and group responses in the society at large.

While controversy exists within society, in general, and the medical community, in particular (as exemplified by the struggle in the American Psychiatric Association over the continuation of labeling homosexuality as a mental illness or behavior disorder), it appears to this author that healthy growth and development (socialization) of the adolescent who has a homosexual orientation is ignored. The issue needs to be explored if the homosexually oriented adolescent is to make choices as an adult that will promote autonomy, intimacy, and self-worth.

ADOLESCENT SOCIALIZATION: RELEVANT THEORIES

The health care professional's background in growth and development places her in a unique position to assess the needs of the adolescent who has a homosexual orientation. She should focus on the ways in which these young people experience disruption in the socialization process at a critical stage in their development. Utilizing the major theoretical models of development to analyze the breakdown in the psychosocial process may result in a clearer understanding of the adolescents' needs and wants. In this chapter, the theories of development postulated by Erikson (neo-analytic) and Maslow (organismic) are used, along with interviews appropriate to the content of these theories. Assessment and intervention considerations follow the theoretical background and correlative case histories.

Identity vs. Role Confusion

According to Erikson, the stage of adolescent development is one of *identity vs. role confusion*.[5] The adolescent develops different behaviors for different situations according to what he defines as appropriate. Out of these varied roles, the adolescent develops an integrated sense of who he is as distinct from others. If the development is healthy, the emerging personality is coherent and personally acceptable. Following this developmental pattern, Berne describes the process in concrete behavioral terms:

> *Adolescence means high school and college days, driver's license, bar mitzvah, initiation, having your own thing and your own things. It means hair here and there, brassieres and menstruation, shaving and maybe an undeserved affliction that blows your plans and your mind—acne. It means deciding what you are going to be for the rest of your life, or at least how to fill in your time until you do decide . . . It means now you really are on the spot to answer the question, because if you don't you may not make it . . .*[2]

Disruption of this process results in what Erikson labeled *role confusion*.[5] Continued confusion about who he really is may result in the development of a "negative identity" or more severe psychopathological problems.

In this frame of reference, two key concepts emerge: trying out roles and making choices. The interpersonal activities necessary for "trying out roles" are established by our society as being primarily heterosexual activities, e.g., dating, or sex-specific ones, e.g., sports.

Mark,* age 17, illustrates the conflict in developing his identity in this milieu as follows:

> . . . I wasn't athletically inclined, but, of course, I still had to take P.E. in high school. This gave me a lot of anxiety because I knew I would probably get "turned on" in the showers to several of the guys in my class. I was still trying to be "cool," and I was afraid I would be embarrassed. Lots of girls were attracted to me; they taught me how to dance and talk to them, but I just couldn't get it on with anyone of them. What I really wanted to know was how to relate with guys, but who ever heard of a gay prom.

The choices available to Mark were, from his point of view, limited, if possible at all. Without an opportunity to explore his own developing sexuality in a less than threatening environment, he saw his only alternative as withdrawal from close social contacts with either males or females in his peer group, at a time when sharing life experiences was critical in developing his identity through trying various roles and making choices about these roles.

Mark, like many other homosexually oriented individuals interviewed by this author, was well aware of the taboo in our society regarding choice of a love object of the same sex. This knowledge in and of itself did not mitigate his being powerfully drawn to members of the same sex. What did happen was the inhibition of a full exploration of what his real sexual feelings were. The result was short-term encounters and promiscuity in an effort to establish an identity and move toward intimacy. Both behaviors are equally self-defeating.

Self-Actualization Hierarchy

Maslow does not assign age-specific stages to his developmental hierarchy of basic needs (Fig. 16–1). Rather, he formulates the thesis that one level of needs must be met to an acceptable degree before the individual can progress to the next level. However, it is not to be assumed that the hierarchy is to be viewed rigidly. New needs emerge before previous needs are satisfied, and the basic needs do continue throughout life. Additionally, Maslow has proposed that along with the basic needs, the individual has "metaneeds"—i.e., goodness, beauty, justice, unity, and order—that are growth needs. Metaneeds are

---

*All personal identifying information has been changed to provide confidentiality.

inherent in the individual and when not fulfilled result in alienation, apathy, anguish, and cynicism.

All levels of basic metaneeds other than the first level are still developing during adolescence. The basic needs are more potent than the metaneeds. Deficiencies occurring in these needs result in neurotic (and, at the extreme, psychotic) behavior patterns and life styles. Maslow defines neurotic as

> ...rather related to spiritual disorders, to loss of meaning, to doubts about goals in life, to grief and anger over a lost love, to seeing life in a different way, to loss of courage or of hope, to despair over the future, to dislike for oneself, to recognition that one's life is being wasted, or that there is no possibility of joy, or love, etc.[12]

This Maslow perceives as a falling away from the full blooming of human nature. He states, "It is a falling short of what one could have been, and even, one could say, of what one should have been . . . if one had grown and developed in an unimpeded way."[12]

The key concepts in this frame of reference are (1) the need to belong — to find a place in the group (level 3 in the hierarchy — love and belongingness) and (2) to do so with esteem for self and other (self-esteem, self-respect, and esteem by others).

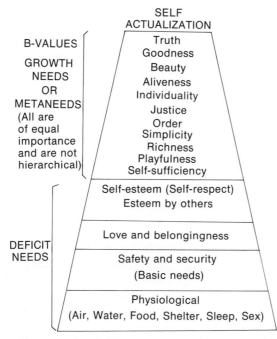

Figure 16-1. Abraham Maslow's hierarchy of needs.

NEED FOR SELF-ESTEEM

George, age 19, discussed the importance of belonging and self-esteem as follows:

> . . . *When I was in grade school and junior high, I had lots of friends and I had a great time. But when I started high school, my friends—girls and boys—began to relate to each other in a different way. The guys started talking about girls and getting turned on. The girls were calling me and them on the phone and trying to get us to go out with them—alone. I realized that I wasn't interested in the girls that way and I was concerned. Then I began to realize that I was becoming more interested in guys—that I was thinking about them in the same way they were talking about girls—I wondered what was going on—if I was inadequate, if I was OK. I was pretty anxious, but there wasn't anybody to talk to. I used to stand around with the guys and try to look interested in all their gas about this girl and that so I wouldn't be alone, and so they would think I was OK. All the time I'd be thinking about one or the other of them. By the end of that first year I was really down on myself. It seemed like I didn't belong—well, not in a way that was important, anyway. I was on such a bummer with myself I'm not sure what would have happened if I hadn't met B, before I lost self-respect totally.*

For George, as well as other adolescents interviewed by this author who became aware of their same-sex preference during high school, the issue of self-respect (self-worth or self-esteem) was of vital importance in their continuing growth and development. The matter of self-worth was inextricably tied to the need to belong and to give and receive affection. Barnett states,

> *Teenagers are hungry for understanding and affection, simply because they are human beings, and human beings are built that way. It isn't being sentimental or indeed unscientific to say that people die, in a deep sense, for lack of love and understanding. . . . Teenagers characteristically need the chance to offer and accept tenderness; to express affection in word and deed becoming more explicit, more intense, as the relationship deepens. . . .*[1]

Disruption of these basic growth needs almost always results in interferences in developing deep, mutually satisfying interpersonal relationships. This disruption was experienced by a high percentage of older adolescents and young adults who shared their concerns with this author.

Reaching the adolescent who has a same-sex orientation at this critical stage of his life, therefore, should be the primary focus of the health care professional. This requires an emphasis on the assessment process—the "how"—of collecting and identifying this information as the sine qua non for the subsequent intervention.

ASSESSMENT OF ADOLESCENT NEEDS

While this author acknowledges that there is no single method that will guarantee the open and honest sharing of information, the following guidelines are recommended:

1. Creating a climate in which the adolescent can, perhaps for the first time, begin to take the risk of self-disclosure. This is done by providing a relaxed private setting; explaining the purpose of the interaction and eliciting acceptance; and by structuring questions in such a way that both the health professional and the adolescent can identify what they need to know.

2. Focusing on each of the human needs and finding out how the adolescent has met or attempted to meet these needs. Deprivation of needs and unsatisfactory or inappropriate fulfillment of needs can more readily be identified by both the health professional and the adolescent in this nonjudgmental way.

3. Checking out the meaning for the adolescent of key words used or behaviors described. This keeps the focus on what is important to the adolescent, since his perception of what has happened or is happening has a greater influence on behavior than the actual situation itself or the health professional's interpretation.

4. Showing unqualified care and concern by using "I value you" comments, to reduce the need for the adolescent to earn approval; passively or aggressively withdraw; suppress information about thoughts, feelings, and desires; or otherwise artificially limit the interaction, thereby reducing the energy available for problem solving. Additionally, the health professional shows care and concern by her handling of sensitive information shared by the adolescent.

The data elicited in the assessment provide the focus for the furtherance of the relationship.

INTERVENTION

The relationship between need fulfillment and development of a confident, competent adolescent moving toward autonomy and intimacy should be of vital concern to the health professional.

Brown and Fowler state, "It may be necessary to designate basic human needs that must be fulfilled, whatever their category, as a precursor to meeting more mature needs. Efforts to stimulate advancement must be based on an accurate assessment of the current status of a person's needs, which will serve as a baseline in evaluating change and the direction of change."[4]

Intervention in this context, then, includes any aspect of the helping relationship that provides the opportunity for a greater understanding of self, insight about goals and desires, and alternatives available for problem solving or goal attaining. The author recognizes that any comments on intervention must, of necessity, be general owing to the uniqueness and variation of characteristics, experiences, and needs of each individual adolescent. However, within the framework of his developmental stage and the met or unmet developmental needs, the health professional has a basis for understanding the adolescent and for determining the disruption in his life. This framework, then, is used to offer direction to intervention, based on the following identified needs (Maslow's):

1. SECURITY

The insecurity and ambivalence in developing role identity during adolescence is well documented. When this is further complicated by sexual identity concerns, the resulting anxiety may take the form of withdrawal or rebellion. The health professional can provide the stable predictable environment in which the adolescent can talk about his experiences, evaluate his feelings, and explore outcomes in comfort.

2. BELONGINGNESS AND LOVE

In addition to unqualified acceptance of the adolescent as a person, the health professional can aid him in taking safe, graduated risks in spontaneous and creative interactions within the family and social group. These encounters should be ones identified as having a high predictability for success. The accumulation of successful interactions increases the "belongingness" and allows the adolescent to consider widening his social contacts by appreciating people of the same sex and relating warmly and affectionately to the opposite sex and to create alternative support groups in which to grow and develop the role that is congruent for him.

3. ESTEEM NEEDS

These needs are expressed in two categories—esteem for self (self-worth) and esteem from others. The esteem for self comes from experiencing success for effort expended. The development and maintenance of self-esteem usually takes place in the context of interpersonal relationships. The health professional can guide the adolescent in identifying his needs, the choices available to meet these needs, and the selection of behaviors likely to bring success. As risk taking increases, the adolescent can be guided to engage in those behaviors that focus on esteem for self and other. The result is the development of autonomy by taking care of oneself, being responsible for one's behaviors, sharing interests and concerns, and giving up patterns of behavior that are irrelevant, self-defeating, or inappropriate to living. James and Jongeward point out that "an autonomous person risks friendships and intimacy when he decides it is appropriate."[10]

SUMMARY

Negative social attitudes about homosexuality are beginning to change. However, the process of change is slow. Many health professionals, along with the general public, deal with homosexuality as if it did not exist. Hoffman states, "One might consider this a psychological conspiracy of silence, which society insists upon because of its belief that it thereby safeguards existent sexual norms."[8] Within this social milieu, the adolescent who has or is developing a strong same-sex orientation has not been understood or reached out to by the health professional. This chapter offers a frame of reference and some considerations for intervention to the health professional who works with adolescents and is concerned with their developing as fully self-actualized adults.

REFERENCES

1. Barnett, Leonard. *Homosexuality, Time to Tell the Truth.* London: Victor Gollancz Ltd., 1975.
2. Berne, Eric. *What Do You Say After You Say Hello.* New York: Bantam Books, 1973.
3. Bieber, I. Homosexuality—An Adaptive Consequence of Disorder in Psychosocial Development. *Nursing Digest* Vol. III, No. 2, March/April, 1975.
4. Brown, M. and G. Fowler. *Psychodynamic Nursing,* 4th ed. Philadelphia: W. B. Saunders Co., 1971.
5. Erikson, E. H. *Childhood and Society,* 2nd ed. New York: W. W. Norton & Co., 1964.
6. Ford, C. S. and F. A. Beach. *Patterns of Sexual Behavior.* New York: Harper, 1951.
7. Goble, Frank. *The Third Force.* New York: Pocket Books, 1972.
8. Hoffman, Martin. *The Gay World, Male Homosexuality and the Social Creation of Evil.* New York: Basic Books, 1968.
9. Hoffman, Martin. The Roots of Homosexuality. In *Human Sexuality: Contemporary Perspectives,* Part IV. Palo Alto, Calif.: National Press Books, 1973.
10. James, M. and D. Jongeward. *Born to Win: Transactional Analysis with Gestalt Experiments.* Reading, Mass.: Addison-Wesley Publishing Co., 1971.
11. Marmor, J. Homosexuality and Cultural Value Systems *Nursing Digest,* Vol. III, No. 2, March/April, 1975.
12. Maslow, Abraham. *The Further Reaches of the Mind.* New York: Viking Press, 1971.
13. Mead, Margaret M. *Coming of Age in Samoa.* London: Jonathan Cape, 1929.
14. Mead, Margaret M. *Sex and Temperament.* London: Ballaneg, 1935.
15. Mead, Margaret M. *Male and Female.* New York: William Morrow, 1949.
16. Plato. *Symposium.* (trans. B. Jowett) Indianapolis: Bobbs-Merrill Co., 1956.
17. West, O. J. *Homosexuality.* West Drayton, Middlesex: Penguin Books, 1974.

17

HUMAN SEXUALITY AND AGING

Lucille Gress, R.N., M.A.

Human sexuality and aging are universal facts of life; their existence should be acknowledged by every human being. Human sexuality is more than the sex act itself; it is the total expression of the person, male or female, during his life span. Individual rights hinge on the worth and dignity of the human being, including his sexuality. Difficulty arises when an individual's rights as a human being are violated, whether it is through his own ignorance and lack of understanding or through this lack in others. In any case, to disregard sexuality is to deny the very essence of life itself; to disregard aging violates a principle that interferes with the person's will to meaning.

While questions relating to human sexuality and aging may occur at any point along the developmental continuum, the focus of this chapter is on those arising among individuals 60 years of age and older and those persons concerned about their well-being.

RIGHTS OF OLDER PERSONS

A point of reference to use in looking at some of the rights of aging persons is the Declaration of Aging Rights, formulated during the 1971 White House Conference of Aging. Participants stated:[4]

Humanity's fundamental rights are life, liberty and the pursuit of happiness. They are rights that belong to all, without regard for race or creed or sex. We declare that all people also inalienably possess these rights without regard for age.

Among the rights defined by the elderly are the following:

The right to maintain health and well-being through preventive care and education.
The right to receive assistance in times of illness or need or other emergency.

The right to peace and privacy as well as participation.
The right to live life fully and with honor — not for their age, but for their humanity.

The declaration concluded with the following statement:

This declaration is the sense of overwhelming numbers of older Americans on the occasion of the 1971 White House Conference on Aging, and to it they dedicate their solemn purpose.

This Declaration of Aging Rights is one means of creating an awareness of the perceptions and expectations of older persons. Since it was drafted by the elderly themselves, its validity is unquestioned.

Jacobson, sensing the problem of the elderly person with respect to his rights as a sexual being, wrote a Bill of Rights to Guarantee Sexual Freedom.[2] These rights are expressed in the following statements:

The right to express yourself as a sexual being.
The right to be self-confident and self-directing in regard to your sexuality.
The right to become the person you would like to be.
The right to select and be with a sex partner of your choice, whether it be of the same sex or of the opposite sex.
The right to be aware of the influence your sexuality can have on someone else and to use it in a constructive and therapeutic manner.
The right to encourage your peer group members to function as sexual beings.
The right to assist others in asserting and expressing their sexuality.
The right to be accepting and tolerant of another's sexual attitudes and preferences.
The right to assist men and women of all ages to recognize their sexuality as an integral part of their personality, inherited at conception, molded and tempered by environment, sustained by health, threatened by disease, and reversed by choice.

To ensure these rights of the elderly requires knowledge and understanding of human development. A system of beliefs, attitudes, and values that facilitate's acknowledgment of sexuality as a naturally inherent quality of the human being is also essential.

THE VALUE OF SEXUAL ACTIVITY FOR OLDER PERSONS

While the focus on human sexuality has tended to be directed toward the sexual behavior of young people, there is evidence of increasing awareness of the meaning and pattern of sexual relationships among older people. Sexual activity among the young is considered essential, primarily for the purpose of procreation. Among older persons, sexual activity tends to be valued more for its therapeutic benefits, both physically and emotionally. Elderly individuals do not necessarily have a monopoly, however, on the pleasurable aspects and therapeutic benefits of a sexual relationship. In a sense, the taboo against sex for any purpose other than procreation has affected acknowledgment of sexual activity among both old and young. While both can enjoy sex as a means of affirming sexual identity, there has been little recognition of this function of the sexual relationship among the elderly. However, studies and recent journal articles reflect increasing attention to sexuality and aging.

Some of the more important aspects of sexual relationships in the elderly are companionship and communication. Intimacy with another person involves communication through the use of touch. Touch can convey tenderness and concern; it can communicate the sense of love and belongingness essential to well-being that is often lacking in the lives of older persons. It is important that the elderly themselves, as well as others concerned for their welfare, be knowledgeable and accepting of the meaning of human sexuality throughout life. The changes of aging affect sexual response and have implications for teaching and learning as well as for counseling and guidance. Moreover, it is important to recognize and accept variations of sexual behavior as a vital part of the total expression of human sexuality among the elderly.

Older persons themselves can help update the knowledge of sexual relationships and activities among the elderly and can assist in increasing the appreciation of human sexuality in the later years. An example is an older man's account of his first sexual experience at the age of sixteen, which he described to a small group of men and women attending a conference on aging.[5] The gentleman said his first sexual experience developed out of circumstances over which he felt he had little control. Because of his ethnic and cultural background, he was bound to respect the wishes of his elders. In this case, the wishes of an older woman whose husband was out of town frequently culminated in a sexual relationship. As a young man seeking work, he found a job driving individuals home when overindulgence in alcoholic beverages made the task unsafe for them. This particular time, he was asked to drive a lady home; he had no reason to question the request. When he saw the lady safely to the door she asked him in, overriding his objections. Reluctantly entering the home, he was asked to wait while the lady bathed; when she had finished, he was requested to bathe also. Continuing to question why he should carry out the lady's wishes, yet hesitant to disregard them, he complied. When the first sexual overtures were made, he reacted by saying that he felt nothing and that he was not interested. The lady again persisted in overriding his better judgment, telling him that she would show him how to experience sexual arousal. Thus, the young man was introduced to a means of expressing his masculine sexuality.

Reviewing the experience, the gentleman elaborated on the meaning of his first sexual encounter. The experience undoubtedly would be interpreted in some cultures as the rape of a young man; he chose to view it as a positive experience, a rite of passage into manhood. As this man related the initial incident and subsequent encounters with the lady, he expressed appreciation for what she taught him. He counseled the men in the audience to take their time and to be intent on satisfying their partners. His major theme was the need for a mutually satisfying experience in the sexual relationship, which involves marked concern for the needs of the other person. He related that he and his wife continue to be sexually active. Through his premarital experience, this gentleman felt he was better prepared to meet the needs of his wife and thus sensed a positive rather than a negative outcome from the encounter. He emphasized the value of sexuality in the later years and its continued meaning in spite of the changes of aging.

During the group session in which this older gentleman recounted his initiation into manhood, other men began to describe some of their experiences and feelings to the mixed audience. One spoke of testing his sexual potency after hearing a speaker relate that diabetes mellitus often interfered with a man's capacity for sexual relations. The gentleman said that he had proved to himself, and wanted to share with the group (if his wife agreed!), that impotence was not always the case in the diabetic.

The foregoing accounts of the experiences of these elderly men were highlights of the conference. The ease with which these men spoke of the intimate details of their sexual experiences, and the way in which they did so, elevated the level of discussion to a much higher plane than is often the case when sex is the topic. A sincerity of purpose and willingness to share their feelings and actions left the audience hushed for a moment, almost in awe. There seemed to be a sensing of the spiritual aspects of human sexuality and intimate relationships that exceeded inhibitions and taboos which often seem to reduce sex to the level of gutter language and ribald response. The openness of the group facilitated discussion; most persons seemed comfortable in the situation. This kind of sharing can raise the level of consciousness about human sexuality and, it is to be hoped, will increase appreciation of its creative and rejuvenating force throughout the life cycle.

PHYSIOLOGICAL AND PSYCHOLOGICAL CHANGES

Given the function of human sexuality in conception and human development, it seems logical to consider changes of aging that influence the individual's ability to cope with his sexuality. While primary changes of aging alter the way the individual responds to his environment over time, they do not necessarily take away his desire to continue as an active participant in life's events, including sexual activities. Nor do secondary changes of aging, those occurring with disease or injury, necessarily diminish the desire to be involved in the mainstream of life. Only recently have relational, emotional, and physical aspects of the sexuality of aging begun to be explored. This development indicates a need to examine more carefully the primary and secondary changes of aging and the way they affect the older person's response to his sexuality.

Masters and Johnson sought answers to two basic questions relating to the physiologic and psychologic response of both male and female to sexual stimulation:[3]

> 1. *What phsycial reactions develop as human male and female respond to effective sexual stimulation?*
> 2. *Why do men and women behave as they do when responding to effective sexual stimulation?*

Masters and Johnson discovered marked similarities in the responses of both sexes. These similarities are categorized into four phases:[3]

1. Excitement phase — the response that develops from any source of stimulation, whether somatogenic or psychogenic.
2. Plateau phase — the phase in which sexual tensions are intensified and reach the extreme level that may culminate in orgasm.
3. Orgasmic phase — the period of involuntary climax resulting, in part, from vasoconcentration and myotonia.
4. Resolution phase — the period when tension is released and the return, through the plateau and excitement levels, to an unstimulated state takes place.

These four phases of sexual response point up the basic potential for human sexual response inherent in human beings, irrespective of sex.

PHYSIOLOGICAL CHANGES SPECIFIC TO
WOMEN

Findings of the Masters and Johnson study have implications for health professionals. Norms of the sexual response of aging women and men, established partly through the study, can be used for health education and counseling and guidance programs. Selected findings that illustrate some of the changes of aging in women that are of interest to both the elderly and health care personnel include the following:[3]

Breast. In the excitement phase, erection of the nipples, the first external evidence of increased sexual tension, is seen shortly after any form of effective sexual stimulation is begun. Additional evidence of physiological response is the production of vaginal lubrication; in the later years, there is a marked decrease in the amount of mucosal secretion. Less vasocongestion and incremental change in breast size occurs in older women than in younger women.

In the plateau phase, there is less engorgement of the areolae in older women, and it may occur in only one breast.

In the orgasmic phase, no specific reaction of the breast has been identified during orgasm.

In the resolution phase, there is loss of sex tension flush, if it has occurred. Loss of nipple erection occurs slowly. and there is rapid detumescence of the areolar tissue.

Clitoris. The clitoral response in older women is similar to patterns seen in younger women. The clitoris increases in diameter as sexual tensions rise during the excitement phase. In the plateau phase there is retraction of the clitoris and flattening of the shaft, decreasing the length of the clitoral body by approximately 50 per cent. No established reaction occurs during the orgasmic phase. During the resolution phase, retraction of the clitoris is terminated.

Bartholin's Glands. Secretory activity of the Bartholin glands is lessened, with a concomitant decrease in secretory output, after the female is several years beyond menopause.

Vagina. Involutionary changes are reflected in the thinning of the mucosa and a shortening of the vaginal length and width. There is also reported loss of expansive capacity.

Contractions of the orgasmic platform (the outer third of the vagina and the labia minora) are lessened and occur only three to five times in older women, as compared with five to ten times in younger women. The orgasmic platform is a transitory constriction of the vaginal outlet in the outer third of the vagina that helps retain seminal fluid in the vaginal barrel through a stopper-like effect. Rapid vaginal wall collapse (inner two-thirds) occurs in the resolution phase in aging women. This may be due to increasing rigidity and lack of elasticity in the vaginal barrel. Uterine contractions (cramping) with orgasm continue in aging women and may become painful.

Sexual capacity including effective sexual performance can continue well into the later years with exposure to regular, effective sexual stimulation, but because of steroid starvation, the rapidity and intensity of the physiologic response tends to be slowed.

Urethra and Urinary Bladder. Postmenopausal women may complain of burning on urination within a few hours after coition, especially if the connection is continued for extended periods of time. This distress, referred to as "bride's cystitis" in younger women, results from the mechanical irritation of the urethra and the urinary bladder by the thrusting movement of the penis. Because of the thinning of the walls of the vagina after menopause, there is less protection of the urethra and bladder from the mechanical irritation of active coition. This irritation is more likely to occur with increasing frequency if there is also lack of adequate lubrication. Many older women have a sense of urinary urgency and must urinate immediately after coition. Burning and frequency may continue for two or three days postcoition.

Knowledge of these changes of aging and understanding of their potential influence should be useful to health professionals seeking to educate and counsel aging women.

THE SEX DRIVE IN OLDER WOMEN

Evidence is increasing that the strength of the sex drive of the woman often becomes greater in the postmenopausal period. There often is an increase in sexual activity immediately postmenopause; this may be attributed partly to the androgen-estrogen hormone ratio. With decreasing estrogen levels, the androgen is thought to overcome the inhibitory action of estrogen, resulting in increased sexual desire. Lack of male partners because of physical infirmity or death becomes a problem in the 70-plus age group. Extramarital partners are less available to women in the later years. Approximately 10 per cent of women never marry, adding to the increasing number of aging women without men, which becomes a problem for elderly females desiring heterosexual relationships.

Healthy older women have sex drives that deserve attention in the assessment of needs and the planning of care. With a 4:1 ratio of women to men in the later stage of maturity, a different approach will be needed for resolution of the problem. Health professionals must be cognizant of the needs of aging women, and of the norms of human sexual response, in order to effectively discharge their responsibility to these aging persons.

THE SEX DRIVE IN OLDER MEN

According to Masters and Johnson, the major difference between the sexual response of the aging male and that of the younger man is the duration of each of the four phases of the sexual cycle.[3] The older man, especially after age 60, is slower in achieving erection and in the completion of the sex act. After age 50, there is also a lengthening of the resolution-phase refractory period; 12 to 24 hours may elapse before the male can achieve erection and ejaculation again. Nevertheless, sexual response of the male, although somewhat slowed, normally continues throughout the later years.

PHYSIOLOGICAL CHANGES SPECIFIC TO MEN

Selected findings from the Masters and Johnson study on the sexual response of older males is presented in the following paragraphs.[3] The same organizational format of the four phases of sexual response is used as was used in presenting material on the sexual response of aging women.

Penis. In the excitement phase, penile erection time is at least doubled from the three to five seconds in young males; it may triple as the male reaches the sixties and seventies. Erection may be maintained for some time without ejaculation.

In the plateau phase, penile erection may not be attained until just prior to ejaculation.

In the orgasmic phase, expulsive penile contractions are achieved through the regularly recurring contractions of muscles that expand and extend the penile urethra. The seminal fluid is forced out through the urethra and urethral meatus. Force of the ejaculatory response is decreased.

In the resolution phase, penile erection diminishes more rapidly in the older man; there is also less recognizable staging of the ejaculatory process. The refractory period is lengthened.

Scrotum. Vasocongestion of the scrotum is decreased in the older man. There are no identified specific scrotal responses in the plateau and orgasmic phases. Since full vasocongestion may not occur, a definitive resolution pattern does not occur.

Testes. After the mid-fifties, testicular elevation is lessened in the excitement and plateau phases. With spermatic cord relaxation, the contractile tone of the cremasteric musculature is lost more rapidly. There is no specific testicular reaction in the orgasmic phase. Resolution occurs more rapidly.

Ejaculation. Ejaculation is the expulsion of seminal fluid, the biological expression of the male orgasm. Usually the act involves cortical activity, but it may be reflex activity. In the older male, expulsive penile contractions are decreased in intensity and duration. Psychosexual pleasure may be lessened for the elderly male.

FACTORS IN DECREASE IN MALE SEXUAL ABILITY

Numerous physiologic and psychologic factors are involved in the involution of the aging male's sexual ability. General categories of basic alteration identified by Masters and Johnson are:[3]

1. Monotony of a repetitious sexual relationship (usually boredom with partner).

2. Preoccupation with career or economic pursuits.
3. Fatigue, mental or physical (mental fatigue is the greater inhibitor of sexual responsiveness).
4. Overindulgence in food or drugs (alcohol is the greater problem).
5. Physical and mental infirmities of either the individual or his partner (less acute problem for the man than for the aging wife with a physically infirm husband).
6. Fear of unsatisfactory performance associated with or resulting from any of these (emotional upsets or negative feelings about the sexual partner may be used as an escape mechanism).

These factors are of concern because of the male's sensitivity regarding his ability to perform sexually; he faces possible rejection if he should fail. Regular sexual activity can be carried out by a man in reasonable health well into the later decades of life. This knowledge is of importance not only because it is the basis of the male ego but also because there is a likelihood that the male will be married. The potential problem of "disuse atrophy" should be realized, because it is possible that loss of sexual capacity may occur, which could have a profound effect upon the man and his partner.

EDUCATION FOR THE OLDER PERSON
REGARDING CHANGES

The preceding paragraphs revealed findings that were in keeping with primary aging changes, such as the decrease in vaginal lubrication and thinning of the vaginal wall in older females, and the slowed response in achieving penile erection and lengthening of the resolution-refractory period in males. There is a need to educate aging adults about these expected changes, about differences in the sexual response of aging men and women, and about measures that may be used to minimize the effects of these changes. For example, the aging woman needs to know that estrogen replacement therapy may help overcome problems with painful intercourse and urinary problems caused by the mechanical irritation of the thrusting penis on the thinning vaginal wall. The aging man needs to know about the slowed response in terms of penile erection and about changes in the refractory time so he will be less apt to become depressed about these normal phenomena. Psychological reaction to changes in sexual response may contribute to problems with sexual performance (e.g., impotence) that are not totally related to sexual capacity.

SEXUAL COUNSELING FOR THE OLDER PERSON

When disturbances arise because of changing physiology, counseling and guidance may be effective. Elderly persons are usually resilient and can cope with changes if they know what to expect and how these changes may affect them. With assistance, they may work through negative feelings about changes that necessitate some adjustment in living patterns and habits of daily living. Physical changes need not be devastating. In fact, it may be that the slowed sexual response of the older man contributes to a greater sense of satisfaction for his partner. Foreplay, for example, often of short duration in the earlier years because of the rapidly building sexual tension in the male, can now be prolonged, affording the female more time to respond more fully. The longer resolution-refractory period of the male tends to decrease the frequency of sexual relations. The aging female may welcome less frequent sexual intercourse, since it may also lessen episodes of urinary problems. If both male and female can begin to understand and accept some of the physiological changes, they may experience a greater measure of physical and emotional well-being. Counseling and guidance can be a means of pointing out some of the positive aspects of aging changes and ways to continue developing a meaningful relationship, in spite of these changes. Grown children may also benefit from counseling that increases their understanding of the behavior of aging parents, as well as their own sexuality.

Another question that bears consideration is: "What are the effects of the secondary aging changes on the individual's sexual response to effective stimulation?" While it is important to have knowledge of the effects of primary aging changes on sexual response, it is also important to explore the secondary changes of aging and the influence of these changes. The aging person often struggles with his feelings about his altered self-image on the basis of primary aging changes, such as wrinkling of the skin and balding; he may become very depressed if disease conditions further alter his appearance or normal body functioning, or both. An example is the individual who has cancer of the colon that requires surgery and a permanent stoma. It becomes extremely important to explore the individual's knowledge as well as that of the partner, of what is happening; their feelings about the situation; how it is going to affect them; and ways of coping with the alteration. In one case, the wife of the patient could not accept the fact that her husband had cancer and required surgery. She refused to look at the stoma or to participate in his care in any way. A sister learned the necessary procedure for colostomy irrigations and stomal care. The man's feeling of rejection was evident. He felt guilty because plans for world travel would have to be cancelled; his wife refused to consider traveling because of the change in her husband's body function and the related daily routine. Thus, a combination of the primary and secondary changes of aging may compound the problems of the aging person and his family; comprehensive care is indicated.

Anticipatory counseling and guidance cannot be initiated in the same way with individuals experiencing secondary changes of aging as with those experiencing primary changes of aging. Disease or injury cannot be predicted to the same extent as changes occurring simply with the passage of time can be. Nevertheless, counseling and guidance can be supportive if geared toward meeting the needs of aging persons whose problems associated with primary or secondary aging have exceeded their ability to cope.

CHRONIC ILLNESS, AGING, AND SEXUALITY

Most older persons have two or more chronic conditions to contend with in addition to the "normal" aging changes. It is advisable to obtain a history that reflects life style and patterns of coping, as well as the problem areas and action taken in regard to them. Not the least of the problems may be the effects of treatment, such as prescribed medications, that interfere with sexual response. Elderly individuals may maximize their potential for continuing functional development in spite of primary and secondary changes of aging. To cope with multiple problems effectively, however, they may require assistance from health professionals in such areas as health education, procedural skills, community resources, and counseling and guidance. Many older persons have a great deal of functional ability in spite of chronic disease conditions.

The aging individual with rheumatoid arthritis is an example of a person struggling with a secondary change of aging that is superimposed upon the normal aging process. Usually, the victim is a female who is dealing with the "ravages" of time in relation to appearance, as well as with the menopause. Body image is disturbed and often has a great deal of psychological impact, whether the changes being experienced are visible to others or not.

In addition to the factors just cited, there is the effect of illness on sexuality. With arthritis, immobility caused by inflamed, painful, or stiff joints tends to affect the expression of sexuality. When there is limitation of ability to abduct and rotate the hips, it is difficult for a woman to participate in genital sex in the supine position. Medications such as tranquilizers and antihypertensives may also affect sexual response. Prolonged periods of hospitalization may create problems related to "disuse atrophy" in terms of sexual activity and capacity. These factors, coupled with a relationship that may also be strained because of the changes in the life of the partner (i.e., change in work role status and hormonal changes), have the potential to disrupt the sexual relationship further. It is essential to make a thorough assessment of the impact of chronic disease upon the affected individual and his partner as a preliminary to developing a plan of action.

Another reason for carefully assessing the individual with arthritis is to determine his capacity for sexual activity as a form of physical exercise. Evidence also suggests that regular sexual activity may help individuals with rheumatoid arthritis, probably because of the adrenal gland production of the hormone cortisone, and because of the physical activity involved.[1] Alternatives in terms of positioning and types of sex techniques used may facilitate sexual activity. This may result in less physical discomfort for the arthritic and less psychological discomfort for the partner, whose fear of increasing pain may be very distressing. Timing of pain medication, use of a warm bath prior to intercourse, and changing the time of sexual activity are additional ways of helping offset the problems. Regardless of the affected person's disability, there is a likelihood of increasing his capacity for sexual response through attention to his needs.

When there are prolonged periods of separation or of exacerbations of acute pain as well as sore muscles, masturbation may be suggested as a way of relieving sexual tension. This method of coping through manual stimulation of the sex organs can be used by either the affected individual or his partner. It is one means of avoiding the problems of disuse atrophy. Masturbation has another advantage: it generally requires less energy than the sex act itself. When physical problems are energy depleting, masturbation can be helpful as a viable option for release of sexual tension, if older individuals and health care professionals can come to an acceptance of the technique.

One of the tasks of the aging adult, as well as of the health professional, is to learn that while aging may decrease the strength of the sex drive, age itself is no detriment to the capacity for sex. Regular sexual activity with an available and interesting partner and reasonable health have been identified as crucial components of continuing sexual performance during the later years. Thus, knowledge of the primary or "normal" aging changes and their effects is essential to understanding human sexuality and aging. In addition, knowledge of the secondary changes of aging, such as cancer and arthritis, is useful in assessing sexual abilities of affected persons and assisting them with alternative ways of maximizing their capacities. Secondary changes of aging are superimposed on the primary changes and may compound problems, but measures can be taken that may enable the individual to have a meaningful experience.

CONCLUSION

Human sexuality in aging is no less real than human sexuality in youth, but it is expressed differently and serves a different purpose. Instead of the primary purpose being focused upon procreation, sexuality among the aging tends to focus upon intimacy, joy, and fulfillment, arising out of the need to relate to another human being through the sensual experience of touch. Changes in the way the four phases of sexual response are experienced need not distract from or negate the value of the intimate sexual relationship. If problems arise, the health professional should point out that there are no absolutes in sexual behavior. Rather, the emphasis should be on the value of open communication in the intimate relationship. The goal of a sexual relationship need not be coitus, but may be the pleasuring and gratification that can be exchanged by elderly persons in a reaffirmation of their humanness.

Human sexuality is an inherent quality that seeks expression in the total personality of the individual. With the increase in marriages between older persons and the questions that may arise among individuals who have been married many years, it is increasingly apparent that health professionals need to be prepared to consider continued human sexuality as a part of the normal process of aging. They must also be prepared to act accordingly, so that the rights of older persons as sexual beings may be respected.

It is important to recognize the norms of sexual capacity and performance in human beings throughout the life cycle. Human sexuality is expressed differently among older persons, but it can be enjoyed and valued as an end unto itself long after the questions and problems of procreation are inconsequential.

REFERENCES

1. Butler, Robert, N. and Myrna I. Lewis. *Sex After Sixty*. New York: Harper & Row Publishers, 1976, p. 32.
2. Jacobson, Linbania: Illness and Human Sexuality. *Nursing Outlook*, 22:52, 1974.
3. Masters, William H. and Virginia Johnson. *Human Sexual Response*. Boston: Little, Brown and Company, 1966.
4. Declaration of Aging Rights. *NRTA Journal*, November-December, 1971.
5. Presented by a participant, Hawaii Governor's Bicentennial Conference on Aging, Honolulu, Hawaii, June 7–14, 1976.

CHAPTER
18

THE ROLE OF RECONSTRUCTIVE SURGERY IN HUMAN SEXUALITY

Frank W. Masters, M.D., and Mani M. Mani, M.D.

The surgical correction of developmental abnormalities of the human sexual organs has been performed for many years. Congenital abnormalities of both the male and the female genitals have challenged the reconstructive surgeon. A variety of techniques have been developed to correct both developmental and acquired defects of the genital organs, with the ultimate aim of producing an acceptable reconstruction that can function both sexually and procreatively.

In recent years, these reconstructive horizons have been expanded with the recognition of other associated defects that are intimately related to individual sexuality but are not necessarily developmental or traumatic deformities of the external genitals per se. A great deal has been written about the surgical management of intersex problems and of gender dysphoria syndromes and the correction of a multiplicity of defects of body image that psychologically may adversely affect an individual's sexuality. This chapter reviews the evaluation and management of some of the more common defects of the external genitalia, some of the more frequently treated problems of body image, and the management of intersex and gender dysphoria syndrome. Although each is considered individually, the relationship of these entities is so close that many of the social, sexual, emotional, and procreative problems are common to all.

SURGICAL CORRECTION OF DEFECTS OF THE EXTERNAL GENITALIA

The vast majority of defects of the external genitalia are of either congenital or traumatic origin, and are associated with emotional and social as well as surgical problems. Regardless of type, it is essential to discuss the individual defect in depth either with the parents of the congenitally deformed child or with the traumatized adult. This discussion should include the description of the problem in understandable language, details of the surgical procedure contemplated, and the ultimate goals of reconstruction. Appearance and sexual and procreative ability should be reviewed, as well as the routine problems that can occur with surgery. This in-depth review is essential before any attempt at surgical reconstruction is undertaken. Both the patient and the medical team must be satisfied that a complete understanding of the goals of therapy has been established and must recognize as well those areas where the ideal may not be achieved.

The general principles of genital reconstruction include the creation of a normal-appearing organ that will function both sexually and procreatively. Even though the ideal correction is not possible in all cases, every effort should be made to approach it as nearly as possible.

Reconstruction of the Male External Genitalia

The most common congenital defects of the male genitals that are amenable to surgical reconstruction are: (1) phimosis, (2) hypospadias, and (3) epispadias.

PHIMOSIS

Phimosis is a congenital defect of the foreskin that does not allow normal mobility of the foreskin over the glans. There is often associated entrapment of smegma or other detritus, which may produce a balanitic infection of major severity. The diagnosis is best established by attempting to move the foreskin back until the entire glans is exposed. If this cannot be readily accomplished, surgical correction by either dorsal slit or circumcision is essential.

HYPOSPADIAS

This condition is due to embryonic failure of closure of the genital folds, producing an abnormal urethral opening on the ventral surface of the penile shaft anywhere from the glans to the perineum. There are two abnormalities in hypospadias that require correction: (1) abnormal opening of the external meatus on the ventral surface of the penile shaft and (2) ventral curvature of the shaft, called chordee. The surgical procedure for hypospadias should correct these two abnormalities if normal appearance and function are to be achieved. In 10 per cent of the cases of hypospadias, there is an associated upper urinary tract abnormality. Endoscopic and radiological studies should be performed routinely to rule out these defects.

Stenosis of the abnormal external meatus is presented in about 25 per cent of patients. This will need correction at an early age. Otherwise, children with hypospadias are left alone until the age of five years or just before starting school, at which time the definitive reconstruction is done. Circumcision *should not* be performed on children with hypospadias, since the preputial skin is vital to the reconstruction.

Surgical correction of hypospadias is usually performed in stages. The first stage is correction of chordee and the transposition of the preputial skin to the ventral surface of the shaft to cover the open areas. Techniques described by Edmunds[6] and Nesbit (cited in Wood-Smith[8]) are used to bring the preputial skin ventrally. Correction of chordee must be complete, and all tight bands of tissue between the hypospadiac meatus and the glans must be divided. This will, in all cases, cause the external urinary meatus to be recessed to a more proximal position. The parents must be warned of this prior to surgery. Bladder drainage is obtained by catheter through the external meatus, and both the catheter and the sutures are removed in five to seven days.

The second stage occurs six months later. At this time, urinary diversion is needed, and a perineal urethrostomy is performed as the first step in this stage. A skin-lined urethral tube can be constructed by one of many techniques. Duplay (cited in Wood-Smith[8]), Broadbent,[3] Bucknall (cited in Wood-Smith[8]), Ombrédanne (cited in Wood-Smith[8]), and Browne[4] all used skin flaps of various designs for the reconstruction. McIndoe[10] and Horton[7] described reconstructive techniques using free split-thickness and full-thickness skin grafts. Whatever the technique used, the aim of reconstruction is to achieve a penile shaft without any curvature during full erection and with the urethral opening at the tip of the glans in the normal position, and a urethral tube without strictures, fistulae, or diverticula. With careful surgical technique, absolute hemostasis, prevention of infection, and tension-free skin closure, the objectives of repair should be achieved. If this defect is not corrected, problems with self-image and peer adjustment can develop. There may also be difficulty in sexual intercourse and ejaculation if surgical correction is not done at an early age.

EPISPADIAS

Epispadias is a much less common congenital defect that consists of a failure of fusion of the anterior abdominal wall, the symphysis pubis, and the dorsum of the penile shaft. This defect, commonly associated with exstrophy of the bladder, is extremely difficult to correct surgically.

A wide variety of techniques have been described, the majority of which are aimed at the correction of the urologic defect and closure of the abdominal wall. Reconstruction of the penis is always less than ideal. Although the reconstructed organ occasionally functions sexually, it is far from normal in appearance, and procreative function is usually disturbed. This problem, however, is so rare that in-depth discussion is not warranted here.

GENITAL TRAUMA

Avulsion of genital skin is almost always due to entanglement of the victim's clothing in some type of rapidly revolving machinery. The clothing becomes twisted, and the skin of the penis and scrotum is included and is torn away with the twisted garments. Avulsion may be partial or complete and also may involve the skin of the perineum and thighs. It usually occurs in the areolar tissue plane superficial to Buck's fascia and the urethra. Pain and blood loss are not major problems in this form of injury.

Treatment of Penile Skin Avulsion. Split-thickness skin graft is the treatment of choice for repair of penile skin loss. After adequate débridement and hemostasis, a split graft measuring 20 cm. by 10 cm. and 0.020 inch in thickness is taken with a Padgett drum dermatome. The graft is sutured to the pubic area and around the corona. The seam of the graft is interdigitated and placed along the ventral line to obviate the possible complication of contracture and ventral chordee. The ends of the suture are left long and are used for a tie-over dressing in the long axis of the penile shaft. The grafted penis is dressed with a bulky dressing to maintain the organ in an erect position. The bladder is drained by an indwelling Foley catheter.

The graft is inspected after five days, and the catheter is removed two to three days later. Sexual activity may be permitted after two months.

In some instances, concomitant injuries or the patient's general condition precludes definitive repair at the time of injury. If this happens, the penile shaft is buried in a tunnel of the pubic area, and the glans is brought out through an incision in the anterior abdominal wall. This will provide adequate coverage and prevent infection. Definitive skin grafting can then be done when the patient's condition has improved.

Both the patient and his sex partner will need counseling regarding the feasibility and safety of resuming sexual intercourse. Just to say that intercourse may be resumed after a specified period of time is not adequate. Both persons will need to know exactly how the surgery was performed. Prior sexual practices should be defined so that the couple can be assured that resumption of them is safe.

Treatment of Scrotal Skin Avulsion. Scrotal avulsions may be partial or complete. In partial avulsions, the remaining skin should be brought together and sutured primarily. Scrotal skin will stretch, and in this instance primary closure under tension is justified. Split skin grafts over the testes will contract and should not be used except as the last resort. In total scrotal skin avulsion, the bare testes are best treated by liberating the cords and burying the testes in pockets above the superficial fascia of the thigh to protect spermatogenesis. Care should also be taken to create these pockets on the anterior medial aspect of the thighs and to place them at different levels. This will prevent pressure on the testes when the thighs are brought together.

In the situation of either total or partial scrotal avulsion, the patient and sexual partner will be in need of counseling. The loss of all or part of the scrotum can cause problems of self-image for the male and sexual adjustment for both the male and female. The scrotal sac is very sensitive to touch, and with damage or removal of the sac, pleasurable sensations from touching this area may be diminished or absent. It is important for the couple to know that sexual fulfillment can be achieved with patience and understanding and with experimenting in stimulating many areas of each other's body.

Reconstruction of the Female External Genital

Congenital absence of the vagina is an unusual condition of unknown cause, occurring once in 4000 live births. Acquired vaginal loss that may necessitate surgical treatment can result from fibrosis due to infection and injury, or from surgery for malignant disease of the rectum or vagina.

Congenital absence of the vagina is associated, in 25 per cent of cases, with other anomalies of the urinary or genital system. Although the ovaries are usually normal in appearance and function, the defect is usually accompanied by an absent or infantile uterus, which militates against ultimate procreative function.

The majority of such patients present at about the age of 16 or 17 with the history of absence of menstrual flow, although some may present earlier with a painful mass in the lower abdomen that increases with each menstrual cycle. In secondary cases, an appropriate history of postpartum infection, injury, or major surgery will be self-evident. Regardless of the cause, the surgical approach to vaginal reconstruction remains the same.

The reconstruction of the vagina requires the construction of an epithelium-lined tube which ideally would measure about 10 cm. in depth, and would be both elastic and distensible without discomfort, particularly during intercourse.

A wide variety of procedures have been described, many of which have proved to be unsatisfactory and have been discarded or utilized only very rarely. The most common methods of reconstruction at the present time are the use of intermittent pressure with a series of graduated obturators and operative creation of a vaginal canal, which is then lined with a split-thickness skin graft.

OBTURATION

This technique may be particularly useful in those congenital defects in which a persistent though tiny tract exists or there is a definite perineal dimple at the normal site for the vaginal opening. By the use of frequent intermittent pressure with graduated obturators, it is possible to produce sufficient stretch of the pliable perineal skin to allow the creation of a vaginal canal that can function sexually.

SURGICAL CREATION OF A VAGINAL CANAL

The surgical construction of the vaginal canal with split-thickness skin grafts was first described by Abbe in 1898 and his method, modified by McIndoe and others, remains the treatment of choice. Since regular and frequent intercourse keeps the new vaginal passage patent, most authorities recommend that the surgical procedure be done just before the patient's marriage.[1, 11]

The operative procedure consists of the creation of a blind pocket between the rectum and bladder, which is then lined with a split-thickness skin graft, taken usually from the buttock or thigh, and maintained in position by an indwelling stent. These molds or obturators may be constructed of a variety of materials, but must be constructed so that both the urethra and the rectum are protected from injury due to pressure.

Since all split-thickness skin grafts tend to contract within the first six months postoperatively, stricture and stenosis of the new cavity will occur if dilation is not continued for at least six to eight months following reconstruction. Thus, postoperative obturation is essential to maintain the reconstructed canal. An internal stent must be worn constantly for at least three months, and thereafter daily dilation by either obturation or an active sex life continues to be necessary to maintain patency.

If the uterus and ovaries are normal, menstruation may be possible, and also conception. If conception does take place, delivery should be accomplished by cesarean section.

CORRECTION OF SEXUALLY ORIENTED DEFECTS
OF BODY IMAGE

The entire field of aesthetic surgery has developed as a result of an increasing demand for the correction of a wide variety of defects in body image. Since there is no functional indication for the correction of these psychologically oriented defects, reconstruction is predicated upon the creation of a new image that is aesthetically pleasing to the individual.

As for all socially, sexually, and emotionally oriented deformities, patients exhibiting concern over defects in body image require careful preoperative evaluation and preparation. This evaluation must include realistic discussion of the limitations of the procedure, as well as the patient's expectations from surgery. Motivation, needs, and emotional goals must be part of the overall preoperative review, and the health care team must be as certain as possible that the patient desires body image alteration because of an innate need rather than because of pressures exerted externally by partner or peers.

Sexually oriented defects of body image other than those associated directly with the external genitalia are generally associated with abnormalities of both the male and female breast, and again the method of reconstruction will vary widely depending upon the individual defect.

Reconstruction of the Female Breast

The demand for aesthetic reconstruction of the female breast has increased markedly in recent years with the development of the nonreactive silicones that have been widely used in breast augmentation and in breast reconstruction following mastectomy. This increasing interest in breast reconstruction has also increased the number of requests for the reduction breast plasty. This new demand has, in turn, produced a variety of new techniques that allow generous reduction of the massive hypertrophy while at the same time allowing a socially and sexually acceptable appearance which preserves shape and sensation.

MICROMASTIA

The augmentation breast plasty is without a doubt the most frequently performed of all aesthetic reconstructions of the breast. This defect of body image has been intensified by the modern advertising agencies that promote the "full figure," in total contradistinction to the so-called flapper era of the 1920's, when the flat-chested look was in vogue and the young women even bound their chests to reduce their figure. As a result of the interest in the larger breast, modern clothes are designed for women with a well-defined figure.

The vast majority of women who seek augmentation are in the age range of 23 to 33 years, are married with at least one child, and do not usually desire reconstruction to improve sexual relations, but to correct their own dissatisfaction with their appearance and their inability to look well in clothes. If a woman comments that she is having breast augmentation to please a husband or boyfriend or to enhance sexual relations, this couple may be in need of marital counseling to better understand their relationship.

The procedure involves the careful, symmetrical insertion of a silicone-gel prosthesis into a pocket created immediately beneath the breast at the level of the pectoral fascia. Augmented breasts have a variable level of persistent firmness. If care is taken, infection or rejection from any source is quite unusual. Unfortunately, in some areas, the augmentation procedure has fallen into disrepute because of the complications coincident with indiscriminate silicone injection. Such injection is potentially dangerous, because medical-grade silicone is not available for injection into the breast.

Once established within their appropriate pockets, these prostheses have produced little if any difficulty, and the majority of women are quite pleased with the finite contour. Pregnancy and even lactation have not produced untoward results with the prostheses, and there is no evidence that these implants have increased the incidence of malignant disease. Women who have had silicone implants placed beneath the breast tissue should be taught to perform self-examination of their breasts on a routine basis. Because the breasts may be more firm, it may be more difficult to detect a lump in the breast tissue.

MACROMASTIA

The basic indications for reduction breast plasty include disproportionate size, pain in the shoulders from strap irritation, recurrent backache from weight of the breasts, and recurrent or persistent pain in the breast. Although size bears no relationship to ability to lactate, there is some relationship to sensuality. The larger breasts do show a marked reduction in nipple sensation, probably on the basis of constant stretch. Although this reduced sensation may not be altered by reconstruction, the sensory deficit is outweighed by the immediate reduction in overall discomfort and the general improvement in the subjective body image defect.

The operative procedures designed to reduce the breast have undergone considerable revision as the demand has increased in recent years. The most widely accepted methods of reduction produce approximately a 50 per cent reduction in breast size, with preservation of the nipple but with the sacrifice of lactation potential. This is because the nipples are transplanted, necessitating the division of the ductile system and negating the ability to nurse.

Massive hypertrophy of the breast does not lend itself well to the usual forms of reduction breast plasty but can be successfully treated with partial amputation and free nipple graft. These procedures do destroy both the ability to nurse and the erotic sensation of the nipple. The comfort factor is so striking, however, that this loss of sensation and lactation is but a minor annoyance. Although all such operative procedures are quite extensive and demand a careful preoperative evaluation, the uncomplicated recovery period is generally short, and the improvement in general well-being is apparent almost immediately.

Gynecomastia

Although a minimal degree of mammary hypertrophy is a normal phenomenon in the male breast during infancy and adolescence, involution usually occurs by the age of 20 years. If involution does not occur, idiopathic gynecomastia is present, providing a multitude of social pressures that necessitate endocrinologic workup and careful surgical mastectomy.

In secondary gynecomastia, the disease is associated with benign or malignant tumors of the adrenal gland, testicular tumors (especially chorioepithelioma), teratomas or other interstitial cell tumors, certain liver diseases, and prostatic carcinoma treated with estrogens. The exact hormonal influence is obscure, and malignant degeneration has not been reported.

Treatment of this condition varies. A conservative attitude should be adopted toward this finding in the younger age group, since this is a normal phenomenon during puberty. Endocrine therapy has been used but is uniformly unsuccessful. In secondary gynecomastia, treatment is directed toward the primary problem.

Surgical treatment is advised if the hypertrophy persists more than two years. Young males affected by gynecomastia are frequently chided by their classmates; the occurrence of this deformity at a critical psychological period of an adolescent's life may result in emotional scars if it is not properly treated.

With this in mind, the surgical treatment that is advised should be carried out in a cosmetic manner. The submammary curvilinear incision introduced 13 centuries ago by Paulus Aeginata has been replaced by the less visible periareolar incision.[5, 13] Pitanguy[12] preferred a transareolar incision, transversely bisecting the areola and the nipple. Though most cases of gynecomastia are amenable to excision with this limited exposure, for the massive ones resembling the female breast, Letterman and Schureter[9] have advised larger oblique resection and transposition of the areola upward and medially, as in the reduction mammoplasty of Dufourmentel and Mouly (cited in Rees[5]). Whatever the incision, a factor that is equally important is the leaving of adequate tissue behind the areola to resemble the normal male contour. This also prevents adhesion of the areola to the chest wall.

The main indication for the surgical removal of an enlarged breast in the male is to rid the patient of the associated psychological stigmata rather than simply to remove an abnormal mass. To achieve this, surgery should be accurate and should leave little evidence to remind the patient of his previous physical condition. A patient operated on for gynecomastia should feel no hesitation in exposing his chest when required.

Surgery is performed under general anesthesia. Although exposure is limted through the periareolar incision, adequate total excision is possible. It is important to leave a disc of tissue behind the areola to maintain vascular viability. Hemostasis should be complete, since hematoma is one of the main complications of resection. Suction drainage and elastic compression are routinely used. If a hematoma develops in spite of these measures, the area should be re-explored under anesthesia. Necrosis of the nipple and adhesion of areola to the pectoral fascia are the other complications.

SURGICAL TREATMENT OF INTERSEX AND GENDER DYSPHORIA

Although quite separate, the problems of intersex and gender dysphoria are often confused and are frequently considered to be the same because the surgical reconstruction is identical. The surgical sex assignment procedures are technically the same whether the individual has a developmental intersex problem or the psychologically based situation that makes up the so-called gender dysphoria syndrome.

Intersex Problems

The pragmatic and operative problems that have euphemistically been categorized under the broad term of "intersex" consist of those congenital abnormalities of both the external and internal sexual organs that produce diagnostic confusion and complicate the sex assignment of the newborn child. Sex assignment generally occurs in the delivery room or the newborn nursery, and it is most commonly based upon a brief and often superficial examination of the external genitalia. This will then be reported to the parents, starting the gender identity wheels in motion as the entire family begins to prepare the child for its newly assigned sexuality.

When there is an apparent abnormality of the external genitalia, all too often sex assignment may be based only upon cellular chromosomal patterns, which give evidence of the predominant endocrine function, and, therefore, of gender, without consideration for externally developed gender identity or the social effects of sexual ambiguity. Whenever there is a question of genital abnormality, definitive decision regarding ultimate sex assigment must be deferred until an ultimate decision can be made based upon scientific evidence, parental consultation, reconstructive feasibility, and underlying pathologic defect, if discernible. This decision must be made as soon as possible, of course.

In general, careful and realistic parental consultation will allow deferral of sex announcement to other family members and friends and will give the time needed to arrive at a definite decision. This may be very difficult for parents to do, and they need assistance from the health care team. The parents can tell friends and relatives that there is confusion about the sex of the infant because of ambiguous external sex organs. They can continue by saying that further studies will be done before the sex is definitively assigned.

The deformity itself may define the necessary reconstructive procedure. As a rule of thumb, reconstruction of female sexual organs, if plausible, is the procedure of choice. The procedures involved are not as complex as those for reconstruction of male organs; fewer stages are involved; and the ultimate result from both an appearance and a sexual point of view is better. Unfortunately, procreative ability is almost always sacrificed if the intersex problem is of sufficient severity to warrant surgical reconstruction.

Gender Dysphoria

Gender dysphoria is the name generally applied to the psychological problems of sex assignment that include transsexualism, or sex role inversion (see Chapter 15), transvestism, and the various forms of sexual assignment denial. The vast majority of these problems do not lead to surgical sex reassignment. In fact, many of these individuals have no desire for sex change procedures but function well within their own particular frame of sexual identification and sexual need.

The transsexual, however, is the leading candidate for surgical sex reassignment. A very careful preoperative evaluation is required, usually accomplished best in an established gender dysphoria clinic with a trained team consisting ideally of a psychologist, psychiatrist, social worker, nurse clinician, internist, gynecologist, urologist, and plastic surgeon.

The true transsexual can be best described as a psychological sexual anomaly, in that the individual has a psychological gender identification of one sex and the physical sexual organs of the other. This "wolf in sheep's clothing" abnormality, if firmly established, can be altered surgically to coincide more closely with the desired physiological gender identification by means of the various well-established sex change procedures.

More important, however, is the preoperative evaluation and preparation of such individuals. Some of the criteria that have been established by various gender dysphoria clinics as indications for sex change surgery include:

1. Careful evaluation of the client's understanding of his condition and of anticipated changes.
2. Careful psychological evaluation and full testing.
3. Complete psychiatric evaluation.
4. Cross-dressing for at least one year.
5. Continued role portrayal for one year.
6. Complete social review of background and living patterns.

Age and general physical condition must also be considered, since such surgery historically has been performed in the majority of instances on patients between the ages of 20 and 30 years. The demand for surgical sex alteration decreases precipitously after 30; the reasons for this decrease are not well understood.

Although all the various ramifications of human sexuality obviously play a very important role in the selection of patients for surgical sex change procedures, it is not within the scope of this chapter to detail all the problems that must be solved prior to approval of any candidate for sex change. Since sex change procedures for gender dysphoria include surgical castration, all such aspects must be considered very carefully before elective surgical reconstruction is begun.

Surgical Sexual Reconstruction

The procedures designed to reconstruct the sexual organs are similar whether the individual problem falls into the broad category of congenital malformations known as intersex or into that defined as gender dysphoria. Although a complete description of the various methods available for such correction is also beyond the scope of this presentation, certain general anatomical principles apply to virtually all such procedures:

1. If possible, the base of the clitoris or penis should be preserved for purposes of sexual stimulation.
2. The urethra must be protected to insure continued urinary continence.
3. Postoperative hormone therapy is essential.

In addition to these general principles, the procedures must vary depending upon the sexual reconstruction that is being performed. If the individual is a genetic male who is being converted into a female, the penile skin is used to reconstruct the labia minora, and the scrotum is used to produce the labia majora. The vagina is usually reconstructed by use of a skin graft, although again penile skin has been utilized in the well-developed transsexual.

The transformation of female to male is a much more difficult program and fraught with many more complications. In general, however, a vaginectomy is performed; unfortunately, this tissue is of little use in the overall reconstructive program. The labia majora can be utilized to reconstruct a scrotum, and Silastic implants are available for testicular simulation.

Reconstruction of the penis is difficult, however, and requires a multistaged tube pedicle transfer from the groin to the pubis, followed by urethral reconstruction with a skin graft. Sexual function can be obtained by Silastic rod implantation, but the tube pedicle is insensitive, and sexual feeling, if any, will be produced by pressures on the residual clitoral elements.

Since the female to male reconstruction is so much more complicated, it is estimated that less than 50 per cent of the female transsexuals undergo the entire gamut of surgical reconstruction.

CONCLUSION

Surgical corrections performed on persons for congenital abnormalities, traumatic injuries, defects of body image, and intersex and gender dysphoria are similar in that they affect how one views oneself and how one relates to others. They are therefore directly related to human interaction and sexuality. Counseling patients and significant persons in their lives is as important as the surgical procedure itself. For if persons cannot adjust to changes that have occurred or will occur because of the surgery, then the assistance for the patients and families is not complete.

REFERENCES

1. Abbe, R. A New Method for Creating a Vagina in a Case of Congenital Absence. *Medical Record*, 54:836, 1898.
2. Blair, V. T. and L. T. Byars. Hypospadias and Epispadias. *Journal of Urology*, 40:814, 1938.
3. Broadbent, T. R., R. M. Woolf, and E. Toksu. Hypospadias—One Stage Repair. *Plastic and Reconstructive Surgery*, 27:154, 1961.
4. Browne, D. Operation for Hypospadias. *Post Graduate Medical Journal*, 25:367, 1949.
5. Doufourmentel, L. cited in Rees, T. D. Plastic Surgery of the Breast. In: Converse, J. M. (ed.). *Reconstructive Plastic Surgery*, 2nd ed. Vol. 7. Philadelphia: W. B. Saunders Co., 1977.

6. Edmunds, A. An Operation for Hypospadias. *Lancet,* 1:447, 1913.
7. Horton, C. E. and C. J. Devine. A One Staged Repair for Hypospadias Cripple. *Plastic and Reconstructive Surgery,* 45:425, 1970.
8. Wood-Smith, D. Hypospadias: Some Historical Aspects and the Evolution of Techniques of Treatment. In: Converse, J. M. (ed.). *Reconstructive Plastic Surgery,* 2nd ed. Vol. 7. Philadelphia: W. B. Saunders Co., 1977.
9. Letterman, A. and M. Schureter. Surgical Correction of Massive Gynecomastia. *Plastic and Reconstructive Surgery,* 49:259, 1972.
10. McIndoe, A. H. An Operation for the Cure of Adult Hypospadias. *British Medical Journal,* 1:385, 1937.
11. McIndoe, A. H. Treatment of Congenital Absence and Obliterative Condition of the Vagina. *British Journal of Plastic Surgery,* 6:89, 1950.
12. Pitanguy, I. Transareolar Incision for Gynecomastia. *Plastic and Reconstructive Surgery,* 38:414, 1966.
13. Webster, J. P. Mastectomy for Gynecomastia Through a Semicircular Intra-areolar Incision. *Annals of Surgery,* 124:557, 1946.

CHAPTER 19

SEX FOR THE CARDIAC PATIENT

R. L. Clancy, Ph.D., and
Mary Quinlan, R.N., B.S.N., M.S.

Although the sex act is an important aspect of living, the attitudes of our society have impeded the acquisition of an understanding of the physiological changes associated with it. Consequently, many health care personnel have avoided counseling the cardiac patient and sexual partner about re-establishing appropriate and satisfactory sexual activity following a cardiovascular accident. Fortunately, society's sexual attitudes are rapidly changing, with the result that many patients and partners want to have the opportunity to discuss the physiological and psychological aspects of the sex act with qualified health care people. Therefore it is important that health care personnel acquire the necessary knowledge to dispel any myths the patient and partner have regarding the dangers of sexual intercourse and to educate them in re-establishing a satisying sex life. The objective of this chapter is to provide health care personnel with information regarding: (1) the cardiovascular and respiratory changes accompanying the sex act; (2) the effects of pharmacological and surgical treatments on sexual activity; and (3) sexual counseling for the cardiac patient and sexual partners.

PHYSIOLOGY OF THE SEX ACT

Although the first published report of the cardiovascular changes during coitus appeared in 1896,[13] very few investigations were carried out in the ensuing 60 years. However, in the last 20 years the results of several studies have appeared in the literature.[1, 5, 6, 10, 11, 14] In general, these studies have involved young healthy subjects performing the sex act with their normal partner. The physiological changes have been correlated with the four phases of the sex act: (1) excitement—erotic arousal or foreplay; (2) plateau or intromission; (3) orgasm; and (4) resolution.[12] Progression through the first three phases of the sex act is

249

usually accompanied by progressive increases in several cardiovascular and respiratory parameters. Littler and coworkers[11] observed the following average maximal increases in seven normal subjects: (1) heart rate—71 per cent; (2) systolic blood pressure—59 per cent; and (3) diastolic blood pressure—42 per cent. Following orgasm, i.e., during the resolution phase, these parameters returned to precoital levels or below in 20 to 120 seconds, the average time being 42 seconds. Fox and Fox[6] observed respiratory changes during the sex act consisting of an increased frequency of breathing and a slight increase in tidal volume. Oxygen consumption increased approximately 500 per cent. Maximal minute volumes occurred during orgasm in males, whereas in the females they were maximal during intromission, with brief periods of apnea occurring during orgasm. The time required for the minute volume to return to a normal level during the resolution phase was usually longer than the time required for the cardiovascular parameters to return to precoital levels. These observations suggest than an oxygen debt occurred during the sex act.

An increase in myocardial energy consumption necessitates the delivery of more substrates and oxygen to the myocardial cells so that energy production can be increased to the same extent as energy consumption. The principal manner in which this is achieved is by an increase in coronary blood flow. If myocardial oxygen requirements exceed oxygen delivery, myocardial oxygen deficiency (hypoxemia) ensues. Myocardial hypoxemia may be manifested as chest pains (angina pectoris) and, if the hypoxemia is severe, may result in cardiac arrhythmias. Cardiac arrhythmias decrease the pumping capacity of the heart, which intensifies myocardial hypoxemia, giving rise to more arrhythmias and possibly ventricular fibrillation. Thus, the capacity to increase coronary blood flow and thereby increase oxygen delivery to the heart is an important physiological adjustment for maintenance of sexual activity.

Although there are no direct measurements establishing the mechanisms of the cardiovascular changes associated with sexual activity, it is likely that they are a result of increased sympathetic activity. It is well established that increases in sympathetic nerve activity increase heart rate, arterial blood pressure, and the inotropic state of the heart. These changes increase the energy consumption of the heart.[3]

Systemic hypoxia, i.e., a decreased arterial oxygen concentration, can lead to myocardial hypoxemia also. One cause of systemic hypoxemia is impaired pulmonary function. A decrease in the rate of delivery of oxygen to the alveoli under resting conditions or the inability to increase ventilation sufficiently when oxygen demands are increased can occur in patients with asthma, chronic bronchitis, pulmonary fibrosis, or pulmonary emphysema. A second cause of systemic hypoxemia is impairment of the movement of oxygen from the alveoli into the pulmonary capillaries. This is the underlying pathologic process in pulmonary emphysema and pulmonary edema. It is conceivable that the latter may become more pronounced during sexual activity because of an increased pulmonary capillary blood pressure. Pulmonary shunting, that is, a less than optimal relationship between ventilation and perfusion of each area of the lung, will result in systemic hypoxia. Finally, systemic hypoxia can result from a decreased hemoglobin concentration (anemia) or an impairment in oxygen combination with hemoglobin. In summary, myocardial hypoxemia during the sexual act may be the result of inadequate coronary blood flow or decreased arterial oxygen content, or both.

The preceding discussion of cardiovascular and respiratory changes accompanying sexual activity is based primarily on data obtained from normal subjects. The factors causing myocardial hypoxemia and cardiac arrhythmias are based primarily on observations in laboratory animals. However, it is reasonable to assume that these physiological changes in the cardiac patient during sexual activity are directionally similar to those of the normal person and that myocardial hypoxemia engenders the same effects as in the laboratory animal.

Very few studies of the cardiovascular changes during sexual intercourse in the cardiac patient have been reported. Hellerstein and Friedman[10] studied middle-aged males suffering from arteriosclerotic heart disease. Sixty per cent of the subjects reported an awareness of extreme tachycardia or the development of angina pectoris during the sexual activity. Continuous electrocardiograph tape recordings over a period of 24 to 48 hours revealed that in some patients sexual activity was accompanied by tachycardia, ST segment displacement, and premature ventricular systoles. Of interest was that in some subjects, comparable electrocardiographic changes occurred during brisk walking or emotionally stressful situations. Presumably these changes were attributable to myocardial hypoxemia resulting from myocardial oxygen consumption exceeding oxygen delivery to the heart.

EFFECTS OF PHARMACOLOGICAL AND SURGICAL TREATMENTS ON SEXUAL ACTIVITY

In the course of treating the cardiac patient by pharmacological methods, sexual activity may be modified.[17] A common pharmacological approach to alleviating hypertension is to modify the activity of the autonomic nervous system. Parasympathetic cholinergic nerve impulses facilitate penile erection in the male and vascular engorgement and swelling of the lower external genital tract in the female. The sympathetic adrenergic nerves promote ejaculation in the male. Consequently, drugs blocking adrenergic nerves (sympatholytic drugs) impair ejaculation, whereas anticholinergic drugs impair penile erection and vaginal engorgement. Ganglionic blocking agents impair both penile erection and ejaculation. Alteration of the female's sympathetic system with reserpine blocks ovulation and may induce lactation. Treatment of the depressed female cardiac patient with antidepressant drugs may enhance sexual drive, but concomitantly these drugs may decrease sexual function because of their effects on the autonomic nervous system. The overanxious cardiac patient may be treated with sedatives or tranquilizers. Such treatment may result in decreased libido, impotence, delayed ovulation, and prolonged amenorrhea. These effects are a result of the drugs' affecting the autonomic nervous systems and the hypothalamus, with attendant changes in certain endocrine glands. The use of the diuretic spironolactone to treat hypertension may produce amenorrhea or impotence.

Surgical procedures for correction of problems affecting the cardiovascular system may have secondary effects on sexual activity. The implantation of a cardiac pacemaker may limit the patient's sexual activity if the pacemaker is not properly set.[4] If the pacemaker is of fixed-rate type, it should be set at a rate equal to or slightly greater than the heart rate attained during sexual activity. In the case of the demand-type pacemakers, the demand set should be sufficient for the heart rate attained during sexual activity. The necessary settings can be established by determining the heart rate requirements for a level of exercise that produces cardiovascular changes comparable to those attained during coitus. The sex partner should be assured that she or he cannot be harmed electrically by the pacemaker.

Cardiac surgery for congenital or acquired heart disease may initially impinge upon sexual activity because of the discomfort associated with tension on the chest incision. However, once the postoperative convalescence period has passed, sexual activity will be normal or even enhanced. Severe atherosclerosis may impair blood flow to the sex organs, resulting in difficulty in producing or sustaining an erection or both. Surgical correction may result in restoration of normal sexual performance.

SEXUAL REHABILITATION AND COUNSELING

Although much of the following discussion relates to the rehabilitation and counseling of the myocardial infarction patient regarding sex, the principles are applicable to patients with other types of cardiac problems. The goals of this program are (1) to restore the patient to an optimal physiological and psychological state in relation to sexual performance and (2) to assist the sexual partner in adjusting her or his sexual role such that it is mutually satisfying.

SEXUAL HISTORY

The first step toward fulfilling these goals is for the health care team to obtain a complete sex history from the patient and partner. The time at which the sex history is taken is very important. Interviewing the patient or partner during the acute phase of a myocardial infarction or before establishing rapport is inadvisable. Alternatively, if obtaining a sex history is delayed too long, the patient or partner may consider sex as being unimportant and may therefore be less cooperative. The patient's marital status—single, divorced, or widowed—should not preclude obtaining a sex history. The attitude of many people that sex is a very private matter may necessitate that the interviewer and interviewee be of the same sex.

Second, questions may need to be very nondirective. For example, an aspect of sexuality can be introduced by suggesting how many people feel about it and then asking the patient or partner how he or she feels about that particular subject. The age, physical condition, and cultural, religious, and educational backgrounds should be considered. Sex terminology should be commensurate with the person's cultural, religious, and educational background. The quality of the couple's relationship and the frequency of sexual intercourse before the illness should be obtained. The health professional must be fully aware of his attitudes toward sexuality and endeavor to prevent these attitudes from affecting his ability to obtain an accurate and complete sex history. One way that the interviewer can enhance his effectiveness in obtaining a sex history is to "role-play" with another health team member. The use of videotape recordings can be of great value in correcting hesitancies, vocal tone changes, and facial expressions that might suggest to the patient or partner that the interviewer is uncomfortable with a particular aspect of sexual discussion.[8]

MASTURBATION THERAPY

In general, physical rehabilitation and sex counseling should be begun after the patient has passed the acute stage of illness. At this time the patient may be depressed because of the fear that he will no longer be able to fulfill his role in society. The patient may compensate for this feeling of uselessness by exhibiting inappropriate sex behavior. The "dirty old man in room 250" and the "lady in the scanty red nightgown" are familiar to most health care personnel. This behavior should be viewed as an improvement in the patient's mental state, and the patient should be encouraged to modify this behavior by showing affection for his partner or by undertaking masturbation, or both.[18]

To achieve these goals, attempts should be made to provide the patient with adequate privacy at set times of the day. The feasibility of encouraging masturbation must take into consideration the patient's attitudes toward masturbation and his physical condition. If the patient accepts masturbation as an outlet for his sexuality, he should be instructed in how to take his pulse. Initially, masturbation can be continued until the heart rate increases approximately 20 beats per minute. The intensity and duration of masturbation can be gradually increased in the ensuing weeks until ejaculation or orgasm occurs. The patient should be counseled that if dyspnea or angina occurs, masturbation should be stopped and a member of the health care team consulted. If appropriate the partner may be counseled about participating with the patient in masturbating. The advantages of a masturbation program are (1) the patient regains self-confidence in his or her sexuality; (2) the transition to sexual intercourse is facilitated; (3) the partner's fears regarding his or her role in the sex act are alleviated; and (4) some physical rehabilitation is accomplished, since the cardiovascular and respiratory stress of masturbating may approach that occurring during normal sexual intercourse.[16]

SEVERITY OF DISEASE IN REHABILITATION

The intensity of the physical rehabilitation program should be based on the severity of the patient's cardiovascular disease. Measurements of oxygen consumption during standardized exercise methods and simultaneous electrocardiographic monitoring can be used as a guide for counseling the patient regarding when sexual activity is permissible.[2] If the patient can attain a level of exercise that increases oxygen consumption five to six times without dyspnea, angina, or significant electrocardiogram changes, sexual intercourse can probably be resumed. Other techniques for monitoring physical fitness can be used if the facilities do not permit this degree of quantification. For example, if the patient can climb two flights of stairs without any ominous symptoms, sexual intercourse is probably permissible. If the patient is judged to be in class I or class II heart failure, normal sexual activity can be resumed. The class III patient should be advised to modify his or her sexual performance by maximizing the use of foreplay and extracoital techniques prior to intercourse. This will result in decreasing the duration of intercourse and thereby decrease oxygen consumption. Sexual intercourse is usually inadvisable for the class IV patient.[10] This patient should be counseled to restrict his or her sexual activity to stroking, caressing, and assisting the partner in masturbation. The patient and partner should be counseled not to engage in sexual activity if the patient has had a large meal within the last three hours, has been drinking alcoholic beverages, is fatigued, or is emotionally upset. The married patient should be informed that extramarital sex is to be avoided, since it is believed that the physiological stress is greater than with the normal partner.[15] For the single, divorced, or widowed patient, sexual activity should be confined to situations that minimize emotional and physical stress.

It is generally believed that the physiological stress of sexual intercourse can be decreased by modifying the body position. For example, the positions of: (1) patient and partner lying side by side; (2) the patient in an armless chair with the partner sitting on his or her legs facing him; or (3) the patient lying on his or her back with the partner kneeling above have been recommended because they decrease the patient's oxygen consumption and cardiovascular stress. However, a recent study indicates that the change in arterial blood pressure and heart rate of the normal male are the same for the "male-on-top" and "male-on bottom" positions.[14] Although these observations have not been confirmed, they suggest that if the male patient feels inferior assuming the "male-on-bottom" position, the sex counselor may want to advise him to try the "male-on-top" position.

DRUGS IN SEXUAL REHABILITATION

It was mentioned previously that sexual inadequacy may result from the use of certain drugs. In many patients receiving these drugs the physiological stresses of the sex act may be of no concern. The health care team should consider counseling these patients in the use of artificial devices. For example, the impotent male might consider using a dildo to achieve a satisfying sex life for himself and his partner.

Drugs can be employed to enhance the sexual performance of the cardiac patient. Nitroglycerin taken prior to intercourse may prevent development of angina by attenuating the increase in arterial blood pressure and thereby reducing the increase in myocardial oxygen consumption.[7] Simultaneously, the coronary vasodilating properties of the drug enhance oxygen delivery to the heart muscle cells. Propranolol administered prophylactically reduces the increase in myocardial oxygen consumption during coitus by lessening the increase in heart rate and arterial blood pressure.[6]

RESPONSE OF PARTNER

A heart attack affects not only the life style of the patient but that of the partner as well. The partner's role in the family unit may be reversed or augmented. The partner may be depressed because he or she feels responsible for the heart attack, particularly if it occurred during sexual intercourse. Alternatively, the partner may respond to new roles by becoming overprotective of the patient. The patient in turn may resent this behavior. The health care team must decide whether to resolve these problems by counseling the patient and sexual partner together or separately. An additional approach may be to place the partner with a group of individuals having similar concerns.[9] This group approach can be beneficial provided that the cultural and educational backgrounds of the members are similar. However, the partner should also be afforded the opportunity of discussing sexual concerns on an individual basis with a member of the health care team.

SEX IN THE ELDERLY

Unfortunately, there are many health care personnel who feel that sexual counseling for the elderly is not important. This may be due to the fallacy that sex ceases with receipt of the first Social Security check. There is considerable evidence that this is not the case. Therefore, it is important that this group be counseled also. The counselor must be aware that the nature and frequency of sexual expression may be different for the older patient or partner. (See Chapter 17.)

The health care team should recognize that their role in sex counseling and sex rehabilitation extends beyond the hospital and the period of convalescence. Therefore, it is important that they establish a means of being available for future counseling. They may wish to establish a program for return visits by the patient or partner, or both. Alternatively, home visits may be appropriate in some cases.

It is possible that upon leaving the hospital the patient's care will be continued by other health care personnel. In this case, it may be advisable to notify these people of the nature of the sexual counseling carried out previously.

Although the foregoing discussion has emphasized the cardiac patient, it should be recognized that the principles of sexual counseling are applicable to other patients. The nature of the counseling program will in part be determined by the nature of the disease.

SUMMARY

There is a consensus that sexual activity is an important aspect of life. It is also well established that increases in heart rate, arterial blood pressure, and respiratory minute volume accompany sexual activity. These physiological changes place an additional stress on the cardiovascular system to the extent that sexual activity may be impaired in the patient with coronary artery disease, pulmonary dysfunction, atherosclerosis, rheumatic heart disease, or hypertension. In addition, drug therapy and surgical correction for cardiovascular problems may decrease sexual competence. The health care team can help patients with these problems to re-establish a satisfactory sex life in the following manner.

A complete history should be obtained, including the underlying pathologic process; the patient's cultural, religious, and educational background; marital status; and sexual attitudes. In addition, the patient's usual sex partner should be interviewed regarding his or her needs for a satisfactory sex life. The members of the health care team involved should be predicated in part on the patient's and the partner's attitudes regarding sex. It is important that the health care team recognize that this information should be obtained irrespective of the patient's age, sex, or marital status; that is, contrary to popular beliefs (1) sexual activity does not terminate upon receipt of the first Social Security check, (2) sexual incompetence resulting from cardiovascular problems is not confined to the male, and (3) the single, divorced, or widowed patient does have normal sexual needs.

Once an adequate sex history has been obtained, the health care team should work together in counseling the patient and sex partner. It is important to recognize that various counseling methods, based on the counselees' sexual attitudes, may be needed to help the patient and partner re-establish a satisfactory sex life. Counseling should consist of informing the patient of the physiologic changes he or she may experience and how to cope with them. This may entail placing the patient on a standardized stress-testing program to ascertain when normal sexual activity can be resumed. The patient should be apprised of those conditions that place an additional stress on the cardiovascular system and consequently adversely affect sexual activity. Of importance is counseling of the sex partner to recognize his or her sexual concerns. With proper physical rehabilitation and sex counseling, the physical aspect of the sex act need be no more taxing, and certainly much more satisfying, than climbing a flight of stairs.

REFERENCES

1. Bartlett, R. G., Jr. Physiologic Responses during Coitus. *Journal of Applied Physiology,* 9:469, 1956.
2. Brammell, H. L. and A. Niccoli. A Physiologic Approach to Cardiac Rehabilitation. *Nursing Clinics of North America,* 11:223, 1976.
3. Braunwald, E. Control of Myocardial Oxygen Consumption. *American Journal of Cardiology,* 27:416, 1971.
4. Cortes, Tara Siegal. Pacemakers Today. *Nursing '74,* February, 1974, p. 31.
5. Fox, C. A. Reduction in the Rise of Systolic Blood Pressure During Human Coitus by the B-Adrenergic Blocking Agent, Propranolol. *Journal of Reproduction and Fertility,* 22:587, 1970.
6. Fox, C. A. and B. Fox. Blood Pressure and Respiratory Patterns during Human Coitus. *Journal of Reproduction and Fertility,* 19:405, 1969.
7. Green, A. W. Sexual Activity and the Post Myocardial Infarction Patient. *American Heart Journal,* 89:246, 1975.
8. Green, R. Taking a Sexual History. In: Green, R., ed. *Human Sexuality — A Health Practitioner's Text.* Baltimore: Williams & Wilkins Co., 1975.

9. Harding, A. L. and M. A. Morefield. Group Intervention for Wives of Myocardial Infarction Patients. *Nursing Clinics of North America,* 11:339, 1976.

10. Hellerstein, H. K. and E. H. Friedman. Sexual Activity and the Post Coronary Patient. *Archives of Internal Medicine,* 125:987, 1970.

11. Littler, W. A., A. J. Honour, and P. Sleight. Direct Arterial Pressure, Heart Rate and Electrocardiogram during Human Coitus. *Journal of Reproduction and Fertility,* 40:321, 1974.

12. Masters, W. H. and V. E. Johnson. *Human Sexual Response.* Boston: Little, Brown and Co., 1966.

13. Mendelsohn, M. 1st das Radfahren also ein gesundheitsgemasse Webung anzusehen und aus arztlichen Gesichtspunkt zu empfehlen. *Deutsche Medizinische Wochenschrift,* 24:381, 1896.

14. Nemec, E. D. and L. W. Mansfield. Heart Rate and Blood Pressure Responses during Sexual Activity in Normal Males. *American Heart Journal,* 92:274, 1976.

15. Veno, M. The So-Called Coital Death. *Japanese Journal of Legal Medicine,* 17:535, 1969.

16. Watts, R. J. Sexuality and the Middle-Aged Cardiac Patient. *Nursing Clinics of North America* 11:349, 1976.

17. Woods, J. S. Drug Effects on Human Sexual Behavior. In: Woods, N. F., ed. *Human Sexuality in Health and Illness.* St. Louis: C. V. Mosby Co., 1975.

18. Woods, N. F. A Sexual Adaptation to Hospitalization and Illness. In: Woods, N. F., ed. *Human Sexuality in Health and Illness.* St. Louis: C. V. Mosby Co., 1975.

CHAPTER
20

CHRONIC ILLNESS AND SEXUALITY

Glenn L. Haswell, M.D.

In recent years, significant accomplishments have been made in the rehabilitation and management of chronically ill patients. Chemotherapeutic agents, prosthetic devices, hormonal replacement, and transplantation procedures have dramatically increased the patients' longevity and functional capacity. Many who were previously disabled are now able to become contributing members of society, despite their physical limitations and dependence upon medical services.

It is easy for health personnel to be so concerned with the physiological rehabilitation of the patient and with management of the chronic disease process that they lose sight of the fact that the emotional and sexual needs of the patient are an essential aspect of his rehabilitation and recovery. Such neglect is not necessarily a reflection of personal embarrassment or lack of sensitivity as much as it may be a consequence of the paucity of published information concerning these areas of patient adjustment. It is the purpose of this chapter to provide useful information about the emotional responses that the patient makes to his chronic illness or disability and to its relationship to sexual function, and how that response influences his sexual interest and performance.

REACTION TO CHRONIC ILLNESS

The individual faced with the realization that something is physically wrong with him reacts either by seeking immediate medical attention or, for a variety of reasons, by delaying such care. Delay acts as a defense mechanism against the patient's fear of the disease itself, with its attendant pain and disability, and also against subconscious anxiety in the face of life-threatening disease. Familiarity with the disease process frequently compounds the delay. Health professionals, for example, are particularly likely to put off seeking help for physical ailments because of their knowledge of the suspected disease. In addition, the patient may postpone diagnosis and treatment because of a basic distrust of others and an unwillingness to place himself under the care of a stranger.[17]

Once the patient is confronted with the reality of serious illness, he usually responds at first with anger, frustration, and hostility. This is later followed by depression, withdrawal, and, finally, dependence upon those around him. After he recovers from the acute phase of his illness and his condition stabilizes, he attempts to establish an adaptive equilibrium, which enables him to function in his environment within the limits of his disability. In doing so, he attempts to resume the responsibilities of a healthy person and re-establish his autonomy and role identity.

Re-establishing Sexual Function

An important aspect of this role identity is sexuality and performance. The degree to which sexual function is re-established depends upon a number of variables, according to Dengrove.[6] These include:

1. *Sexual function prior to the onset of the illness.* The illness may provide an excuse to avoid participation in sexual activities for those individuals who previously achieved little satisfaction or enjoyment from intercourse. In contrast, a previous gratifying sexual relationship may be adversely affected by the physical inability of the patient to return to his former level of function.

2. *The pathophysiological effects of the illness.* Although the patient may be physically capable of sexual intercourse, persistent malaise, fatigue, or pain may suppress sexual desire to the point that participation is impossible. Similarly, significant sensory or motor loss, as experienced in paraplegia, for example, may prevent adequate physical participation in sexual activities.

3. *The patient's emotional response to the illness and its relationship to one's personal concept of masculinity or femininity.* The woman who equates childbearing capacity with personal worth and femininity may experience profound depression and loss of libidinal desire as a result of hysterectomy. Similarly, a man recovering from a myocardial infarction may abandon all sexual activities because of fear that such participation may result in further injury or even death.

4. *The physiological consequences of therapy upon the patient.* Surgical procedures, which may result in unavoidable neurologic impairment; radiation therapy, which may produce local atrophic tissue changes; or medications, which may be depressive or hypnotic in effect, may result in sexual dysfunction such as impotence or impaired ejaculation, and thereby compromise sexual performance and gratification.

5. *The response of the partner to the patient's illness.* The partner may initially respond to the patient's disability in an empathetic, comforting, and protective manner. Such support not only meets many of the immediate emotional needs of the patient himself, but may also provide a compensatory mechanism of expression of unfulfilled needs by the partner. This compensation may be reinforced by nonsexualization of the partner or by purposefully avoiding sexual contact from fear of aggravating the condition. Problems arise in their interpersonal relationship when these mechanisms fail, however. The deprived partner may become resentful and intolerant of the spouse, and the resultant marital discord threatens to disrupt not only their own interpersonal relationship, but the integrity of the family unit as well.

The patient, out of sensitivity to the sexual needs of his partner, may experience considerable anxiety over his inability to gratify those desires. He may, in fact, be fearful of infidelity on the part of his partner as a result of his real or imagined inability to satisfy her. These fears arise from a threatened sexual identity and self-image. Involved in this threat may be such factors as the loss of position as financial provider or "breadwinner" for the family, fear of loss of position of authority in the home, or the fact that his disease has relegated him to a passive-dependent role, which is inconsistent with his self-image as an aggressive self-reliant person.

Despite the fact that the physical participation in intercourse by the chronically ill female may be a more passive one than the male's, emotionally she must face similar difficulties. She may feel an obligation to participate in intercourse with her partner in order to meet his needs, and yet not feel like participating or be concerned that she may have lost her sexual attractiveness as a consequence of her disability. The resultant feelings of shame and inadequacy may further threaten an already precarious relationship.

ANATOMICAL AND FUNCTIONAL ASPECTS OF SEXUALITY

Significant psychosexual problems can arise when the patient undergoes extirpative surgery of the genitalia or reproductive organs.

Surgery of Male Genitalia

Radical amputation of the penis for carcinoma frequently precipitates profound depression. This mental state usually results not so much from a loss of reproductive capacity as from the inability to actively participate in coitus despite normal libidinal desires. A similar depressive response may occur in the partner who is unable to adjust to the loss of coital activity resulting from the patient's disability.[2] Satisfactory sexual activity has been re-established in these patients by the use of plastic surgical procedures that incorporate penile tube grafts. While such grafts lack cutaneous nerve supply, these patients often derive satisfactory erotic gratification from stimulation of other erogenous areas of the body.[2]

Patients with carcinoma of the prostate in whom the lesion is not completely resectable usually undergo bilateral orchiectomy and estrogen therapy. Such a procedure is psychologically more acceptable if the epididymal portions of the testes are sutured into a spherical shape and left within the scrotal sac. The apparent emotional satisfaction derived from being able to palpate some sort of tissue in the scrotum appears to be highly important in the maintenance of the patient's masculine self-image. Despite the institution of estrogen therapy, patients have maintained their sexual potency for some time, and immediate postoperative impotence has not been a consistent occurrence.[2]

As an aside, it is important in discussing impotence with the patient that the physician understand what the patient means by "impotence." The patient may variously define the term as lack of ability to accomplish an erection, inability to maintain an erection, or inability to ejaculate. The latter may be the result of neurologic incapacity or, as in patients who have undergone prostatectomy, may actually be due to retrograde ejaculation as a result of trauma to or removal of the internal urethral sphincter during the surgical procedure. Since a variety of physiological as well as psychological factors may be involved in the patient's potency, it is important that the patient's problem be recognized and understood as he defines it.

In similar fashion, changes in libidinal drives may be multifactorial in origin. Diminished interest may be a consequence of the surgical procedure or may be a drug-related side effect. It may be a reflection of the debilitative effect of the disease process itself. Indeed, it may be a result of the lack of communication by the health professional concerning the relationship of the disease process to the patient's sexual interest and performance. As cited earlier, the patient may be reluctant to participate in sexual intercourse because of fear of aggravating his physical condition. Also, he may erroneously assume that his disability is incompatible with participation in sexual activities. Thus, libidinal desires are voluntarily suppressed, a situation that can result in considerable anxiety and depression.

As previously mentioned, in some individuals, cessation of sexual activities may be intentional. If sexual intercourse was not gratifying or discord existed prior to illness, the patient may welcome the disability as an excuse for avoiding a source of interpersonal conflict. On the other hand, the patient may react to his disfigurement or disability by increased coital activity. Sexual demands may be made on the partner that are inconsistent with previous patterns of sexual activity. This heightened coital interest serves as a defense mechanism against feelings of loss of masculinity.[8]

Surgery of Female Genitalia

Radical extirpative surgery of sexual or sensualized organs in the female also may result in significant emotional trauma. Our society has placed great emphasis on the female breast as a symbol of sexual attractiveness and desirability. Surgical removal of the breast, therefore, often results in depression and feelings of rejection in postmastectomy patients. Such a woman may consider herself mutilated by the operative procedure and therefore unacceptable, not only to her partner, but to the outside world as well. Sexual intercourse may be avoided because she feels that she is no longer as attractive to her partner. If she does participate, she may permit it only if the operative site is covered by clothing or if there is absolute darkness in the room. The partner, in fact, may compound her feelings of rejection by avoiding sexual contact with her out of fear of injury to her operative site.[17]

Patients who have undergone radical vulvectomy and clitorectomy may also experience psychic trauma. The surgical absence of the patient's genitalia may lead her to assume that she lacks adequate physical apparatus to participate in intercourse or, even if participation is possible, to enjoy it. Concerns over the mutilative effect of the procedure as it relates to her concepts of sexual attractiveness may also play a part in her reluctance to participate in intercourse. The patient who feels that clitoral stimulation is necessary, indeed required, for sexual gratification and orgasm may presume that participation in coital activity will no longer be enjoyable or satisfying. Here, education of the patients regarding the pleasurability of vaginal sexual response can be valuable in dispelling such fears.

Shortening of the vaginal vault may result from radical surgical therapy for invasive carcinoma of the cervix because the procedure incorporates partial vaginectomy. Such shortening is an almost inevitable result of radiation therapy for cervical cancer as well. Certain operative procedures for the management of vesicovaginal fistulae may also involve approximation of the anterior and posterior walls of the vaginal apex and will result in the same loss of vaginal length.

While vaginal shortening may not allow the depth of penile penetration that was experienced preoperatively, many couples are able to adjust to this condition by altering coital positions and techniques. Despite these adjustment maneuvers, the patient may experience pain during intercourse because of the scarring that follows therapy. This appears to occur more commonly in women treated with radiotherapy than in those treated with radical surgery. The resultant dyspareunia may be interpreted as a symptom of malignancy recurring, and the patient may therefore avoid sexual intercourse in order to combat her anxiety.[1]

HYSTERECTOMY

Of all the surgical procedures performed upon the sexual organs of the female, none perhaps is fraught with more anxiety and depression than hysterectomy. Drellich and Bieber, in 1958, investigated 23 premenopausal women who had undergone hysterectomy to determine the psychological importance of the uterus and its relationship to sexual function and feminine self-image.[7] One of the major concerns voiced by their subjects was the anticipated loss of childbearing ability. While some women welcomed hysterectomy because it meant a freedom from unwanted pregnancy and from reliance on contraceptive techniques, others felt that the loss of childbearing capacity left them less than a "complete" female, even though they did not desire a future pregnancy.

The resultant loss of menstruation also caused anxiety in some of the patients. A number of them regarded the menstrual flow as necessary for periodic cleansing of their body. Without this excretory mechanism, "poisons" and body wastes might accumulate and affect the person's mind. Furthermore, the cyclic occurrence of menstruation was deemed necessary as a regulating device for maintaining the regular function of other body processes. A number of sexual functions were assigned to the uterus. The womb was considered by some to be the seat of sexual desire and necessary for orgasm. Hysterectomy was considered to result in a loss of sexual interest and to prevent them from responding sexually to their partner. They no longer would be attractive to their partners, who would thus lose interest in them or, worse yet, seek sexual gratification elsewhere. Many feared that if they did resume intercourse postoperatively, they would no longer enjoy it because of pain or failure of the operative site to heal. Others expressed the concern that their partners considered them to be "fragile" inside, and thus they were afraid to resume sexual activity. These feelings compounded the patients' anxiety that hysterectomy would somehow leave them with defective sexual equipment. Preoperatively, many of the patients were concerned about the possible loss of bladder or bowel function. The anatomical proximity of the uterus to the bladder and rectum apparently led to the mistaken assumption that these functions were somehow interrelated.

Other gastrointestinal functions were also confused postoperatively with removal of the uterus. While some patients said they had lost their appetite after surgery, more frequently patients complained of an increased appetite and a subsequent excessive postoperative weight gain. One patient felt "empty" since her procedure and had a compulsive urge to eat "in order to fill up the emptiness."

Finally, some patients manifested guilt feelings after the uterus had been removed. They felt that the surgical procedure was punishment for guilt-laden activities involving the organ. One patient interviewed felt that her increased sexual activity with her husband had caused the cervix to become irritated and had produced the cervical lesion that necessitated hysterectomy. Another patient had previously had an illicit affair with a married man which resulted in pregnancy. When her consort refused to divorce his wife and marry her to support the child, she had the pregnancy terminated by abortion. The subsequent hysterectomy, which occurred for reasons unrelated to the previous affair, resulted in severe depression because of the guilt associated with her manipulative attempts to gain a husband as well as with her ultimate pregnancy termination.

Thus, as Schon has noted, the emotional response by the patient, male or female, who has undergone extirpative surgery depends upon the psychosexual emphasis placed on the removed organ.[17] While the removed organ may not prevent or inhibit involvement in sexual intercourse, the feelings of guilt, sexual inadequacy, loss of femininity or masculinity, or loss of value as a person that the individual associates with the surgical procedure may severely compromise or even terminate participation in future sexual activities.

ADAPTIVE PROBLEMS RELATED TO SPECIFIC CHRONIC DISORDERS

Blindness

The blind population consists of those who are congenitally blind or whose onset of blindness occurs during the neonatal period and those who have subsequently lost their sight after usable vision had been established. An interesting review of the sexual behavior of these individuals has been presented by Gillman and Gordon.[9] While vision had been considered by earlier investigators to be of vital importance in the development of a child's sexual identity, the authors' observations of preschool, school-age, and adolescent individuals failed to confirm this theory. Observations of these handicapped children at play repeatedly showed that their selection of play activities was appropriate to their age and gender. Their choice of play activity, however, was limited by their life experience. The intelligent early teenager exhibited a realistic understanding of sexual anatomy and function. The congenitally blind late adolescent showed the same interests in persons of the opposite sex that sighted teenagers did, although their relationships lacked the sophistication of their sighted peers. It appears to Gillman and Gordon that gender role identity is not dependent solely on visual capacity.[9] For, in the absence of visual ability and information, sexual identity and behavior seem to be learned through language.

The emotional reactions to blindness that occurs after useful vision has been established most commonly involved acceptance, denial, or depression. In general, those patients who react to their blindness with realistic acceptance of the disability may not report any sexual difficulties. On the other hand, the individual who uses the mechanism of denial as a defense against the impact of his disability may manifest his anxiety through aggressive sexual activity or may respond to his disability with withdrawal and depression. Many times he complains of impotence, sexual disinterest, and inhibition. Such reactions and difficulties are a reflection of the threat to the patient's self-image and concept of self-worth that the handicap imposes. Rehabilitation programs for the blind that enable them to establish a realistic acceptance of their handicap should include a sexual focus. This may result in a return to gratifying sexual function by improving the person's feelings of self-worth and value as an individual.

Spinal Cord Injuries

Neurological deficits that result from injuries to the spinal cord or cauda equina frequently involve partial or complete loss of sensory and motion function below the level of the lesion. The ability of the injured patient to participate in coital activities, therefore, depends upon the level and extent of the injury. Such functional capacity cannot be prognosticated on the knowledge of the level of vertebral injury alone. Thorough neurological evaluation involving determination of motor and sensory segmental levels, presence or absence of reflex activity, and completeness or incompleteness of the lesion must be done.[3]

SPINAL CORD INJURY IN MALE

The neurological examination for the male involves determination of light touch and pinprick sensation over the skin of the penis, scrotum, and saddle area bilaterally; determination of the bulbocavernosus reflex; and rectal examination, in which the presence or absence of intrinsic sphincter tone, as well as volitional control of the external rectal sphincter, is noted.[3]

According to Comarr and Gunderson, on the basis of these findings, the following four categories of lesions may be described.[4]

1. *Complete upper motor lesion:* Loss of cutaneous sensation or of volitional control of the rectal sphincter in the presence of positive bulbocavernosus reflex or maintenance of intrinsic sphincter tone or both.

2. *Incomplete upper motor neuron lesion:* Partial loss of pinprick sensation or only light touch sensation and loss of volitional sphincter control. Sphincter tone or bulbocavernosus reflex, or both, is maintained.

3. *Complete lower motor neuron lesion:* No cutaneous sensation, tone, or volitional sphincter control and absence of the bulbocavernosus reflex.

4. *Incomplete lower motor neuron lesion:* Partial sensation remains but otherwise there is loss of rectal sphincter tone and voluntary control. Bulbocavernosus reflex is also absent.

It is important to recognize that accurate prognostication of the injured patient's sexual potential cannot be made immediately after the patient has been injured. The extent of functional recovery is related to time and the level of injury. To quote Comarr, "Usually the patients with upper motor neuron sexual potential will have their answers within a few weeks to six months after the injury, whereas patients with lower motor neuron sexual potential may have to wait as long as three years."[3]

On the basis of considerable experience with patients with nerve cord and cauda equina injuries, Comarr states that 93 per cent of his patients with complete upper motor neuron injury are able to have reflexogenic erections, either spontaneously or by external penile stimulation.[3] However, only 72 per cent of those who attempted coitus were successful. This was because those who had spontaneous reflexogenic erections either were unable to attain an erection when their partner was available, or were unable to maintain it long enough to achieve intromission. This latter experience also explained the failure of successful coitus in those patients in this group who were able to achieve an erection by external penile stimulation. In addition, the majority of patients with complete upper motor neuron lesions were unable to ejaculate or have an orgasm.

Whether the patient with an incomplete upper motor neuron lesion is able to experience orgasm and ejaculate depends upon the extent of the lesion. Such potential for psychogenic erections and ejaculations varies inversely with the level of the neurological defect. In Comarr's study, the majority (74 per cent) of men with complete lower motor neuron lesions were unable to have an erection or experience orgasm or ejaculation. Those able to experience a psychogenic erection had lesions below T12. The patients with the best prognosis for return of sexual ability were those with incomplete lower motor neuron lesions. Comarr's studies indicated that 83 per cent could have psychogenic erections, 90 per cent were successful if they attempted coitus, and 50 to 70 per cent ejaculated and experienced orgasm.

SPINAL CORD INJURY IN FEMALE

Women who have experienced neurologic injury resulting in paraplegia or quadriplegia have not been studied as extensively as men. The injury does not appear to interfere with normal menstrual function or reproductive capacity, regardless of the level or completeness of the injury.[10] Pregnancies usually result in vaginal delivery of healthy infants unless pelvic measurements were inadequate. The mothers were more likely to develop urinary tract infections during pregnancy, however, and had a higher incidence of premature labor.[10] While women with complete cord lesions are unable to experience orgasm, tactile stimulation of body areas above the level of the lesion frequently results in gratifying sexual stimulation.[10]

SEXUAL REHABILITATION

The sexual rehabilitation of the cord-injured patient is multifaceted and requires that the individual understand the limitations upon his sexual function imposed by the injury. Altered techniques of sexual arousal and coital positioning, as well as realistic expectations for performance, are vital aspects of this process. Of particular importance is the encouragement of the patient to confidently communicate his sexual needs and desires to his partner.[14] Such understanding and communication can do much to dispel the patient's feelings of inadequacy and rejection and can help establish his necessary self-confidence.

Diabetes Mellitus

Disturbances of sexual function were a common problem in diabetic patients in the pre-insulin era. Diabetic women frequently were unable to conceive, and men were troubled with erectile impotence. The advent of insulin replacement therapy has enabled diabetic women to conceive, but their pregnancies are complicated by high fetal wastage, congenital malformations, toxemia, large infant size, and increase in neonatal death.[11]

IMPOTENCE

Impotence continues to be a well-recognized problem in diabetic men. According to Rubin, impotence may occasionally be the presenting complaint in men who are later diagnosed as having diabetes mellitus.[15] His study of 198 diabetic men revealed an incidence of impotence 2 to 5 times greater than that in the general population. Studies by Schöffling et al. indicated that 51 per cent of their 314 male diabetic patients complained of erectile impotence.[16] The fact that their impotence is not a result of sexual disinterest is borne out by studies of Rubin's patients: almost all of them reported little or no decline in libido, despite their loss of coital capacity. Both Rubin and Schöffling et al. reported that the incidence of impotence was not related to duration of the disease process, nor did it correlate well with the incidence of neurovascular complications such as retinopathy, peripheral vascular disease, or neuropathy. In addition, the incidence of this dysfunction did not appear to be a reflection of diabetic control.[15, 16]

The mechanism of diabetic impotence is uncertain. Urinary 17-ketosteroid excretion is usually low in diabetic men and approaches castrate levels. However, there does not appear to be good correlation between these low levels and the incidence of impotence.[15] Similarly, diabetic men have been noted to have low levels of excreted gonadotropin, but these too have been inconsistently associated with impotence. The reason for this diminished gonadotropin excretion is not currently known.[16]

SEXUAL DYSFUNCTION IN FEMALE DIABETIC

Sexual dysfunction in diabetic females has not been investigated as thoroughly as that in diabetic men. Prior to data presented by Kolodny[11a] in 1971, no published studies were available concerning the problems of sexual function in diabetic women. His well-controlled studies of 125 sexually active diabetic females between the ages of 18 and 42 revealed a 45 per cent incidence of complete absence of orgasmic response during coitus during the year preceding the investigation. This was in contrast to an incidence of 6 per cent among the 100 nondiabetic controls for the same time period. In addition, all the anorgasmic nondiabetic women had never experienced orgasm before, while 91 per cent of the anorgasmic diabetic patients had been orgasmic previously. The onset of the dysfunction had in all cases been gradual and had occurred after the onset of diabetes. As noted with diabetic men, there was little relationship between sexual dysfunction and such factors as patient age, degree of sexual interest, or severity of disease process (as measured by insulin requirement or neurovascular complications).

Thus, it appears that significant problems exist in the area of sexual function in diabetic patients. The mechanisms responsible for such impairment are not yet clearly defined. Further investigation is needed into the etiological factors involved as well as the therapeutic measures necessary to rehabilitate these patients.

Renal Failure — Hemodialysis and Transplantation

Little is known about the effect of chronic hemodialysis and renal transplantation upon sexual function. Studies by Levy, based upon a voluntary mail questionnaire, revealed that considerable deterioration of sexual function was experienced by hemodialysis patients, especially men, as well as by male transplant recipients.[12] Sexual dysfunction as defined by Levy meant impotence in the men and a decline in frequency of orgasm with intercourse in women. These patients were comparing their present functional capacity with that experienced prior to the onset of uremia. As expected, sexual function deteriorated with the onset of uremia, prior to hemodialysis. However, initiation and maintenance of hemodialysis was associated with deteriorating sexual function in a significant proportion of patients (35 per cent of the men and 24 per cent of the women). Only 9 per cent of the men and 6 per cent of the women experienced improvement in sexual function, despite overall physical improvement.

In this study, there were a number of sources of possible error, which the author himself recognized. Of importance, however, is the fact that impotence was defined as inability to achieve or maintain an erection *or* a decline in sexual interest to the extent that the patient recognized it as "a problem." This broad definition probably explains the high incidence of "impotence" prior to the onset of uremia reported in the study population.

Dialysis by its very nature contributes to a feeling of dependence — in particular, having to rely on hospital staff or, in the case of home dialysis, family members, usually the spouse, for carrying out the procedure. Such dependence is compounded frequently by role reversal, with the ill husband having to remain home while the wife becomes the breadwinner. These factors, along with the physiological consequences of chronic uremia, may readily explain the high incidence of male sexual dysfunction in this population of patients.

It is difficult to understand why significant sexual dysfunction after transplantation remains a problem in the patients surveyed. It is the personal experience of this author that successful transplantation usually results in complete rehabilitation of the patient and that it resolves many of the psychosexual difficulties inherent in the disease process.

SUMMARY

Chronic illness results in a number of emotional changes in the patient, including fear, anxiety, depression, withdrawal, and dependence. Not only must he deal with the acute physical threat of the disease, with its attendant fear for survival, but, once the immediate danger has passed and his condition has stabilized, he must also adjust to the chronic disability associated with his illness. The emotional adaptation that the patient makes will depend upon how he views that disability in relation to his concept of body image, self-worth, and sexual role identity. That response will significantly affect his interpersonal relationships with his spouse and other members of the family unit. In addition, it can profoundly affect his sexual interest and performance.

It is the responsibility of health professionals to educate the patient and his partner about the emotional and sexual conflicts that he may encounter in his adjustment to a chronic illness as well as to educate him about the disorder itself. A supportive relationship should be fostered by the health professional. Such things as telephone calls, home visits, and clinic visits to talk about problems related to the condition will help enhance such a relationship and, it is hoped, will help alleviate much of the anxiety that results from the unknown.

REFERENCES

1. Abitol, M. and James Davenport. Sexual Dysfunction After Therapy for Cervical Carcinoma. *American Journal of Obstetrics and Gynecology,* 119:185–188, May 15, 1974.
2. Amelar, R. D. and Lawrence Dubin. Sex After Major Urologic Surgery. *The Journal of Sex Research,* 4:267–273, Nov. 1968.
3. Comarr, A. E. Sex Among Patients with Spinal Cord and/or Cauda Equina Injuries. *Medical Aspects of Human Sexuality,* 7:222–228, March 1973.
4. Comarr, A. E. and Bernice B. Gunderson. Sexual Function in Traumatic Paraplegia and Quadriplegia. *American Journal of Nursing,* 75:250, Feb. 1975.
5. Crigler, L. Sexual Concerns of the Spinal Cord-Injured. *Nursing Clinics of North America,* 9:257–264, Dec. 1974.
6. Dengrove, E. Sexual Responses to Disease Processes. *The Journal of Sex Research,* 4:257–264, Nov. 1968.
7. Drellich, M. G. and Irving Bieber. The Psychologic Importance of the Uterus and Its Functions. *Journal of Nervous and Mental Diseases,* 26:322–335, 1958.
8. Ford, A. B. and Alexander P. Orfirer. Sexual Behavior and the Chronically Ill Patient. *Medical Aspects of Human Sexuality,* 1:58, Oct. 1967.
9. Gillman, A. E. and Arlene R. Gordon. Sexual Behavior in the Blind. *Medical Aspects of Human Sexuality,* 7:49–60, June 1973.
10. Griffith, E. R., Michael A. Tomko, and Robert J. Timms. Sexual Function in Spinal Cord-Injured Patients: A Review. *Archives of Physical Medicine and Rehabilitation,* 54:541, Dec. 1973.
11. Hellman, L. and Jack Pritchard. *Williams Obstetrics,* 14th ed. New York: Appleton-Century-Crofts, 1971, pp. 791–792.
11a. Kolodny, R. C. Sexual Dysfunction in Diabetic Females. *Diabetes,* 20:557–559, Aug. 1971.
12. Levy, N. B. Sexual Adjustment to Maintenance Hemodialyses and Renal Transplantation: National Survey by Questionnaire: Preliminary Report. *Transactions of the American Society for Artificial Internal Organs,* 19:138–143, 1973.
13. MacRae, I. and G. Henderson. Sexuality and Irreversible Health Limitations. *Nursing Clinics of North America,* 10:587–597, Sept. 1975.
14. Romano, M. D. and Robert E. Lassiter. Sexual Counseling with the Spinal Cord Injured. *Archives of Physical Medicine and Rehabilitation,* 53:572, Dec. 1972.
15. Rubin, A. Sexual Behavior in Diabetes Mellitus. *Medical Aspects of Human Sexuality,* 1:23–25, Dec. 1967.
16. Schöffling, K., K. Federlin, H. Ditschuneit, and E. F. Pfeiffer. Disorders of Sexual Function in Male Diabetics. *Diabetes,* 12:526, Nov.-Dec. 1963.
17. Schon, M. The Meaning of Death and Sex to Cancer Patients. *The Journal of Sex Research,* 4:282–302, Nov. 1968.

21

RAPE COUNSELING: PERSPECTIVES OF VICTIM AND NURSE

Ann Wolbert Burgess, R.N., D.N.Sc., and Jane Huntington, B.A.

If it had to happen . . . at least I was in a place where rape was beginning to be dealt with and where there was an awareness of the problem.

How many rape victims are able to make this statement? And how many nurses have enough awareness of the problem to be able to therapeutically negotiate crisis care for the victim?

Women, breaking through silence, prudery, and misconceptions by relating their experiences as rape victims, have pressured the American society to begin to examine their feelings and reactions to the crime, the victim, and the offender. Indeed, progress has been made in the past decade, from small groups of women speaking out on the issue to concentrated efforts to organize and implement rape crisis centers.[1] The latest accomplishment has been gaining national support with the establishment of a Center for the Prevention and Control of Rape.[2] Mandates have concurrently appeared for health facilities and community mental health professionals to be able to provide adequate bio-psycho-socio-legal services to rape victims.

As the momentum to provide services has increased, so has the professional literature on the treatment of victims. However, clinical articles on specific therapeutic techniques usually have a one-sided bias—the clinician's view—and thus may miss important views of the client. Therefore, in an attempt to provide perspective to this article on rape counseling, we are presenting a joint approach including a theoretical framework for victim counseling and the victim's and nurse-counselor's interpretations over a three-year period.

CONCEPTUAL FRAMEWORK FOR RAPE COUNSELING: RAPE CRISIS CONCEPTS

The process of victim counseling is built on crisis concepts in the professional literature and concepts that have evolved from research on the victim's perception and reactions to the crime. The concepts we have found most useful for rape crisis counseling may be identified briefly as follows.

1. Rape, a forced violent sexual attack, is usually perceived by the victim as a life-threatening or severely stressful experience. Human response to this stress calls for coping behavior in an attempt to function during the rape.[7]

2. The stressor or life-threatening situation usually has four time phases: early awareness of danger, before the rape, during the rape, and after the rape. Coping tasks may be identified in each time phase and multiple coping strategies may be employed.[9]

3. Rape precipitates an externally imposed crisis for the victim, the family, and often the community. The life style of the victim is disrupted in four major areas: physical, emotional, social, and sexual. The rape trauma involves two phases: (1) an acute phase of disorganization of life style, and (2) the long-term effects, in which a reorganization process occurs back to a previous level of health.[3]

4. The crisis the rape victim faces can be analyzed by looking at the interaction between the developmental phase the person is in and the externally imposed event of the rape. The rape takes on significant meaning for the victim according to the crisis issue involved in the person's developmental stage.[3]

5. A legal process recapitulates the rape crisis. Going to court is as much a life-style disruption as the actual rape. Several psychological responses are triggered. Time becomes suspended; the rape is relived through the process of retelling the experience in court; silent suspicion is felt by the victim; the victim may be betrayed either deliberately or unwittingly by people she believes are supportive of her.[11]

6. Rape has the potential for triggering additional crises. One external crisis event has the potential for activating additional crisis situations, both internal and external.[10]

CASE HISTORY

THE CRIME: ARMED ROBBERY AND RAPE

It had been a pleasant Thanksgiving weekend thus far. I had just returned to my new apartment the day after Thanksgiving to wait for my friends, who said they would be right over. I was lying on my bed listening to my stereo—it was about 1:30 in the afternoon. The outer door to my apartment rang, and I pushed the buzzer to let my friends in and opened my apartment door. Instead of my friends, I saw three young men, one of whom had a paper in his hand and who said, "This is for you." I looked at them and froze. Instinctively, I knew something was wrong. I said, "Oh, no, thank you." I stepped back into my apartment. I attempted to close the door, but one of the men pulled a gun, one grabbed me, and they all pushed their way into my apartment. They threw me to the floor, verbally assaulted me, and kicked and hit me. They held the gun to my head and threatened to shoot if I didn't keep quiet. I thought at first this was the kind of thing that happened on TV, not to me. I was terrified and sick to see them gathering up my things to take with them. And I really didn't know what to do. I yelled and was kicked; I argued and I was hit. Every sentence of theirs was laced with profanities.

I just wanted them out of the apartment. I told them to take everything—my TV—just go. One said, "We don't want your crappy old TV—we're going to tie you up with the cords." I kept praying my friends would arrive. Finally one said, "Let's call a cab and get out of here." But then the one that had been hitting me all along said, "I'm not leaving till I get my nuts off on this white bitch." It was then I realized rape was to be part of the robbery.

I was yanked up off the floor and frisked, and my pants were ripped off. One took me into a small closet because he "couldn't fuck in front of his friends." He choked me so hard that he cut off my wind. He wasn't able to get an erection, which infuriated him, and he kept choking me, saying, "Do you want to fuck or die?" I couldn't do as he was ordering me to do and he said, "All right, I'll throw you on the bed and we'll all have you." All three then raped me—one forced me to perform fellatio while one raped me and one hit me. After the rapes, they threatened to cut off my breast with a knife from my kitchen. I think my terror amused them, and they did not carry through with their threat. They tied me with cords they had cut from my radio, TV, and lamps, and they taped my mouth and put a pillow case over my head. Almost three hours after they had entered my apartment, they called a cab and left with over $8000 worth of my personal possessions. I felt completely devastated and numb. My body felt like limp spaghetti. I gathered enough energy to get myself untied, thinking it would take a long time to die by starvation because of the big Thanksgiving dinner I had just had. My instinct for survival carried me through this process. The rapists gave me the idea to call the police when they said, "We're going to rip out the phone—don't want you calling no cops." In their haste to leave, they forgot to tear out the phone. I dialed the police and told the person I had been robbed and raped and gave my address. Within a very short period of time, the police arrived and this action set into motion my pressing charges and receiving medical and counseling attention.

A MODEL OF RAPE COUNSELING

Short-Term Issue-Oriented Model

Victim counseling is an issue-oriented crisis treatment model. The focus of the initial interview and follow-up is on the rape experience, and the goal is to aid the victim to return to her previous life style as quickly as possible. ("The whole point of counseling is to integrate the experience into your life so that you go back to living how you were living . . .")

Previous problems that are not associated with the rape are not considered priority issues for discussion in counseling. This would include individual or family problems. Victim counseling is not considered psychotherapy. When other issues of concern are identified by the victim that indicate another treatment model, referrals are generally offered to the victim, if so requested.

A face-to-face interview is recommended and usually occurs within a short period following the rape, if not at the hospital where the victim has been taken for medical examination. Crisis counseling can be successfully handled, however, totally by telephone if the victim is secure enough in this model and articulate in being able to report signs and symptoms of trauma reactions.

The nurse gathers data on the rape and also on how other stresses and crises have been handled by the victim. These data provide a baseline on how much stress the victim has previously dealt with and how much additional stress she will be able to tolerate. Information on the network of social support is essential in determining how active the nurse will need to be during the acute crisis period.

In the Boston-based victim counseling program, we used telephone counseling as a primary intervention tool after seeing the victim. There are several reasons why we felt telephone counseling was effective. (1) It provides relatively quick access to the victim; (2) it places the burden on the nurse to seek out the victim rather than on the victim to seek help at a time when she is in crisis and having difficulty making decisions; (3) it allows the victim considerable power in the situation; (4) it encourages the victim to resume a normal life style as quickly as possible; (5) it is cost-effective; and (6) it provides an alternative way to discuss difficult issues other than face-to-face.[5]

In regard to the case illustration, Jane questioned whether she needed psychotherapy because "all my friends were telling me I should see a shrink . . . they all were in therapy and just assumed I should be also." Jane did investigate the various clinics in her home state and filled out the application, which put her on a long waiting list. She later said, "I never went for an evaluation appointment. The vibes weren't right. It was so much of a hassle."

Assessing Coping Behavior during the Rape

Assessment of coping behavior and strategies used before, during, and after the rape is an essential step in the crisis interview. This assessment can be used as a supportive measure. Nurses, in listening to the victim recount the rape, can identify the coping behavior and acknowledge this information to the victim. This support tells victims that they have coped in a positive adaptive mechanism in surviving a life-threatening situation.

Our case illustrates several coping strategies. First, Jane had an early awareness of danger but was unable to shut the door in time. She remained relatively calm and tried verbal tactics of bargaining ("Take everything you want—take my TV and go"); focused on the men's faces in hopes of seeing them again in court; memorized details ("I kept thinking, you guys, you picked on the wrong one this time. I had to think that—it was the only way I could cope."); prayed for her friends to arrive; complied with the sexual demands in the service of survival; pointed out reality ("You guys will be in real trouble if you kill me"); and physically freed herself and called for help.

Part of a rape experience is encountering dangerous people. ("I kept thinking if I get out of this alive . . . I was so unsure . . . they looked crazy . . . one of them had strange Charles Manson eyes . . . I'd never dealt with people like that.")

"Crisis Request" of the Victim

The victim is considered normal, that is, as an individual who was managing adequately in life style prior to the crisis situation. In this context, the victim is viewed as a customer of emergency services who has an immediate crisis request—that is, seeking a particular service from the professional. This clinical concept is taken from the research by Aaron Lazare and colleagues, who developed this approach.[12] They perceived the patient as a customer whose requests for aid are considered reasonable, usually legitimate, and always a key part of the clinical negotiations. Requests are defined as hopes or desires of the patient for treatment or "help."[12]

A study of the crisis requests of the 146 sexual assault victims admitted to the Boston City Hospital revealed five categories:[6]
1. Police intervention: I need police help.
2. Medical intervention: I need medical care.
3. Psychological intervention: I need to talk to someone.
4. Control: I need control.
5. Uncertain: I'm not sure I need anything.

The crisis request is the common ground of communication between victim and counselor or police. Identifying the request on initial interview and understanding the request reduces and contains the sense of helplessness and powerlessness one may feel in dealing therapeutically with the victim. Something *can* be done for the victim provided that one first jointly with the victim figures out what needs to be done and what the priorities are.

Referring back to the case example, Jane's immediate crisis request was for police intervention. Once freed of her wrist ties, she dialed the police. The police officer on duty who took the call later said in court, "I felt so helpless listening to her tell me what happened. I wanted to jump through the telephone to be able to help her." The police immediately responded to her call, and it was the police detective who identified the next crisis request—medical attention. ("It never occurred to me to go to a hospital.") Jane had lacerations of her forehead, wrist burns, neck pain, and genital trauma. Victims may not be aware of their need for medical attention, as in this situation. From an analysis of signs and symptoms of physical and emotional trauma to rape victims, we strongly recommend that all victims receive immediate medical attention for the bruises and lacerations.[8] Victims also need protection from further injury to the body, that is, venereal disease and pregnancy.

Negotiating the Counseling Request

Negotiating the follow-up counseling request is a key factor in the clinical work: the nurse-counselor states that services are available. In studying the counseling requests of the 146 victims at Boston City Hospital on telephone follow-up, five categories were identified.[6]

1. Confirmation of concern: It's nice to know you are available.
2. Ventilation: It helps to talk about this.
3. Advice: What should I do?
4. Clarification: I want to think this through.
5. Wants nothing: I don't need the counseling services.

By learning what the victim wants in terms of follow-up, an important alliance is made, because the victim has been listened to carefully and with respect. The counselor communicates respect to the victim by taking her seriously, by being honest, by listening well, and by regarding the victim as a person instead of an object.

Jane's first counseling request was for ventilation. The mind works in priorities, and Jane's immediate concern was for "all the things I'd lost." Considerable time and energy was put into reviewing the lost items and the disarray her life was now in.

In the acute phase of the crisis reaction, most victims request ventilation or confirmation of concern. However, we often found requests changing, such as shifting to requests for clarification. This observation supported the findings of Lazare et al., who noted that the patient's dominant or primary request frequently changes during the course of several interviews, indicating either progression or regression.[12]

In the reorganization phase, Jane's request changed to clarification. ("Once you can get on with living, which is the whole point of counseling, then you can get back to the business at hand—the influence the rape will have in my life.")

Clinical Assessment of Rape Trauma Syndrome

Assessing, understanding and evaluating the reactions and feelings of the victim following a rape are essential skills for the nurse. A rape experience triggers a two-phased reaction: an acute, highly confusing, and disorganized state, followed by a long-term period in which the victim attempts to put her life back into the order it had prior to the rape. The acute phase includes the many physical symptoms as well as a wide range of emotional reactions that result from being faced with a life-threatening situation. The long-term phase includes changing residence, seeking social network support, dealing with nightmares, and developing transitory phobias.

THE ACUTE PHASE

As Jane said, "It's the kind of flurry that a crisis brings . . . there's a lot of activity and then there's the aftermath . . . to settle down." The counselor needs to assess the decisions quickly as they apply to details of reality such as moving. ("Getting out of that apartment and getting packed; dealing with the silly landlord who asked me why I opened the door; trying not to have my mother too panicked about the whole thing; and feeling very confused.")

Physical symptoms may be quite uncomfortable to the victim. ("Had terrible headaches and neckaches and my wrists hurt from being tied up. I lost my appetite for about six months and lost ten pounds. I required a lot of sleep.") The emotional reaction generally includes minor mood swings and transitory phobias. ("I resumed smoking and chain-smoked and drank wine. Emotionally I was confused and nervous. My hands shook so that I couldn't write for at least a month. And I was terrified. My moods varied dramatically from being glad I was alive to not wanting to be alive if I had to live in such disruption. Sometimes I was unable to go out in the afternoon; everybody scared me. I spent time alone. I was edgy and often irritable with my friends. I might cry—not in front of people—it would just come on. I wrote in my journal to get it out of my system. I felt a prisoner of my fears and confusion.")

Change in *social network* relationships can occur in a variety of ways. Often, friends and family are very upset over the news and rally to support the victim. However, they also have thoughts and feelings that may influence their behavior and that may be unknown to the victim. ("Socially, everything fell apart. I called on all of my friends and family. My female friends became much more fearful themselves. My one friend who lived right down the street took off by herself after it happened and left me and my mother in her apartment. She couldn't deal with the horror of all this—the whole identification that it could happen. Men's reactions varied, with some wanting to avenge my loss.

After initially wanting to hug and be hugged, I withdrew and put a protective shield around myself. I couldn't even touch anyone, nor could I bear to be touched. I couldn't relate to my friend's realities. When I read, I wanted only children's books.") Financial disruption may also occur for the victim. ("I had the hospital bill, lost my earning power, lost one month's rent, had to pay to move, plus all the possessions that were stolen.")

Each victim will react individually to the rape within the framework of co-existing issues. Two major issues Jane dealt with in the acute phase focused on "clichés come true" and the "invasion of privacy."

Clichés Come True. Perhaps one of the major clichés when a crime has been committed is the survival of the victim(s). Jane experienced this when many people minimized the armed robbery part of the crime, saying, "Well, things are just things and they don't matter; thank goodness you are alive." Granted, Jane was glad she was alive, but she also needed time to adjust to the loss of her material possessions, and people failed to allow her to grieve for the items.

Invasion of Privacy. The chain of events linked to the invasion of privacy is most apparent: Three men enter Jane's apartment without permission, and injure and penetrate her body. Then the police enter the picture and, in the line of their investigation, have to examine everything in the apartment, looking for fingerprints and such ("They looked at and read papers on my desk and had to take some of my notebooks") and asking additional questions. Jane next goes to the hospital and, in line with good health care, is subjected to invasive procedures (pelvic examination and antibiotic injections).

REORGANIZATION PHASE

After the acute phase, the "settling down" period may last months or years. One of the factors necessary to start the process is some structure—a need for order—as a way to start putting one's life back into a normal pattern. For example, encouraging the victim to write her thoughts, feelings, and reactions daily in a journal is one suggestion that might help. Encouraging the victim to get back into a routine similar to her style prior to the rape may also be beneficial.

Dreams and nightmares can be very upsetting to the victim. Early in the recovery period, the victim will describe "day mares"—that is, being alone or walking down the street and mentally reviewing the entire scene. Such conscious thoughts are painful, and the victim will say, "I just want to forget—I can't get the thoughts out of my head." Nightmares will also occur. They appear in two versions: First, with the victim still powerless and helpless, and second, with the victim in control and having mastered the situation. The dreams may be thinly disguised, with the issue being interpreted from them. Jane had disguised dreams in which she was still not in control, yet was trying to master the situation. ("I was in my boat and coming back but just couldn't get my boat into its slip—everyone else had docked their boat and I couldn't, but I kept trying.")

Eliciting social network support in the reorganization phase may be a difficult task, as Jane found out. She experienced a variety of reactions, usually linked with the friend's ability to deal with the news. *Once is enough* can be one response. ("People are interested and they want to hear and hold your hand or whatever and express shock, but that's it.") Avoidance and fear may be another response. ("This is your problem, Jane. I don't want Sue to go to the trial—we don't want any trouble from this.") And then there is hostility. ("Don't you think you are indulging yourself in this . . . dwelling on it . . . it's morbid.")

Waiting for Court.   The three men were apprehended one month following the rape, thanks to exceptionally fine police investigation. However, time becomes suspended when a court process is pending. There are the probable cause hearing, the grand jury investigation, and the court trial. In this case, the total time for the three court steps took six months, which is considered quite fast. Jane did not have a job because she had just moved to Boston to find employment. Now she had to move back home and did not have the energy to begin to settle her life *and* to prepare for the trial. She chose to put her energies into preparing for the trial. A successful court process—in terms of getting a guilty verdict for the defendant(s)—is dependent on how well all people involved can work together. However, a significant part will rest with the strength and skill of the victim to be clear, precise, and in emotional control under the stress of the cross-examination. It was during this court preparation that Jane felt most isolated and lonely. The impact of her friends not being able to deal emotionally with the rape issue led Jane to thinking that perhaps her friends were right: that she should not impose this topic on them, and that she must have been doing something wrong in her life for this misfortune to have occurred to her.

It is precisely during this period that the counselor may be of most support to the victim in terms of reviewing her concerns, helping her to bear the uncomfortable feelings that are surfacing, and in some manner conveying to the victim that "we're in it together." The commitment the counselor makes to the victim is precisely this guarantee—to see the case through the court process and for a sufficient period following to insure settlement of feelings and reactions.

The Evaluation

An evaluation of the victim's return to a normal lifestyle is done at 3-, 6-, 9-, and 12-month intervals. On a 3-year follow-up, Jane made the following comments.

Physical life style: "My physical health has been fine."

Emotional life style: "I still have some fears and paranoia. I was on a train and saw three young men sitting and I felt scared and thought I am giving off really scared vibes and everyone on this train knows how scared I am . . . I felt that inside kind of shiver. I was glad to get home. I don't want those feelings." From a counselor's perspective, it is important to reassure the victim, at this point, that those feelings are not constant, as they once were, and that the victim can usually now "ride with the feeling" without having it be disruptive to both emotional and intellectual equilibrium. The victim has moved from the general ("Everyone scares me") to the particular ("Three men in a row scare me").

Social life style: Jane's situation was complex. She had just arrived in Boston and did not have a job. One concrete option that could be offered was the course in progress at the university in Victimology. ("I came to your class every Tuesday and that was the only thing in my life at that time that made sense.") This action had an additional pay-off. Jane, when unable to find employment after returning home, decided to return to college to complete her B.A. degree—after 10 years. She attended one summer session and two academic semesters and graduated magna cum laude in 1975.

Sexual life style: The disruption in sexual life style may well linger the longest. ("I didn't become a man hater, but I became both anxious and suspicious with men I've known and new men I've met. I interpret simple friendliness as sexual aggression.")

SUMMARY

From the nurse's perspective, a main therapeutic task is providing the victim with a non-judgmental person who will listen over and over and over to the rape experience in the attempt to help the victim settle the unbearable feelings that have been triggered by the rape, and to help the victim make some sense of the experience in terms of her total life experiences. The counselor helps to strengthen the victim, focusing her emotionally on the crisis and intellectually on our current limited knowledge about the psychology of rape.

After the acute phase, the settling down period may last months to years. A variety of factors influence the victim's resilient powers to reorganize her life: the number of additional stressors concurrent in her life; the number of supportive ongoing relationships in her life with people who genuinely care; the number of positive, structured, socially reinforced events in her life such as work and school. If the number of stressors is not favorably balanced with relationships or social re-inforcers, the victim will be more prone to depressive symptoma-tology; that is, the phenomenon of loss will present itself in terms of lowered self-image. Victims will be self-reproachful. ("I felt sorry for myself; didn't have much energy . . . found it a big letdown after grand jury . . . was having no luck job hunting . . . thought of suicide . . . would I have the energy to keep going?") The nurse needs to assess feelings and reactions appropriate to the rape crisis and to note those issues that indicate another treatment model, such as psychotherapy.

From the victim's perspective, the nurse is someone to talk to about the rape—an opportunity rarely available. The nurse is just a telephone call away. ("I remember getting shaky when I was home, so I phoned the counselor.") The victim needs a professional—more than just somebody who cares—who can help her to understand that her feelings and reactions are not abnormal and who can provide accurate information. ("Now, two years later, I can talk of my victimization, the counseling, and the prosecution from an emotional distance. The rape and robbery were totally disruptive and devastating to my entire person, and I could not have come back to life, as it were, without enormous help. It took a great deal of work, which would have been much greater had I had to work alone . . . You might be interested to know that the rapists were found guilty on all counts and are now serving life terms in prison. They might not be there if I had not been supported every step of the way.")

REFERENCES

1. Brodyaga, Lisa, Margaret Gates, Susan Singer, Marla Tucker and Richardson White. *Rape and Its Victims: A Report for Citizens, Health Facilities, and Criminal Justice Agencies.* Washington, D.C.: National Institute of Law Enforcement Assistance Administration, U.S. Department of Justice, 1975.
2. Brown, Bertrum. *Research Grants—Rape Prevention and Treatment.* Washington, D.C.: Department of Health, Education and Welfare, 1976.
3. Burgess, Ann W. and Lynda L. Holmstrom. *Rape: Victims of Crisis.* Bowie, Maryland: Robert J. Brady Co., 1974, pp. 37–50.
4. *Ibid.,* 109–119.
5. *Ibid.,* pp. 163–177.
6. Burgess, Ann W. and Lynda L. Holmstrom. Crisis and Counseling Requests of Rape Victims. *Nursing Research,* 23:196–202, May-June 1974.
7. Burgess, Ann W. and Lynda L. Holmstrom. Rape Trauma Syndrome. *American Journal of Psychiatry,* 131:981–986, Sept. 1974.
8. Burgess, Ann W. and Lynda L. Holmstrom. Sexual Assault: Signs and Symptoms. *Journal of Emergency Nursing,* 1:11–15, March-April, 1975.
9. Burgess, Ann W. and Lynda L. Holmstrom. Coping Behavior of the Rape Victim. *American Journal of Psychiatry,* 133:413–417, April 1976.
10. Burgess, Ann W., Lynda L. Holmstrom, and Maureen P. McCausland. Child Rape by Family Member: Divided Loyalty. (in press).
11. Holmstrom, Lynda L. and Ann W. Burgess. Rape: The Victim and the Criminal Justice System. Paper presented at the First International Symposium on Victimology, Jerusalem, September 1973, and published in the *International Journal of Criminology and Penology,* 3:101–110, 1975.
12. Lazare, Aaron et al. The Walk-in Patient as a "Customer": A Key Dimension in Evaluation and Treatment. *American Journal of Orthopyschiatry* 42:872–883, Oct. 1972.

CHAPTER
22
OLD MORALITY VS. NEW MORALITY

Reverend Jerry L. Spencer
and
Sister Mary Emmanuel Thomas, R.S.M., M.S.N.

The delivery of health care makes many demands upon those who are associated with it, whether client or professional. In the nitty-gritty daily realities of demands for appointments, medications, surgical intervention, written reports, diagnostic studies, counseling, interviews, and so forth, a person's concerns about the behavioral expression of sexuality may never surface. Traditionally, the sexual aspect of a person has been of minimal interest to members of the health team. Often, the sexual aspect was ignored in the interaction between the health care professional and the client, but now it is realized that the omission of this vital aspect of a person's life results in poor communication and inadequate care.

It is a phenomenon of social psychology that what belongs to a person is often viewed in a positive or negative manner by that person and assumes meaning and value for the individual on a personal level. Thus, the choice of a particular life style with a particular behavioral expression of sexuality has meaning for the person who has chosen it or defines it.

It is the intent of the first part of this chapter to portray the personal meaning in a person's choice of sexual expression, as described by some of those involved in various life styles. This chapter also explores some of the behavioral expressions of sexuality found in our American society of the mid 70's. In presenting the personal meaning of a particular choice of sexual expression, we have selected to explore the contemporary sexual atmosphere in terms of various motifs: the behavioral dimension (including social and psychological aspects), the moral dimension, and the spiritual dimension.

LIFE STYLES

Sexual behavior is learned as all behavior is learned, through the complex interaction of cultural and psychological factors.[8] This means

283

that sexual behavior can be expressive of a wide range of nonsexual interests. In contemporary society, the prevailing arrangement for the physical (or genital) expression of sex is marriage. We shall explore various life styles in relation to marriage.

SINGLE LIFE STYLE

Choice of the single life usually involves a variety of motivations. Some of the major reasons include a desire to fully dedicate oneself to a particular professional endeavor; the need of a family member for continuous care and attention; the lack of adequate opportunity to meet a partner; religious motivation; or the appeal of the fun life of a "swinger." The following brief description provides us as members of the health team with a beginning understanding of the persons who may choose to express their sexuality in this mode, differing from the cultural norm.

Baker found that the personal fulfillment of never-married subjects, insofar as it could be realistically measured, did not depend on marriage and parenthood.[1] The never-married subjects in his study expressed no feelings of frustration, no sense of not being a whole person as a consequence of remaining unmarried. Their sense of personal worth came not from their biological function but from what they perceived as their creative contribution to their significant society.

Insemination is a man's biological function and fetal development is the female's. According to young parents involved in the task of rearing children, however, parental fulfillment comes more from subsequent contributions to the developmental needs of the child than from impregnating a woman or giving birth to a child. This view is supportive of Baker's previous findings that sense of personal worth comes not from biological function but from social function as a human being.[1]

One of the major tasks of young adulthood, according to Erikson, is to achieve a sense of intimacy or close affiliation in sexual unions or orgasms, in close friendships, and in experiences of inspiration from persons such as teachers.[4] Many believe that the loss of sexual intimacy inevitably dooms the never-married person to a degree of psychic frustration. In the experience of the authors, persons who do not achieve intimacy in sexual expression report that their needs for close affiliation with others are provided through reciprocal relationships established with family, friends, and co-workers. Erich Fromm offers support of this view by defining love as an attitude or personal orientation toward many others.[7] To become a loving person, one must be related to the world as a whole.

CELIBACY

Goergen describes the person who chooses to be celibate out of religious motivation.[9] This life style presupposes the belief in a God who calls persons to an inner spiritual awareness, which is expressed in an external physical reality of sexual abstinence. Members of various religions, including Hinduism, Judaism, Protestantism, and Roman Catholicism, give evidence of valuing the choice of the single life for the sake of the kingdom in a religious sense. Four levels of motivation for choosing this life style have been proposed by Goergen: (1) The ideal level—to grow in love of God, to witness to a transcendent value, to grow in freedom. (2) The subjective and conscious level—to achieve personal goals of importance to the particular individual. (3) The unconscious level—motivations stemming from the particular developmental history of an individual. (4) The existential level—the individual's choice of the rightness of this life style for himself or herself.

Deciding to choose this life style is never totally explainable. Celibacy, according to Goergen, demands an integration of one's sexuality.[9] A truly "sexual" celibate is a person who appreciates his body and the power of sexual drives and puts this energy into the service of others for the sake of the kingdom.

"SWINGING"

The rebels and swingers described by Willwerth and Kanfer, who belong to the Sexual Freedom League, claim intellectual, philosophical, and sensual motivation for their life style as "swinger."[21] Opportunities to gather with others interested in the same things are provided at dating bars, in apartment high rises for singles only, through computer services, and through travel and resort accommodations.

Accented in this life style is the relationship, and if the relationship is expressed in sexual togetherness, so much the better. Some of those who choose this life style report that the constant round of dating and different partners can begin to resemble "running in circles after awhile," as stated by Judy McKeown, a young Chicago T.V. personality. One male swinger observed that although he enjoyed the freedom to travel allowed by his single status, he was aware of the lack of a person with whom to share his appreciation of something beautiful such as a sunset.

Both Rollo May and Victor Frankl emphasize the need people feel to search for love and for meaning in their lives.[6, 13] Frankl states that a person must give the sexual aspect of his life meaning, and for Frankl, the meaning is in commitment. May advocates achieving personal fulfillment through loving others in total commitment. For May, this type of commitment helps a person to face up to the greatest anxiety, which is the mystery of human death. Some members of society who seek to escape this mystery do so through sexual eroticism.

ALTERNATIVE MARRIAGE FORMS

Trial marriage, or simply "living together," may arise from the need not only for deep personal involvement but also for the comfort of a stable relationship and environment.[17] Persons who choose this life style differ from swingers. They tend to model their relationships after the ideal of a stable marriage. Feelings of liberation from the stigma of extramarital sex taboos and from the imposition of the marriage contract are important to such couples as they learn to become compatible mates in the humdrum day-to-day existence. Those who are able to sustain a sexual relationship are creating the emerging pattern of the extended affair through cohabitation.

Communal living is chosen by some persons who are seeking relationships similar to those found in an extended family. Gathered together in a large dwelling place, they share money, food, clothing, child care, and sometimes sexual partners. Basic to their motivation is a common philosophy of life—to share peace and brotherhood.

Extramarital sexual expression, which was formerly called "cheating," is currently known as an affair. Persons who participate in this type of life style have moved from defending it to proselytizing.[2] They explain that sexual expression agreed upon by consenting adults should be considered an inalienable right. Sex without guilt or restriction is good, pleasurable, and relaxing and promotes a spirit of human closeness, compassion, and good will. Many persons who endorse this life style will also speak of the pervasive loneliness of their marriages, usually due to a serious lack of communication. Finding meaning with someone other than their spouses seems to them to be making the most of their opportunities to satisfy deep human needs.

The brief descriptions of possible personal meanings to be found in the life styles just described are intended to provide a beginning understanding of why or how a client may choose such sexual expression. Members of the health team are becoming more aware of the importance of seeing another's situation from the "insider" perspective in assuring the success of the communication process. However, questions arise in many minds regarding the moral dimension of such behavior. Confusion, acceptance, rejection, and understanding are present in the attitudes of many toward persons with life styles so different from the traditional ones. The second part of this chapter explores the moral and spiritual dimension of contemporary sexual behavior.

ETHICAL PERSPECTIVES AND REFLECTIONS

It is obvious that the decade of the 1970's is witnessing perhaps the greatest sexual revolution of all time. With the combination of "the pill" and the new permissiveness, being single no longer means being alone. Sex has broken out of the confines of marriage, and just about everybody is "letting it all hang out." The sexual revolution that began in the 1950's and flourished in the 1960's has peaked in the 1970's.

The traditional form of monogamous marriage, the nuclear family, and indeed the idea of marriage itself and of relationships between men and women are being challenged and expanded. Sexual mores, attitudes, practices, and expectations are shifting. There is a heightened interest in sexual adequacy and performance, and it is common to hear the view that sexual pleasure is a natural and meaningful part of life — something to strive for — as well as a right. These changes are most visible among young people and adult women, who are questioning the traditional concept of female sexuality.

Now there is a plurality of sexual life and love styles (e.g., group marriage, homosexual liaisons, single-parent families, "swinging"), and each life style has its own rationale, as we've seen. Thus, there are no longer common standards of morality; apparently both the old and the new codes of sexual behavior seem inadequate and in a state of flux.[18] These patterns of behavior prompt us to ask the question: Is there really a new sexual morality today? In a sense, yes. The attitudes and motivations of many people, particularly the young, seem to be changing with regard to sexual activity outside marriage and cohabitation without marriage. Although this phenomenon is nothing really new, it is becoming a prevalent attitude among the young (and even among the not-so-young), so that a serious investigation of the reasons given for this new attitude is highly warranted. We propose to subject to intense scrutiny some of the underlying justifications for the so-called new morality and to see whether or not it successfully challenges some of the traditional views of sexuality and marriage.

SEXUAL MORALITY IN TRANSITION

The younger generation prides itself on being more educated and more honest than any other in history. There is nothing it fears or has hangups about (with the exception of the establishment), nothing it is unwilling to talk about or even experience. This is above all true of human relationships and sexuality. The "new morality," we are told, is more honest, healthy, and open than any in the past. Although experience may be the best teacher (in this case, sexually), it is not the only one, nor is it generally adequate in itself. The studies of Kinsey (1948, 1953) and others provide sufficient data to give a fairly accurate description of the sexual person in operation. The sexual response is as important a part of the phenomenon as the sexual apparatus, and an understanding of the human sexual response is a useful foundation for our theological and ethical reflections (see Chapters 3 and 4).

In spite of a better education, changes in the physical and biological environment, improved communications and so forth, man remains morally about the same. In fact, within himself, man has changed very little (insofar as history shows us). A translated French saying is quite apropos: "The more things change, the more they are the same."

One can perhaps describe sexual morality in transition by means of the following outline, which does not pretend to be exhaustive or chronologically developmental: (1) The "taboo" level: Sexual taboos have emerged in the course of every civilization; some were based on biological convictions and others on socioeconomic factors. These sexual codes (including numerous myths) vary from society to society, from group to group, and from time to time.[10] (2) The "moralistic" level: This might also be termed "ethical" according to one's vantage point, although there can be a distinction. However, it does involve a value judgment in terms of right and wrong, good and evil. Consequently, one can even speak of immoral and amoral in discussing human sexuality. (3) The "realistic" level: Contemporary American society has more than one code of acceptable sexual behavior, different for the young, the old, the wealthy, the poor, the black, and the white. All codes of the various segments of society together have an influence on the attitudes of parents, who in turn shape the attitudes of their children — at least until adolescence, when friends and peer groups become more influential. (4) The "Judeo-Christian" level: This is not intended to exclude the values and insights of other major world religions but to refer to value judgments based on Biblical and ecclesiastical writings. It recognizes the theological teachings about human sexuality that have a definite religious frame of reference. Based primarily on Scriptural references from both the Old and New Testaments, they also include interpretations and commentaries by Jewish, Protestant, and Catholic scholars.

Whatever the shortcomings and deficiencies of the older constraints and moral codes, they did provide man with a restraint on some of his baser instincts and impulses. Hard as it is to admit, modern man has pretty much the same strengths and weaknesses as any of his predecessors. The older codes provided a means of controlling and channeling man's natural selfishness, violence, jealousy, and possessiveness. They provided a structure in which there were clearly defined elements of guilt and praise.

Man, on his own, has a hard time deciding what some limits truly are. Is the only restraint on sexual relations, for instance, that you do not harm the other person, as many of the young claim? The older morality claimed a divine sanction for its defined limits ("Thou shalt not"), but a purely ethical person can have real difficulty knowing the limits of sexual freedom or what actually does harm the human person.[16]

Perhaps historically Christianity went overboard (e.g., St. Augustine) in emphasizing the demonic or Manichean within the sexual and did not stress enough the positive elements of growth, joy, and love. At least this tradition did not deny man's potential capacity for evil. The traditional restraints placed on the sexual did in fact remind man of a boundary beyond which he may not go without injuring himself and others. Whether this boundary was too narrowly conceived is another question. It is precisely this limit to human sexual freedom that is denied by many today.[20]

CONTEMPORARY SEXUALITY

Many of our contemporaries deny that sexuality is replete with feelings of aggression, dependency, and possessiveness and attribute these sexual attitudes to a puritanical hangup from another age. Yet all around us is ample evidence that sexuality, unless correctly used and disciplined, leads to destructive consequences in human relationships. Our society today is obsessed with sexual talk and activity. There are sexual opportunities of every sort for everyone, and yet one of the most frequently heard complaints in the offices of psychiatrists and marriage counselors is that there is no feeling in sex and therefore no fun.[3]

The argument is often given that traditional sexual morality depended mainly on fear for its sanction. Now that the fears of unwanted pregnancies and venereal disease have been removed by the manifold contraceptives and antibiotics, the only moral criteria for sexual behavior, so the argument goes, are mutual consent and interest. College and university people are frequently citing this in attempts to justify much of their sexual experience. But is it so? Can simple moral criteria free man from the exploitative and possessive needs that everyone has? Interestingly enough, more and more empirical data are beginning to pile up to show that some traditional restraints commonly associated with religious values are not so "old-fashioned" after all.

EFFECT ON INTIMATE RELATIONSHIPS

A panel of researchers reported at a session on human sexuality at the 141st annual meeting of the American Association for the Advancement of Science that the sexual revolution is "cooling down." Some of the avant-garde found that sexual variety without affection leads to "frustration, tension, and jealousy." "The movement of American society toward reducing sex to animal-like conduct between people is about to end," said Amitai Etzioni, a Columbia University sociologist.[5] He said the pendulum is swinging back "to a new synthesis, a new middle." He added that people are now "seeking ways to draw a line between sexual freedom and sexual fantasy. It's been discovered in varying degrees that all this sexual spice leads to less satisfaction. There is now more emphasis on things other than 'sexual acrobatics.' " His view was based partly on interviews with 215 single persons in Greenwich Village in New York and 50 couples at Rutgers University who had lived together and had decided to get married.[5]

Kolodny in St. Louis said that his researchers interviewed hundreds of people from all walks of life.[11] Their experiences confirm the Etzioni view: "We have found that a strictly mechanical, hedonistic approach to sex, while espoused by some, is relatively rapidly falling to the wayside." Kolodny noted that many of those who experimented with the hedonistic approach found it "enslaving, not freeing." They are returning to "at least a search for a relationship where there can be a positive emotional return."[11] Etzioni has added: "However, before long there may be a new form of family life—maybe a return to the nuclear family with men and women staying together with the children."[5]

Such views as those of Etzioni and Kolodny call to mind that the major goal of marriage is achievement of intimacy with another person in all dimensions of human existence. Possibly the maintenance of the nuclear family would enhance trust by building and sharing intimacy and experiences. It is very unlikely to develop between a couple who have serious reservations about how long they will stay together. In other words, this intimacy is almost impossible (psychologically) unless there is a permanent commitment to each other in love. Otherwise the relationship does not seem worth the pain and agony demanded of two people trying to make a go of living and sharing together. People are usually unwilling to risk vulnerability, pain, and suffering, which are absolutely necessary for true intimacy and growth, without a definite commitment to each other.

Peter Riga quotes the eminent psychotherapist Alexander Lowen, who has put it in the following way: "We cannot command our body to ignore the deepest truth it knows—that in opening itself to the possibility of pleasure, it stands exposed to the possibility of pain. Furthermore, in the center of our being we are sharply aware that the greater the pleasure we enjoy today, the greater the pain we will suffer tomorrow if we lose the person who gives us the pleasure."[16]

The conscious mind may be willing to accept such a gamble, and desire can propel us into making it. Only if love is present will the body accept the gamble, however. For love is commitment, and with commitment—with faith that today's happiness will return tomorrow—the body opens itself to pleasure. Without commitment, with the clear knowledge that today's pleasure will be denied tomorrow, the body holds back. It remains tense and on guard, and cannot fully respond to another's touch. Thus, love liberates our sexuality.[16]

According to a group of clergymen and physicians who attended a symposium on marital and sexual counseling, trial marriages may be bad psychologically and morally. The majority of the population does seem to realize this. They recognize very clearly that a life without values and order is a meaningless life. Yet in the search for these values, they sometimes embark upon courses doomed to failure and frustration. It appears, then, that the "games being played" produce relationships without commitment.

An opposite point of view is that of Dr. Beverly T. Mead, head of psychiatry at Creighton University. She relates that more people are living together without marriage, and that this behavior pattern probably will grow because it serves many couples who desire close alliances without major responsibilities. This will not bring an end to formal marriage. Most couples will continue to prefer a public declaration of marital vows. However, this does not mean the marriage arrangement will not change. With the emphasis on feminine rights and women working outside the home there may come into general use a more specific legal contract drawn up by a lawyer.

CELIBACY AND THE NEW MORALITY

In this context it is feasible to discuss briefly the charism and experience of celibacy as a life and love style. Obviously, the difference between married and celibate loves is purely sexual. The common factor is love. In marriage, only love keeps sex from taking the lover's mind away from the person of the loved one. In celibacy, only love can put such emphasis on the person that sex cannot intrude on the relationship. The same degree of love that keeps sex in its place in marriage keeps genital sex in its place in celibacy. Without that love, marriage and celibacy are equally meaningless charades. Consequently, celibacy is not freedom from love but rather freedom for love.[15]

Celibate persons can know as much about love as any married person. They can know a great deal about marriage, too, if they are interested in really listening to the couples who are happily married, as well as to those who are disappointed and disillusioned in their marriages. Celibates need not be prejudiced in favor of marriage or alternative life styles, or against them, because of personal experience. They can be detached, objective, and positive — perhaps some of the very few persons who can be.[14]

Traditional morality has been criticized because it emphasized the letter of the law to the detriment of the spirit of the law. Even within this framework, however, many feel that the "new morality" is an "easy" morality, catering to human weakness, and leading to excessive permissiveness and ultimately to immorality and licentiousness. This is unfounded and untrue. In fact, anyone who says or creates the impression that the new morality is an "easier" one simply does not understand it.[12]

Our conviction is that the new morality emerging in contemporary writings is not easy to live by, but very demanding. Norms and laws are necessary and helpful guides, but they cannot substitute for our personal responsibility and "response-ability."

The new morality stresses the central and radical importance of freedom, responsibility, and the interrelatedness of all persons. It does so in a way that makes growth in freedom the goal of life and sees responsibility as a part of all aspects of life.

The new morality seeks to reflect qualities emphasized by the Judeo-Christian Scriptures: faith, conversion, growth, freedom, and love. Traditional morality sought to do the same, in its own way. However, we believe that the new morality reflects the evangelical imperatives more accurately and enables one to live by them more consistently, wholeheartedly, and fruitfully; it is its very justification.

Thus, a traditional Judeo-Christian sexual code, properly understood, would appear to be far from obsolete. In fact, after all the pretenses are discarded and other pragmatic codes are tested and found wanting, such a code could well experience a rejuvenation. In this perspective, commitment and marriage are not simply moral demands; they are moral demands because they are human imperatives.

CONCLUSION

In conclusion, there are predictions being made by such writers as Snider that we feel are very likely to come true. These include the following:

1. There will be a tendency to stick to one partner.

2. Few will continue to defend sex as something to be casually enjoyed with several partners.

3. Free-swinging promiscuity will "cool down."

4. Living together in a meaningful relationship will not necessarily eliminate guilt feelings.

5. Many girls will wrestle with the question of how many such arrangements can be dissolved and new ones started before they become identified as persons indiscriminate in sexual relations.

6. Counselors will find themselves talking to more women seeking guidance about which conditions favor and which interfere with a lasting relationship.

7. There is little fear that the institution of marriage is endangered by unmarried persons setting up housekeeping. Couples who find themselves compatible will eventually marry. A home with children still will be the goal of the vast majority, and no better framework than marriage has yet been found for this.

8. Virginity will not be swept aside by the new trends. The pressures that caused a girl to worry about her normality if she remained a virgin will be eased. New social support will emerge for the girl who fears that in remaining chaste she has failed to prepare herself for the responsibility of love and marriage.

9. A pattern of "secondary virginity" will emerge in which those disillusioned by a period of sex will choose to remain chaste until marriage.

10. There will be a need to consider the agonizing dilemmas experienced by males in their quest for sexual identity.

11. The revolution will have contributed a more satisfying sex life for married couples. Lifting of taboos and sanctioning of more aggressive roles by both partners will reduce conflict. A corresponding drop in divorce rates will follow.

12. Disenchantment will set in with how-to manuals and the books of sexual mechanics now saturating the market. Mechanical striving for perfection will give way to more frankness and tenderness as couples turn to themselves for solutions to their sex problems. There will be increased willingness to seek counseling when needed.

13. Mate swapping and group sex as important sources of sexual satisfaction will decrease.

14. Pornography will continue to lose appeal.

15. The greatest beneficiaries of sexual freedom may be the geriatric set. Expect the new view of society to be admiration rather than condemnation for aged who maintain an active participation in sex.[19]

Admittedly, these are bold predictions for brave new horizons, and only time will test their validity. We believe that the insights shared and the trends noted reveal man's indomitable search for meaning in life. As members of the health care community strive to serve the health needs of people in various settings, they cannot ignore the spiritual dimension of the total personality. This can refer to a person's religious orientation and formation, but it can also be concerned with his quest for intangibles which cannot be measured by empirical data. In the midst of this real sexual awakening is there not also a real spiritual awakening? Is there not present here the age-old search for Love?

REFERENCES

1. Baker, Luther G. Sex, Society and the Single Woman. In Kirkendall, Lester A. (ed.). *The New Sexual Revolution.* New York: Donald W. Brown, Inc., 1971.
2. Bell, Robert R. and Michael Gordon. *The Social Dimension of Human Sexuality.* Boston: Little, Brown and Company, 1972.
3. Dedek, John F. *Contemporary Sexual Morality.* New York: Sheed and Ward, 1971.
4. Erikson, Erik. *Childhood and Society,* 2nd ed. New York: W. W. Norton & Co., 1964.
5. Etzioni, Amitai. Quoted in End of Sexual Hedonism Seen. *Kansas City Times,* January 30, 1975.
6. Frankl, V. *The Doctor and the Soul: From Psychotherapy to Logotherapy,* 2nd ed. Translated by Richard C. and Clara Winston. New York: Alfred A. Knopf, 1965.
7. Fromm, Erich. *The Art of Loving.* New York: Barton, 1963.
8. Gagnon, John H. and William Simon. *The Sexual Scene.* Chicago, Aldine Publishing Company, 1970.

9. Goergen, Donald. *The Sexual Celibate.* New York: The Seabury Press, 1974.
10. Kennedy, E. C. *The New Sexuality — Myths, Fables and Hang-ups.* Garden City, New York: Doubleday and Company, 1972.
11. Kolodny, Robert C. Quoted in End of Sexual Hedonism Seen. *Kansas City Times,* January 30, 1975.
12. Lohkamp, Nicholas. *The Commandments and The New Morality.* Cincinnati: St. Anthony Messenger Press, 1973.
13. May, Rollo. *Love and Will.* New York: W. W. Norton & Company, 1969.
14. McGoey, John H. *Dare I Love?* Huntington, Indiana: Our Sunday Visitor, Inc., 1974.
15. Raguin, Yves. *Celibacy For Our Times.* St. Meinrad, Indiana: Abbey Press, 1974.
16. Riga, Peter J. *Problems of Marriage and Sexuality Today.* New York: Exposition Press, 1973.
17. Salisbury, Winfield and Frances Salisbury. Youth and the Search for Intimacy. In Kirkendall, Lester A. (ed.). *The New Sexual Revolution.* New York: Donald W. Brown, Inc., 1971.
18. Schultz, LeRoy G. Ethical Issues in Treating Sexual Dysfunction. *Social Work Journal of NASW,* 20:126–128, March 1965.
19. Snider, Arthur J. Sexual Mores: What Next? *Kansas City Times,* March 11, 1975.
20. Taylor, Michael J. (ed.). *Sex: Thoughts for Contemporary Christians.* Garden City, New York: Doubleday and Company, 1972.
21. Willwerth, James and Stefan Kanfer. Rebels and Swingers. In *Sex in the 60's.* New York: Time-Life Books, 1968.
22. Wright, Beatrice A. *Physical Disability — A Psychological Approach.* New York: Harper and Row, Publishers, 1960.

INDEX

Page numbers in *italics* refer to illustrations. Page numbers followed by (t) refer to tables.

295